Sociology of Education

Second Edition

Sociology of Education

An Introductory View from Canada

Second Edition

Joyce Barakett
Concordia University

Ailie Cleghorn
Concordia University

PEARSON
Prentice
Hall

Toronto

Library and Archives Canada Cataloguing in Publication

Barakett, Joyce
        Sociology of education : an introductory view from Canada / Joyce
Barakett, Ailie Cleghorn. — 2nd ed.

Includes bibliographical references and index.
ISBN 978-0-13-225549-3

        1. Educational sociology--Canada. I. Cleghorn, Ailie II. Title.

LC191.8.C2B37 2007   306.43'0971   C2007-900041-X

ISBN-13: 978-0-13-225549-3
ISBN-10: 0-13-225549-9

Editor-in-Chief, Vice-President of Sales: Kelly Shaw
Acquisitions Editors: Christine Cozens and Kathleen McGill
Sponsoring Editor: Carolin Sweig
Marketing Manager: Toivo Pajo
Developmental Editor: Charlotte Morrison-Reed
Production Editor: Katie Hearn
Copy Editor: Allegra Robinson
Proofreader: Emmanuelle Dauplay
Production Coordinator: Avinash Chandra
Composition: Laserwords
Art Director: Julia Hall
Cover Design: Geoff Agnew

    8   14

Printed and bound in Canada.

Contents

Chapter 3 The Organization of Teaching and Learning   57

Chapter 4 Critical Perspectives on the Politics of Teaching and Pedagogy   83

Chapter 5 The School as an Informal System of Socialization   112

Chapter 6 Globalization, Schooling, Technology, and the Curriculum   127

Figures and Tables

Figures

Tables

Preface

This book is written for undergraduate students who seek a sociological understanding of the educational process. It is especially written for students in education or sociology, who, as future educators, will need to be knowledgeable about current sociological debates in education in general and in Canadian education in particular. In order for students to gain this knowledge, they will need to learn about sociological concepts and theoretical perspectives and understand the ways in which the formal and informal aspects of the educational system are connected to the political, economic, legal, religious, and other sectors of society. It is of paramount importance that teachers and other educators acquire the knowledge and skills that will be needed if they are going to respond with good judgment to the constant pressures to introduce various changes, including the new technologies, into their schools. This book asks them to remember that education is essentially a social process that is ultimately about people.

Although the focus of this book is on the Canadian educational system, it is not simply a sociology *of* Canadian education. As the title suggests, we present a view *from* Canada. This is important for several reasons. First, we believe it is important to illuminate to the now highly multicultural student population, which includes many international students, what distinguishes Canada's educational system from that of other countries. Second, we would like to convey that which is particular to the Canadian vision of *how society ought to be organized*, even if the reality may fall short of this vision. Here we have in mind what appears to us as a particularly Canadian way of looking at ethnic, linguistic, racial, and other *differences* with a sense of the right of those differences to exist, to persist, and even to flourish. Although not everyone would agree with us, we believe that Canadians are in general agreement about the promotion of *unity in diversity* through the promotion of biculturalism, French and English bilingualism, and, wherever possible, official support for the maintenance of other first languages. We go further and suggest that, most of the time, Canadians are comfortable with the consequences of these policies—the necessity of negotiating mutual understanding in a civilized manner across multiple social boundaries.

In this book we draw on studies carried out in Canada, the US, Britain, and France to show how the field of sociology of education has developed. From time to time, we also draw on far-reaching examples from various parts of the globe to locate the Canadian system within the broader context of issues, trends, and practices, and to help students take an objective stance towards their own system of education. Since people tend to take for granted the system that educated them, it can be difficult to see its components and effects clearly; many of the particulars have been internalized. To understand that which is familiar, it sometimes helps to take a look from afar. Therefore, although we have written this book with a Canadian readership in mind, it would make an equally useful text for American or British students, providing them with a different "world view," and thus illuminating their understanding of their own educational systems and their experience within them.

The decision to write the first edition of this book grew out of our combined experiences teaching in sociology of education, comparative education, and issues of difference at Concordia University. As instructors, we found that the few available Canadian texts soon went out of print, and we had little choice but to assign American or British texts or readers, none of which provided the perspective that we felt was necessary for understanding Canadian education in its broader context. In response to our students' experience with the first edition and our reviewers' comments, we have made many changes for this second edition, re-writing significant sections of Chapters 1 to 5. Chapter 6 is completely new.

We know of no other current Canadian text that attempts, in the manner that this one does, to link theory and practice to an analysis of the controversial issues in education that affect the Canadian system in the context of a rapidly changing world. This book is a response to our concern that it is no longer enough to educate teachers for Canada alone. If their perspective is not broadened beyond their own borders, they will not be prepared to adapt to and teach in situations where the school structures, rules, and expectations of teachers and students may be unfamiliar. Increasingly, these unfamiliar situations, as described throughout the text, exist in our own society and are also encountered when students and teachers travel to teach in other parts of the world. Thus we hope that this book reflects not only the range of historical and theoretical perspectives that affect education in Canada but also new ways in which educators can develop strategies for future educational and social change.

Probably every academic textbook purports to represent "the state of the art" in its field. We believe that this goal is best accomplished by signalling to the reader that some "old" ideas are fundamental to current thinking and therefore still valid. State of the art means linking the best thinking in the field—no matter how old—as intelligently and coherently as possible to new thinking. It means avoiding faddist jargon, since this obfuscates understanding. It means drawing on our own considerable experience teaching at the university level and conducting educational research in Canada and elsewhere.

The table of contents reflects the overall aims of the book and of each chapter. The chapters are organized around major themes and are designed to clarify the relationship between school and society. To make this text both interesting and meaningful, we have included illustrations, tables, case examples, and current Canadian data.

Chapter 1 provides the basic terminology and an introduction to the main concepts in the field of sociology of education. This chapter also discusses the structure of the Canadian educational system in terms of system goals and governance, showing how the Canadian system is either similar to or different from education in an international context. In this edition, the chapter has been expanded to include a history of Canadian education and educational goals. The educational experience of Canada's First Nations people and Canada's French-speaking population is then discussed. The chapter ends with an introduction to sociological research in education.

Chapter 2 provides a historical overview of present-day thought in the field, then reviews the major theories that have been put forth to explain the nature of the relationship between schooling and society. In this edition we have added a discussion of anti-racist theories put forward by various Canadian and other researchers.

Chapter 3 looks at the organization of teaching and learning in terms of the formal organizational features of the school. We have added a discussion of the various attempts to reform the organization of teaching and learning. Here we also examine the policy context of Canadian schools, in particular Canada's policy of multiculturalism. The norms of the teaching profession and the roles of teachers, as well as that of the principal, are also presented. The question of whether or not there is a crisis in teacher education, and the context of trends and debates in teacher education in Canada are examined. This discussion is followed by an overview of current models of teaching.

Chapter 4 points to the influence of the work of Paulo Freire's work in the field of education. It distinguishes between teaching and pedagogy and the politics of education through a discussion of critical, feminist, and critical multicultural pedagogy, along with the pedagogy of whiteness and anti-racist pedagogy.

Chapter 5 provides the reader with an overview of the role of the school as an informal system of socialization and moral and political socialization. Here the student will gain a more thorough understanding of the meaning of the hidden curriculum, teacher expectations and typifications of student behaviours, the influence of the peer group and popular culture, and their implications for teacher education.

Finally, Chapter 6 looks at education in Canada today in the context of globalization, technology, and curriculum issues. Several critically important ideas and issues are raised for the consideration of future teachers and educators as we move further into the twenty-first century. These include the influence of globalization on the content and format of text materials, as well as the need for technological and social literacy.

Guide for Instructors

We believe that the autonomy of the instructor to use the book in the way that serves him or her best is to be encouraged. However, our experience is that this book works well when used as the main text in a one-term, twelve-to-fourteen-week undergraduate course. Although the text is organized into six chapters, we do not believe that any of these can be covered properly in a single week. Rather, we find that two weeks are sometimes required for the teaching and discussion of each chapter, especially if the suggested readings at the end of each are assigned in whole or in part throughout the course. One piece of advice we do have for instructors is to refer to the table of contents when developing an outline for a particular class.

At the end of this book you will find a glossary of terms as well as a list of web links. The glossary is intended to provide the reader with a quick reminder of the main idea of a concept or term; however, for a complete definition as applied to the field of sociology of education, the student will need to turn to the chapter in question.

The list of weblinks represents a concession on the part of the authors to social and technological change. The intention is that these links will be helpful and add to the knowledge provided in each chapter; however, given the nature of the internet, the authors cannot insure the future presence, quality, reliability, and content of the weblinks. Many of those provided in the first edition can no longer be found. We encourage students to do their own searches in areas that are of particular interest to them and to share these with their peers and instructors.

In addition, a series of **PowerPoint slides** has been created for the new edition of *Sociology of Education*. These slides offer helpful summaries of key points and can be used to augment lectures and in-class discussions. Instructors can download the slides from a password-protected location on Pearson Education Canada's online catalogue (**vig.pearsoned.ca**). Simply search for the text, then click on "Instructor" under "Resources" in the left-hand menu. See your local sales representative for details and access.

Acknowledgments

Many people have helped, directly and indirectly, with this book. First to be mentioned are the hundreds of students we have taught, especially in sociology of education, comparative education, and gender and education courses. We have drawn many lessons from them in designing a book that would be both readable and informative.

Second, we want to thank several people for their individual contributions. Judith Leonard and Deborah Baverstock-Angelus, now both graduated from Concordia's educational studies masters program, very kindly gave of their time and energies to go back to their theses and contribute to the inserts on the use of teacher narratives in teacher education in Chapter 3 and The Alternate School in Chapter 4. We would also like to thank the anonymous individuals who reviewed the first edition and provided Pearson Education with helpful comments and suggestions for this second edition.

About the Authors

Joyce Barakett is a professor in the education department at Concordia University. Her doctoral degree in sociology of education, social psychology, and sociology of women is from the Université de Montréal. She has a B.A. from Concordia University and an M.A. in Sociology from McGill University. Her courses include undergraduate and graduate teaching in sociology of education, issues of difference, school and society, popular culture, and media and education.

Ailie Cleghorn is a professor in the education department at Concordia University. Her doctoral degree in the comparative sociology of education was completed at McGill University in 1981. She holds a B.A. from McGill University in sociology and anthropology and an M.A. from Concordia University in educational studies. She teaches undergraduate courses in comparative education. At the graduate level, her courses include literacy and development, and introduction to research methods in education.

chapter one

The Nature of Sociological Inquiry and the Study of Schooling

CHAPTER OBJECTIVES

The aim of this chapter is to provide

- an introduction to the major concepts in the field of sociology of education
- a brief section on the history of education in Canada
- a discussion of the ways in which the Canadian education system is both similar to and different from other systems around the world
- an introduction to sociological research in education

SOCIOLOGICAL CONCEPTS

By the time students are in their third or fourth year of university, they have come to realize that the educational system to which they have been exposed over the previous 15 or so years is complex, but few of them really understand the extent or the details of this complexity. It is therefore our purpose to provide you with an understanding of the ways in which educational systems, structures, and processes connect with various aspects of society, including dominant values, political goals, and ideologies. To understand the scope of the field of sociology of education we must first define some basic terms. Before we move on to the sociology of education, we need to have a clear understanding of the field of sociology.

Sociology is a social science discipline that explores and explains the organization and functioning of society. It is a field of study that looks at the social groups (social classes, ethnic, linguistic, and racial groups) and institutions that make up a particular society. By institutions, we are referring to the family, the economy, and the legal and political systems. Sociology is also concerned with the relations between the social groups as well as the position or status of the individual within the group, groups, or institutions that he or she belongs to. The **ideologies** (beliefs, values, norms, and ways of understanding the world) that underlie the functioning of society's institutions, as well as its various groups, are a major part of the field of sociology.

Sociology of education is a subfield of sociology with two major foci. First, it focuses on the relationship of schooling processes, practices, and outcomes to the organization of society as a whole. Second, it focuses on the school system and the school. That is, sociology of education is concerned with social groups (teachers, students, parents, school administrators, school board officers, ministries of education), the relations between them, and the academic as well as social results of in-school processes. Sociology of education is thus particularly concerned with such matters as the way in which educational processes ensure, for example, that individual students come to abide by the norms and values of society at large, and the role that the educational process plays in recreating society's social structure as this relates, in particular, to the division of labour and the hierarchy of power.

To further understand sociology of education we need to distinguish between everyday or **informal education**, which normally takes place within the family, and **formal education**, which takes place in institutions (schools) designed for that purpose. Formal education refers to the set of organized activities that are intended to transmit skills, knowledge, and values as well as to develop mental abilities. We can also talk about **non-formal education**, which refers to organized instruction that takes place outside of school settings (e.g., girl scouts, music lessons, sports groups). Our main interest in this book is in both the formal and informal education that takes place within regular school settings.

Education is sociological because it involves a network of interrelated societal institutions and a **social process**, and because it has sociological functions, both intended and unintended. That is, education takes place within an established institutional structure (a school system) that is connected to other institutions in society—the economy, the political system, the legal system, and the family, as well as the belief or religious system. The dominant norms and values of society are reflected in all of these institutions.

Education is also a sociological process in another way. Education involves human beings and requires them to interact in order for the intended knowledge, skills, and values to be transmitted and their mental abilities to be developed. The main participants in this process—the teachers and the students—bring to the classroom their prior life experiences, their **social class** background (a combination of parents' education, occupation, and income), their language background, their racial origins, their gender, their beliefs about the value and purpose of education, and their notions of how girls and boys are supposed to behave in classrooms. What goes on in classrooms is therefore greatly influenced by these factors or variables, or, more accurately, by the social meaning that is attached to such matters as language, ethnicity, race, and gender.

It is important to note that some school settings are more complex than others with regard to the variables just mentioned. For example, because of large numbers of immigrants, especially since the end of the World War II in 1945, schools in major cities in Canada are now very multicultural and multilingual, as they are in other countries such as the United States, Britain, and Australia. This **diversity** of the student population makes it more important than ever before for teachers to be educated and prepared to teach children who may bring to the learning situation many different kinds of prior experiences stemming from their varied social class, language, and cultural backgrounds. In turn, these differences will mean that in any single classroom children can be expected to vary considerably in their learning styles, attitudes towards school, and expectations regarding the roles of teachers and students. Thus it is not only the **social context** of teaching and learning that is important but the context of the experience that each child brings to school. To *contextualize* instruction is to attend to both of these aspects of the culture of schooling.

The Functions of Formal Schooling

The functions of schooling can be categorized as either **intended** (manifest) or **unintended** (latent), though there is considerable overlap between the two. The unintended functions of education are also considered to be part of what is known as the hidden curriculum (Mifflen & Mifflen, 1982).

Intended Functions of Schooling

By intended or manifest functions we are referring to those aspects of schooling that come immediately to mind when we ask ourselves what it is that schools do. It seems simple at first. As we already stated, schools transmit knowledge, skills, and values and develop mental abilities. Apart from the other obvious fact that elementary schools do different things than universities, is this all there is to it? Let us look first at four intended functions of schooling.

1. Schools transmit generalized as well as specialized knowledge.
2. Schools transmit the existing culture from one generation to the next and to new members of the society.
3. Schools transmit new knowledge that is produced in universities and in industry.
4. Schools provide opportunities for social mobility.

To elaborate on the first function (the transmission of generalized and specialized knowledge), we teach children to read, write, and calculate—that is, to be **functionally literate**—providing them with the general knowledge they will need to take part in society, work, and learn other things. At a more specialized level, we teach many facts in subjects such as history, geography, art, music, and literature, as well as procedures in subjects like science and mathematics. Nowadays we teach computer and other skills that will be useful in specific jobs. These are the kinds of obvious things that come to mind when we ask what it is that schools do. The situation is not so simple, however, when we begin to ask *whose* knowledge is taught in school, and *who has decided* what is to be taught, at what level, and *to whom*. We will return to these important sociological questions later.

What do we mean when we say that schools transmit the society's existing culture (the second function mentioned above), including the accumulated knowledge and the dominant values, from one generation to the next and to new members of the society? By **culture** we are referring to the ways of perceiving, thinking, believing, and behaving that characterize the members of a particular social group. Culture also includes the artifacts that distinguish one group from another (e.g., clothing, technology, type of housing). In complex, multicultural settings the transmission of culture through the school is not a simple, straightforward matter because of the multicultural makeup of many classrooms. That is, the culture that is transmitted in school reflects the values and attitudes of the so-called **dominant group**. Here we are referring to those people (mostly men) who hold key decision-making and leadership positions in society as well as those who are closely associated with them, professionally or through friendship. This includes those who are in charge of the school system. Sometimes the dominant group's culture differs in important ways from the home culture of many or even most of the students. Thus we see that schools play not only a socialization role from one generation to the next but also a role in the acculturation of the children of newcomers (immigrants) to the norms and values of the dominant society. **Acculturation** refers to the changes that occur within a group through culture contact and through the process of adapting to and taking on the values, attitudes, and ways of behaving of the culturally dominant group. Some refer to this as the process of integration. **Culture contact** occurs when members of more than one culture or ethnic group live in proximity to each other. The group that arrived first or has been in the region the longest tends to include those who hold the important and powerful positions in the society's institutions (including the school system).

Although Canadian law includes provisions for religious and ethnic minorities to establish their own schools, it is generally the culture of the dominant group that is transmitted through the public schools. In this way, cultural transmission involves acculturation. By bringing together young people from various backgrounds within a single societal institution for a number of their formative years, schools play an important role in establishing loyalty and consensus over what the society values most (i.e., a sense of national identity or citizenship). In some countries schools promote national loyalty overtly, with daily saluting of the nation's flag, for example. In countries such as Canada acculturation tends to be subtle, contained within federal multicultural policies, which are in turn expressed through school festivals that celebrate diversity.

Cultural transmission also involves **cultural diffusion**. For example, Western culture, values, and schooling practices, including curricula, have been spread or diffused to communities in the Canadian North as well as many parts of the still-developing world through colonization and its aftermath. Cultural diffusion also refers to the dissemination throughout society of new knowledge that is produced in universities as well as in industry (the third intended function of schooling). Cultural diffusion may be increasing globally through the textbook industry, which tends to be controlled by Western capitalist interests (Apple & Christian-Smith, 1991).

Cultural production refers to the role that higher education institutions play in producing new knowledge in technology, science, the social sciences, the humanities, business, art, and other areas. Through a complex decision-making and implementation process, new knowledge is incorporated into the school curriculum. In due course, it is passed on to the next generation and to new members of the society (Werner, 1987).

Before proceeding to discuss the fourth intended function of schooling, social mobility, it is important to clarify what we mean by social structure. **Social structure** refers to the way people's relations in society are organized to form patterns or networks. The social structure of a complex society like Canada is made up of multiple systems or institutions—the economic, political, family, religious, and education systems.

Every society, from the smallest and most simply organized to the largest and most complex (such as that of Canada) is stratified, or has a system of **social stratification**. That is, every society is organized in a hierarchy based on people's access to and possession of whatever is most valued in the particular society. Individuals (and the groups they belong to) are accorded prestige and power (status) based on such matters as education, income, occupation, race, ethnicity, religion, language, and gender. Canadian society is stratified on the basis of ethnic and linguistic background, occupation, education, and income (Porter, 1965). That is, the system is stratified according to both **ascribed status** and **achieved status**. While the Canadian system of stratification is considered to be "open," allowing movement up through the strata from the lowest to the highest on the basis of achievement, the extent to which such **social mobility** is actually possible is still limited by ascription (characteristics acquired at birth, such as gender, ethnicity, and social class). In other words, there are limits, albeit ill-defined ones, on the extent to which achievement in school can compensate for ascribed characteristics; academic achievement tends to be patterned by ascribed characteristics, although individual exceptions can often be found.

A society's system of stratification is also related to the **division of labour**, the differential distribution of jobs that need to be done in order for the society to maintain itself economically. Every society has unwritten rules as well as formal criteria (the required credentials) that determine who may perform which tasks. The unwritten rules are generally based on such matters as gender, ethnicity, family background, and the like, and every society has some tasks that are considered more important or desirable than others. Similarly, some occupations are more highly valued than others and pay accordingly. Since it is not possible for all qualified people to perform highly desirable tasks, and there are fewer desirable jobs than qualified people, there has to be a selection process. In fact, some theorists would argue that there has to be a way for a society to ensure that achievement is distributed unevenly (patterned). There also has to be a way for people to accept their lot. We must ask, then, how is it that people "accept their place" and agree to perform even the most menial of tasks? How do individuals get ahead? How is the system of social stratification perpetuated?

In Canadian and North American society in general, we find a widely held belief that schools are places for people to acquire the credentials that will allow them to move up the social ladder. It is widely believed that there is **equality of educational opportunity** (equal access to schooling, equal treatment within schools, and the potential for equal results). This is a popular but ill-defined concept, and more of a myth than a reality. If educational opportunity were truly equal for all, there would be no differential distribution of educational results: achievement would be distributed evenly from one social class to another, from one racial and ethnic group to another, and between the sexes. While not all people are equally able to achieve well in school, there is no scientific evidence whatsoever to suggest that some individuals are more intelligent than others based on their social class, race, ethnicity, or gender. That is, there is no biological or genetic reason why one group or another should be overrepresented among either those who succeed or those who fail in school (Ogbu, 1991; Slavin, 1991).

In addition, there is a related set of myths. One myth states that those who achieve well in school have done so through hard work and by being evaluated according to objective and "fair" (universalistic) principles. This is to say, there is a popular belief that we live in a **meritocracy**, where individual effort and ability lead to higher achievement in school, and therefore to higher social status. Another myth suggests that a student's performance in school is not affected by his or her family's social class, racial origin, language spoken at home, or other particularistic criteria. As we shall see later on in this text, these myths do not reflect reality. At this point, it is important to understand that myths serve the important function of building and maintaining consensus and social cohesion, but that this comes at a cost to individuals who are members of certain groups (Aronowitz & Giroux, 1993).

The same set of myths or beliefs is used to explain why some students fail in school, take up menial jobs, and do not move up the social ladder. To take this reasoning a bit further, if girls fall behind boys in mathematics, there must be a good reason for it; if special education classes are made up of a disproportionate number of children from minority backgrounds, there must be a good reason for this also. This kind of commonsensical understanding or belief, which justifies or rationalizes the way things are and thereby supports the status quo, is called a **legitimating ideology**.

Although the majority of people have enough intelligence to achieve quite well in school and perform a variety of occupations, there is some truth in the fact that not all individuals are equally suited to a given task. In addition, the distribution of jobs to be done does not necessarily match the distribution of abilities. There are fewer interesting and prestigious jobs than there are intelligent people. Thus there has to be a way to select some people to perform certain kinds of roles and persuade others to perform low-status jobs. This process is part of the **selection and allocation function** of schooling. Although manifest and intended at one level, the selection-allocation function of schooling is difficult for many to see, since we have all been socialized to believe that the system is fair and just. It is for this very reason that it is extremely important for teachers to know about this function of schooling. It is one of the main concerns of the field of sociology of education.

Closely related to what we have just said about social mobility is the fact that, through the process of schooling, young people learn a lot about the occupational structure of society. Schools introduce young people, both directly and indirectly, to many occupations as well as the types of position and roles within them. For example, children learn early about the hierarchy of power when they find out that serious infractions (both behavioural and academic) get referred "up the line" to the principal of the school. Similarly, they learn that there are complex rules associated with competition, cooperation, and achievement; sometimes chatting in groups in the classroom is cooperative learning; at other times chatting in class is considered disruptive behaviour. In such ways, children eventually become familiar with society's rules for getting ahead, what constitutes fair competition, what counts towards academic achievement, and what does not. Thus, through observation of repeated patterns of interaction between all the actors in the school—the principal, the teachers, the librarian, the parent volunteers, the janitor—children are introduced to occupational roles. They also discover who has authority over whom and what kind of behaviour is acceptable under what circumstances. It is through such mechanisms that children also come to accept the results of tests that are said to be objective and therefore fair. The belief that testing procedures are unbiased and fair is an important precursor to later acceptance of the fact that the rewards of society are distributed unevenly—some people get ahead and "deserve" to, while those who do not can only "blame themselves." We will discuss this legitimating ideology in more detail in Chapter 2.

Unintended Functions of Schooling

There are several functions of schooling that are considered unintended, or less obvious and recognized than the preceding intended or manifest functions. We will discuss the following four: (1) social control; (2) custodial; (3) establishment of social relations and subgroup maintenance; and (4) promotion of critical analysis. (See Mifflen & Mifflen [1982] for a more complete discussion of manifest and latent functions.)

Social control is not only about the control of undesirable behaviour; it is about the definition and imposition of the expected behaviours of boys, girls, blacks, whites, teenagers, university students, and so on. Social control refers to the role that the school plays in perpetuating social class differences; it refers to the unwritten rules that define who is expected to get ahead and who is not. These are the rules that sometimes result in subtle or not-so-subtle rejection of an individual who "steps out of line" by showing an interest in entering an occupation that requires years of higher education despite, for example, the modest educational achievements of his or her parents. These are the rules that lead some girls to suddenly lose interest in science or mathematics at about the age of puberty and other students to rebel against the system in ways that conform to popular racial or ethnic stereotypes (Dei, 1996; Ogbu, 1991). The functional theorists, who will be discussed more fully in the next chapter, would say that it is through social control that the social structure is maintained in a kind of equilibrium.

Schooling can also be said to have a **custodial function**. This refers to the fact that elementary schools, at least, are places for children to be looked after, to be guaranteed the same safety they enjoy at home, from about nine o'clock in the morning until at least three o'clock in the afternoon. Nowadays many elementary schools recognize the importance of their custodial role by providing care for children during parents' working hours, from early morning until late afternoon. The custodial function of schools is reinforced through a variety of laws that place a legal responsibility on the school and the teachers to substitute for parents (*in loco parentis*) during the school day (Dickinson, 1995). Schools and teachers are held responsible for the safety and care of the child, but, interestingly, they are not (yet) legally responsible when children fail academically: failure belongs to the individual and can easily be explained according to the myth and belief system discussed above.

The custodial situation in high schools is not quite so clear. While schools may have a legal responsibility to provide a safe environment for young people, they do not always do so. In fact, some high schools are dangerous places for students and teachers alike—drugs, violence, rudeness, defiance, and truancy appear to be increasing everywhere.

We realize how important schools are for developing social skills and establishing social relations when we imagine children learning everything they need to know at home in front of a computer. Not only do schools teach children how to get along with their peers and work in groups, but, by virtue of their location in residential neighbourhoods, schools tend to draw children from similar social class and ethnic backgrounds. Over time, the friendships that develop become part of a community's adult network of social relations, reinforcing and maintaining the cohesion of particular ethnic, linguistic, social class, and other subgroups within the society.

It may be another myth that schools teach students to think critically about the society they live in as well as about global issues. While there are a few reports of experiments in high schools to promote critical analysis (Norris & Phillips, 1990), it appears that very little instruction in it actually occurs until the graduate level of university. It is important, therefore, for sociology of education students to ask themselves why critical thinking is so rarely encouraged at earlier stages of schooling. What kind of education would teachers need to have in order to integrate critical thinking into the curriculum?

Although elementary and most secondary schools are quite conservative institutions, they are also places where social changes are felt and technological changes are tried out. Thus one of the functions of higher education is to carry out research and reflect on the changes occurring in society and how these affect the educational process. Schools now have to deal with many different kinds of change, such as a vastly increased divorce rate (deemed a problem by most teachers), immigrants who adhere to religious practices that are unfamiliar to members of the host society, and computers, which are being adopted as a new panacea for every conceivable educational problem. These are but a few of the changes that require study, critical reflection, and consultation with teachers, teacher educators, school administrators, the education ministry, and others. These are also the kinds of issues that academics take up in sociology of education courses with pre-service teachers and others interested in the field of education.

THE HISTORY OF EDUCATION IN CANADA: WHOSE HISTORY?

The first part of the title to this section, *The History of Education in Canada*, suggests that there is only one story to be told, with the emphasis on key influences and important events. There are, however, three points we would like our readers to understand from the outset.

1. The history of education in Canada reflects and parallels the social history of the various groups that have come into contact, and conflict, since the first settlers from Britain and France encountered Canada's **First Nations**[1] groups in the early 17th century.
2. There are many histories of education in Canada, depending on whose history is being told.
3. Three tensions have marked this history from the beginning and continue to do so today—the tension between uniformity and diversity, stability and change, and power and equality (Levin & Young, 1994).

Most accounts of Canadian history state that there were two "founding groups," the French and the English. This points to the "standard" or generally accepted view of history that is infused with the ideology of Canada's dominant group, since it was neither the French nor the English who discovered Canada; rather it was "discovered" by its **aboriginal** peoples thousands of years ago with the first ancestors' crossing of the Bering Strait from Asia. Nevertheless, there are clearly many histories to be told in a country that has had 10 provincial systems of education, a federally controlled system for **Native peoples**, constitutionally guaranteed rights to education in the religion of one's choice (with the only choices being Roman Catholic or Protestant!), and huge demographic changes in the population over the last 50 years. (Now there are 13 separate education systems, 10 provinces, and three territories.) All this is to suggest that the telling of history is always open to interpretation and debate, a debate we would like you, the reader, to join. So that you can do so properly, we ask that you refer to the list of references as well as to the questions and discussion points that appear at the end of this chapter.

Several hundred pages would be required to do this topic justice; thus this section is limited to a conventional and brief review of the major influences and events in the development of Canada's provincial education systems. Here we illustrate that a political and religious struggle for power and control has been at the centre of this development. This is followed by two examples of the ways in which the focus of the education historical narrative differs according to

[1]We use the term "First Nations" to refer to the aboriginal peoples of Canada, including Indians, Inuit, and Metis groups. The term "Indian" is often used by the Canadian government to refer to people who have the legal status of registered Indian as defined by the *Indian Act* (first passed in 1876 and revised several times since). Throughout this chapter we use the terms aboriginal, Native, First Nations, and Indian interchangeably, and as appropriate to the particular context of the discussion.

a particular group's experience. The first example reflects the experience of Canada's First Nations peoples; the second looks at the experience of Quebec's French-speaking population. As you will discover in these accounts as well as later on in this book, from the start social control, allocation, and **legitimation** have been at the heart of schooling in Canada, as elsewhere in the Western world. That is, schooling has been and remains a system for inculcating the ideology and values of those in power (e.g., the dominant group) into "the people," those with little or no power (Bowles & Gintis, 1976).

How Canada Acquired 10 Systems of Education

The standard account of the development of education in Canada begins in the early nineteenth century with political struggles in Upper Canada/Canada West and the work of John Strachan and Egerton Ryerson. It was mainly through these two educators that Canada's education system came to be influenced by Britain and the United States (Levin & Young, 1994).

Strachan came to Canada in 1799 from Scotland. In reaction to an already established small school system mainly for the upper classes ("grammar schools") in what is now Ontario, Strachan saw to the establishment of "common" schools. Thus, early on in Canada schooling was influenced by the British model, with the grammar school curriculum for children of the upper classes emphasizing the classics and the common schools for children of the working class emphasizing learning by rote and appropriate behaviour (learning to be on time, dress neatly, carry out routine tasks as required). Strachan, an Anglican bishop, taught in this system. Although there were reformers and dissenters amongst Roman Catholics and others who sought to reduce the Anglican influence, overall the emphasis remained a commitment to Christianity, instilling the "correct" set of values and supporting the already established system of stratification (i.e., social control and a concern with social stability).

Egerton Ryerson, originally from the United States, had been greatly influenced by Horace Mann, a Massachusetts politician and innovative educator. Ryerson brought this influence to Canada. As chief superintendent of education in Upper Canada in 1846, Ryerson sought to reduce the Anglican control of schooling and to introduce Mann's ideas about tax-supported free schooling and secular schools within a centralized education department, all of which were being established in the United States. That is, Ryerson was important for his contribution to the development of public schooling for the masses in Canada.

By this time, the system of separate schools (Protestant and Catholic) had already been prompted by the Durham Report of 1839 and the Common Schools Act[2]. The principle of dissent within the Act allowed minorities to establish their own state-supported schools. Ryerson brought separate schools under state control with the Separate School Act of 1853, which then became incorporated into the Constitution Act (formerly called the British North America Act) of 1867. By 1867, the four original provinces—Ontario, Quebec, Nova Scotia, and New Brunswick—had elementary and secondary school systems supported through

---

[2]The Common Schools Act, 1865, entitled *An Act Respecting Common Schools*, provided for free, non-sectarian public schools. The Act authorized the appointment of schoolmasters, a superintendent of education, and a general board of education. It also allowed the governor to appoint local school boards, which were to serve in an advisory capacity. The general board of education was empowered to establish school districts, examine and appoint school teachers, set curricula, and prescribe textbooks. The superintendent of education—who served as the board's chief administrative officer and ex-officio secretary—was responsible for visiting and inspecting all schools that came under the jurisdiction of the Act.

the still-controversial issue of property taxation. Quebec had separate systems for Protestants (English) and Catholics (French), as did Ontario, though the system in Ontario for speakers of French was small. This pattern was adopted as the other six provinces were established. The one exception was Manitoba, which revoked the right to separate schools in 1890, an event that had long-lasting repercussions for the schooling and lives of the relatively large number of French speakers who had settled in the West, the majority of whom were Roman Catholic.

Section 93 of the 1867 British North America Act (later the Constitution Act of 1982) made education the sole responsibility of the provinces and also established guarantees to public education in the religion of one's choice. As you will see later on in this chapter, this had implications for the language of schooling in Quebec. Each province thus developed its own ministry or department of education; this structure remains to this day. Unlike the United States, Canada does not have a federal department of education; however, the federal government plays a fiscal role, especially in higher education, with a complex system of equalization payments to the provinces in the name of promoting equality of educational opportunity in a country with huge regional disparities in economic and geographical conditions between one province and territory and another.

The Experience of Canada's First Nations Peoples

The history of education for Canada's First Nations peoples is a very different story from what has just been recounted. Unlike the structure of education in the provinces, the education of Canada's First Nations peoples has been controlled by the department of Indian and Northern affairs in Ottawa and its bureaucratic predecessors. First Nations education is covered by treaties between Canada and the particular First Nations groups through a policy adopted bilaterally in 1973, the policy of Indian Control of Indian Education.

This is a history of culture contact and conflict, and on the part of Canada's dominant French and English speaking groups, racist attitudes and failed attempts to assimilate and control the Native population. The process of trying to control and assimilate the Native people began not with the development of Canada's provincial structure in the early 1800s but at least two hundred years prior to that when the early settlers from France and Britain first came to this country. The first contact between the groups brought the Native people diseases they had never encountered before: estimates are that 95% of the original population of aboriginal peoples in North America died out in the first 130 years after initial contact (Dobyns, 1983 as cited by Ennamorato, 1998, p. 95). An eighteenth-century governor general of British North America is quoted as having recommended deliberate infection "with sheets upon which smallpox patients had been lying, or any other means by which may serve to exterminate this accursed race" (Ennamorato, p. 96). Control (subjugation) of the Native population was accomplished by the nineteenth century by isolating Native children in residential schools, forcing a European curriculum on them, denying them their beliefs and language, and, eventually, severing them from close family relations (Barman, 1987; Cardinal, 1977). The influence of parents and knowledge of the community's language and customs was to be interrupted, replaced by "Christian" values and the learning of English or French. The last residential school was closed as recently as 1984 (Banasik, 2002; Royal Commission on Aboriginal Peoples, 1996).

When the early European settlers first encountered Native peoples, they observed an indigenous, non-formal, and oral system of education that was closely tied to the people's need for learning survival and subsistence skills. As Cardinal wrote, "The Indian method...

was designed to prepare the child for whatever way of life he was to lead—hunter, fisherman, warrior, chief, medicine man, or wife and mother... to become a functioning, contributing part of his society..." (Cardinal, 1977, p. 52). Although some of the Europeans settlers realized that the Indians and Inuit offered useful knowledge and skills for hunting, trapping, fishing, and survival in the woods and wide-open tundra, as the following quote indicates, the missionaries amongst the settlers were affronted by what they considered as sacrilegious rituals and behaviour; they sought to "save" the "natives" by converting them to Christianity.

> So long as the children are allowed to be running wild about the streets, and even joining the nightly yelling and dancing, of which there is very little cessation the year round—so long as they are not trained to any habits of order—it is not to be expected that they will make much progress in learning, which necessarily requires thought, application, and restraint—exercises to which they have never been trained.
>
> Missionary Register, 1828, pp. 284–285

The following excerpts from the writings of a member of the Mohawk community remind us that the obstacles to cultural renewal and autonomy persist to this day.

> I began my education by attending an Indian Day School run by the Department of Indian and Northern Affairs in Kanehsatake, a one-room schoolhouse, to grade three... All children were then bused twelve miles away to attend a provincial elementary school in St. Eustache and I still have the "history" book I was required to use in grade five, entitled "Pages from Canada's Story" (Dickie & Palk, 1951, first published in 1928)... The book contains a play for children to act out about an attack by Iroquois. While denigrating the Iroquois in racist terms the book also encourages the reader to "develop a worthy pride in his country's progress."
>
> David-Cree, 2004, p. 9

In 1990 an educator and member of the Mohawk community wrote

> There was a hunger to learn the language, culture and rich history of our [Mohawk] nation. With three children we demanded and obtained funding for an immersion Mohawk program. Lacking didactic materials, the teachers began with the ancient way of teaching... Walks in the woods and mountains with Elders to identify plant and animal life... Artists drew the first books that had the likenesses of the children... they saw themselves...

And 11 years later in 2001

> ... with about 40 children we moved into their new school amid the towering pines... a magnificent place for renewal.
>
> Anonymous, 1990

Although unrelated to the particular situation just cited, a 1998 Health Canada report suggests that those in power in Ottawa—that is, those who hold the purse strings on First Nations schooling—are not yet very willing to permit such autonomy. The tension between power and equality persists.

> The Aboriginal Head Start for on-reserve children, funded by the Federal Government... will strive to achieve excellence, while meeting or exceeding relevant, applicable, provincial and territorial child care and preschool standards... *until First Nations have developed their own standards and licensing regulations* [emphasis added] (Health Canada, 1998).

There are also many personal accounts of how difficult it is to be a good parent when one's parents and grandparents were not only removed from their families and thus deprived of good parenting themselves, but were denied their own languages and often physically abused as well (Banasik, 2002; Battiste & Barman, 1995; Barman, 1987; Cardinal, 1977; Jaenen & Conrad, 1993). When a group loses its ability through oppression to pass on its language and culture to the next generation, this is what is known as **cultural genocide.**

The efforts to destroy the First Nations' way of life through inappropriate residential schooling invariably failed; however, these efforts were successful in undermining the self-esteem and cultural identity of several generations of individuals (Cardinal, 1977). Cultures disintegrated, languages disappeared, and traditional ways of ensuring survival were replaced by guns and skidoos. Non-formal, oral ways of transmitting indigenous knowledge were taken over by a definition of knowledge that values only that which is written down in books.

The effects of this history are still seen today in many aboriginal communities, with high rates of alcoholism, suicide, and school dropout (Fletcher, 1999). The situation is improving rapidly, however. In 2000, at the start of the twenty-first century, about 28% of the aboriginal population living on reserves had less than a grade 9 education, compared to about 5% of the total population, and only 1% of non-reserve aboriginal peoples had a university degree, compared to about 11% of the total Canadian population. Six years later, in 2006, the high school completion rate for First Nations students living on-reserve was well over 40%. This represents an increase of over 10% in five years, while the increase in high school completion rate for the non-Native population during this period is about 7%. First Nations and Inuit participation in post-secondary education has also increased rapidly. From 1987 to 2001, the number of registered First Nations and Inuit students enrolled in post-secondary education funded by Indian and Northern Affairs Canada almost doubled from approximately 14 000 to about 26 000. Finally, the First Nations population (on- and off-reserve) with a post-secondary certificate, diploma, or degree increased from 20 to 23% from 1996 to 2001. The population of all Canadians with post-secondary qualifications increased from 35 to 38% (Statistics Canada, 1993; 1996; 2001).

In addition to the above rapid improvements in educational attainment for the First Nations population, the number of band (Indian)-operated schools, which are managed directly by First Nations, has increased 33% from 372 to 496 (2001 statistics). These schools use appropriate curricula, specially trained teachers (including more and more aboriginal teachers), aboriginal languages for instructional purposes wherever possible, and a school year adapted to the hunting and fishing economy. Yet gaps persist: while 80% of Indian and Northern Affairs-funded students in grade 1 attend First Nations schools, by grade 12, 55% of students are attending provincial schools.

Change is occurring in other ways as well. In at least one community (the Dene), indigenous environmental knowledge is being systematically tape recorded, indicating a preference to store knowledge orally, rather than "burying" it in books (Fletcher, 2005, personal communication). In addition, several universities have contributed to these developments by offering Native teacher education programs while others have included cultural knowledge in the courses for non-Native teachers. But training teachers, Native or non-Native, does not address two serious problems—the difficulties in deploying teachers to isolated communities and the frequency of teacher turnover in those communities. These are serious problems that undermine the quality of education for Native peoples as well as the morale of school staff (Banasik, 2002). Furthermore, well-trained Native teachers may find themselves among the more educated members of their communities and thus under pressure to take on leadership positions outside the field of education (Banasik, 2002, p. 65). As a result, their potential contributions to classroom teaching are lost. This loss is critical, since there is considerable evidence that Native teachers are often better able to interact in culturally familiar ways with Native students than non-Native teachers, with the result that their teaching is considered to be more effective (Mohatt & Erikson, 1981; Lipka, 1991; 2002; Stairs, 1991).

In the territory of Nunavut, there is also promise. Nunavut was formed in 1999 out of about two-thirds of the Northwest Territories. The majority of the people in the local government are Inuit, and they, along with some imaginative Inuit teachers, have had a major hand in the planning of the education system. Due to the increased number of Native teacher training programs at Canadian universities, there are now many native teachers in Nunavut primary schools. The number of native teachers at the community-based high schools is also beginning to rise. In Nunavut the general goal is to enhance Inuit culture and language through an adapted Alberta curriculum, with a strong science core that includes indigenous knowledge and perspectives. Since there are suddenly numerous new white-collar, administration, and construction jobs to support the new Nunavut government, there is now evident reason for young people to complete trade school or high school. In addition, the first venture into post-secondary education has begun with Arctic College in Iqaluit. Arctic College has agreements with several universities in the south to launch and staff a number of innovative programs, including a transitional, pre-college, pre-university bridging program and an executive Masters in Business Administration, offered by St. Mary's University in Halifax (Fletcher, 1999).

Today, we find amongst the First Nations communities different types of schools, such as Mohawk immersion schools, depending on the wishes of each particular community and its success in negotiating self-determination with the department of Indian and Northern affairs in Ottawa. In general, however, it can be said that the main current effort of the First Nations communities is to provide a culturally and linguistically relevant education, one that retrieves or revives ancient cultural values and ways of knowing while also providing the bridges to the world beyond each community that young people so often need to get along in today's world.

Despite these positive developments, for many First Nations groups schooling remains a mixed blessing. On the one hand, there are many shared, bitter memories; on the other hand, schooling is now seen as necessary to future survival. Most of the teachers are still non-Native and not fully able to compensate for culturally embedded differences in learning styles (Lipka, 1991; 2002; Stairs, 1991). The curricula and teaching materials are still not adequate for life in the North. Ways to establish comfortable bicultural competencies still need to be found, but the following quote does sum up the current trend.

> Our world is changing. Let us put our minds together. Take the best of both worlds and make a better life for our children.
>
> Medicine, 1995, p. 45

The Experience of Canada's French-Speaking Population

The history of education for Canada's French-speaking population is intimately tied to the history of the English-French language issue in Canada as a whole. Again, this is a history that cannot be told or understood fully without much more detail than space in this chapter allows. This is because language has been an issue in Canada since at least the early part of the nineteenth century. To this day the telling of history in English and French Canadian textbooks differs: for example, the fact is not always emphasized that French-speaking colonists preceded English-speaking colonists and had already established an agriculturally rooted way of life with its own traditions and religion by 1763, when the French territory was ceded to the British.

We mentioned earlier that Section 93 of the Constitution Act (BNA Act) of 1867 provided the basis for access to public education in the Protestant or Catholic religions. In the last 30 to 50 years this provision has been redefined in terms of language rights, now set out in Section 23 of the Canadian Charter of Rights and Freedoms of 1982. Section 23 gives parents who speak the minority official language of their province the right to have their children educated in that language "where numbers permit." The Canadian courts have thus been faced with several challenges to the different provincial definitions of the meaning of "where numbers permit." The courts have also yet to resolve to everyone's satisfaction the distinction between "entitlement" and the need for parents to "demand" and establish their case to have their children educated in the official minority language.

In Quebec, the focus of this section, the experience of the French-speaking population not only reflects a number of landmark legal decisions at the federal and provincial levels, but also the history of the changing role of the Roman Catholic Church in French Canadian society. This is a history about the contact and shifting power relations between the French- and English-speaking groups, and the identity, values, and goals of Quebec's French-speaking population as a '*nation*' (fr), with common roots, common ties to the land, a common religion, and a common language (Magnuson, 1980).

The late 1950s and the 1960s brought major social and political change to Quebec in a period of time that is referred to as The Quiet Revolution. The Quiet Revolution coincided with other changes—an increase in secularism along with a reduction in the role of the Roman Catholic Church in French Canadian society; an increased demand for higher education; the establishment of a public system of higher education, the *collège d'enseignement général et profesionnel* (CEGEP); and a lowering of the birth rate to less than the national average. Up until this time, the Catholic Church had considered educational matters as belonging to the family, not the state, and with the Church in control of schooling for the French-speaking population, this institution in effect replaced the State. State-supported schooling was viewed as an intrusion on Church matters. Moreover, until this time, the Quebec economy had been agriculturally based and impoverished, and families were very large. This caused the schooling of girls to lag far behind that of boys, since girls often left school early to help raise their many siblings. Thus family, schooling, and religious matters had been fused.

The Quiet Revolution also reflected an increased awareness in North America of the rights of minorities, women, and blacks, especially in the United States. Thus a new awareness of the integrity and the fragility of the French language and culture in Quebec in the face of the North American "sea of English" brought a number of proposals and legal efforts to reinforce the French language and culture in Quebec.

The changes just described came with a power shift in politics and business from the sociologically dominant English-speaking numerical minority to the French-speaking majority. In 1964 a secular ministry of education was established, officially ending the formal control of the Church in Quebec schooling. Several acts and bills were passed in the late 1960s and early 1970s, culminating in Bill 101 in 1977. Bill 101 established French as the sole language of instruction in Quebec with the exception of a small English system for children who had acquired historical rights to English education through a parent who had been educated in English in Canada. All others, including the non-English and non-French-speaking children of immigrants, were henceforth to attend French-medium schools. Thus began a topic of debate that remains alive and well in Quebec society at large as well as in university classrooms. Similarly, the fact that the story being told differs according to the linguistic vantage point of the teller is evidenced by continued public debate over the content of the new history and citizenship education course in Quebec secondary schools, as well as debate over the terms of 2002's Bill 104, which further restricts access to English-medium schools (Carroll, 2006).

Although the language laws of Quebec may be difficult for some readers to comprehend, as educational sociologists we would suggest that their apparent strangeness may lie in the tacit assumption that the position of the English-speaking majority of the country ought to prevail, despite the fact that education is under the control of the provinces and the majority language group in Quebec speaks French. When we consider that French, as spoken in North America, may be a language at risk of dying out, the measures of Bill 101 make sense. In addition, until the mid-1960s, the English-speaking people in Quebec, although only 20% of the province's population, were a sociological majority in terms of their power in the society, especially in the business sector. With the Quiet Revolution in the 1960s, there came a collective push on the part of many French-speaking people to be "masters of their own house" (*maîtres chez nous*). The result was the just-mentioned series of new language laws, the most important being the 1977 Bill 101.

Table 1-1 summarizes the key legal and policy proposals for educational reform. The reader will note an interplay between the federal and provincial proposals for reform, evidence of the ongoing tensions referred to earlier in this chapter, especially between uniformity and diversity, and power and equality.

In sum, the links between educational change over time and the social order have been viewed differently by members of the English-speaking and French-speaking communities in Canada. The emphases are different, as are the concerns and goals. For a straightforward narrative that describes Quebec's early educational laws, the reader is referred to Wilson, Stamp, and Audet's 1970 *Canadian Education: A History.* Elsewhere, you can find interesting documentation of convent education and the role of Roman Catholic nuns in the education of girls in Quebec. According to Danylewycz (1987), nuns not only idealized poverty and reinforced women's inferior status in society, but also, in apparent contradiction, played an important role in their communities by providing social services and even supporting feminists in their campaign for women's higher education in Quebec.

Finally, our readers are reminded that this section of the chapter has not dealt with the educational history of the many different minority/immigrant groups that have formed in Canada, especially since the end of World War II in 1945. The stories of these **voluntary minorities** will be found to differ markedly from those of **involuntary minorities**, both in Canada and elsewhere (Ogbu, 1991). Briefly, a voluntary minority group is one that has formed because the members of that group are assumed to have left their countries intentionally, in hope of a better life. Involuntary minority groups are those that have formed as a result of oppressive colonization. More information on this topic will be found in later chapters as well as through students' own independent research.

TABLE 1-1	Key Legal and Policy Proposals for Educational Reform	
Year	Commission/Reform	Purpose/Result
1963	Royal Commission on Bilingualism and Biculturalism (Federal)	Attempt to address rights of French-speaking minority across Canada and to defuse emerging unrest in Quebec
1964	Ministry of Education established (Provincial)	Catholic and Protestant committees reduced to advisory role
1966	Royal Commission of Inquiry on Education (Parent Commission) (Federal)	Critical of existing elitist education; overemphasis on literary studies at the expense of science
1967	CEGEP system established (Provincial)	Increased opportunity for post-secondary education and professional training
1973	Gendron Commission (Federal)	Recommended measures to encourage the use of French, especially in the economy
1974	Bill 22 – The Official Languages Act (Federal)	Declared Canada as officially bilingual: Federal services to be offered in French and in English in all provinces
1977	Bill 101- Response to Bill 22 seen as decreasing the role of the French language in Quebec (Provincial)	Established French as the sole official language in schooling, work and politics in Quebec: the language of instruction for all except for a small minority with historical rights to education in English
1982	Canadian Charter of Rights and Freedoms (Federal)	Section 23 provides access to public education in each province's minority language 'where numbers permit'
1988	Quebec Education Act (Provincial)	Specified who is allowed to attend French or English schools

THE CANADIAN EDUCATIONAL SYSTEM IN AN INTERNATIONAL CONTEXT

University students may not initially realize what is different about the Canadian educational system, or, alternatively, in what ways it is similar to other systems throughout the world. In this section we will try to paint a broad picture of how the Canadian system is located according to a number of factors that tend to vary from one educational system to another.

Educational systems vary worldwide in many ways, but some of the more obvious differences relate to structure, governance, goals, and historical influences (Thomas, 1990). Structure refers to the formal organization of schooling—the number of years allocated for primary and secondary education, the grade levels, and the specific learning goals to be reached by the end of each. Structure refers as well to the presence or absence of any formalized pre-school such as kindergarten, as well as the total minimum number of years that school attendance is compulsory. **Governance** refers to the way the education system is controlled and operated.

Structure and Governance

Canada's system of education is unique in terms of governance. At a national level it is highly **decentralized**, while within each of the provinces it is **centralized**. This means there are 10 systems of education in Canada, in addition to the three education systems in each of the territories (Northwest, Yukon, and Nunavut), which, until recently, were controlled by the federal department of Indian affairs. The territories now have their own equivalents to education ministries; however, funding of their school systems is still federal. Each of the ten provincial systems normally allocates six or seven years for primary schooling and five or six years for secondary schooling. Most elementary schools contain kindergartens, although these are not legally mandated, and attendance is not compulsory.

In Canada we have universal access to elementary and secondary schooling and require by law that young people remain in school until the age of 15 or 16 (about grade 9), depending on the province. This is not the case everywhere; there are many countries that do not yet provide universal access to elementary schooling and many countries that do not have laws requiring children to attend school; nevertheless, there is no lack of demand for formal schooling throughout the world. Parents everywhere want their children educated; however, when faced with economic constraints, they tend to educate their sons for longer than their daughters (Gordon, 1997; Lindsay, 1990; UNESCO, 2000; UNICEF, 1994).

Figures 1-1 and 1-2 outline the basic structure of the Canadian education system, showing that there is minor variation from one province to another. While the Canadian systems provide a similar secondary education for all—through grade 11 in Quebec and grade 12 in the other provinces—interesting differences in education structures may be observed in the systems of Japan, Russia, Germany, and France, for example (Thomas, 1990).

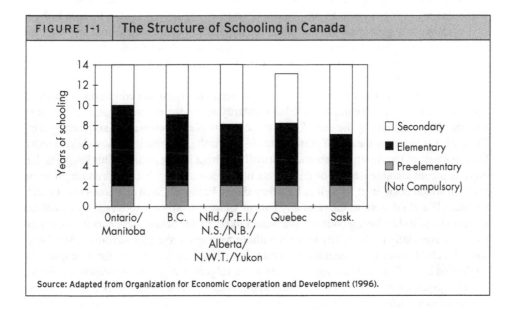

| FIGURE 1-1 | The Structure of Schooling in Canada |

Source: Adapted from Organization for Economic Cooperation and Development (1996).

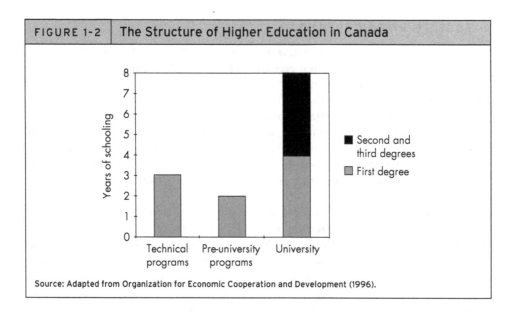

FIGURE 1-2   **The Structure of Higher Education in Canada**

Source: Adapted from Organization for Economic Cooperation and Development (1996).

Updated information about the education system in different countries is easily available through UNESCO, UNICEF and related websites on the internet.

Another factor that varies from one country to another is the length of the school year. Table 1-2 shows that the length of the school year varies from a reported 251 days in China to 172 days in Portugal, with Canada's average being 185 days. Recent cross-national studies of educational achievement do not suggest, however, that performance in mathematics or science, for example, is significantly related to the length of the school year (Orpwood & Garden, 1998). Other factors such as teaching strategies are more important.

Another way to compare education systems is to look at the length of the school day. While this factor varies considerably across Canada, as Figure 1–3 shows, there is little, if any, evidence to suggest that differences in the length of time spent in school are reflected in achievement. Again, it appears that achievement is more closely tied to the subtleties of *how* things are done in classrooms, rather than how much time is spent there (Stigler & Stevenson, 1988/89).

Although Canada has 13 different and legally separate systems of education (10 provincial, three territorial), there is a remarkable similarity across the country from one system to another. What is taught by the end of primary school in New Brunswick is sufficiently similar to what is taught by the end of primary school in British Columbia to allow a child to move from one part of the country to another, normally without losing ground. This suggests that there is a considerable degree of consensus in Canada about what children ought to be taught at which grade level, as well as how they should be taught. Such consensus is not cross-national. If a child were to move to any part of Canada from an impoverished education system in a still-developing country, she would likely be far behind her peers in some subjects, but especially in the ability to learn without relying on rote memorization. Similarly, should a child move to a Canadian province from Japan or Singapore, for example, she might find herself ahead of her age-mates in some subjects (Stigler & Stevenson, 1998/99).

The governance of different education systems can also be studied and compared. It is important to ask *who organizes* the system, *who controls it,* and *how it is controlled.* Where

TABLE 1-2	Length of School Year in Various Countries	
Country		**Days**
China		251
Israel		215
Switzerland		207
Italy		204
England		192
Canada (average)		185
United States		178
France		177
Portugal		172

Source: Adapted from international comparisons from a selected sample from National Center for Education Statistics, Washington, D.C., for 13-year-old students.

does Canada fit into the range here? While the majority of countries have highly centralized systems of education, there is still much variation, and the trend internationally is towards decentralization. The educational system in France is among the most highly centralized, while the system in the United States may be the most decentralized. Canada lies somewhere in the middle.

As we mentioned earlier in this chapter, under the terms of the British North America Act of 1867 (the Constitution Act), education falls under the control of the provinces and territories, not the federal government. While the Canadian federal government deals with issues relating to the equalization of funding for education between the provinces, all other

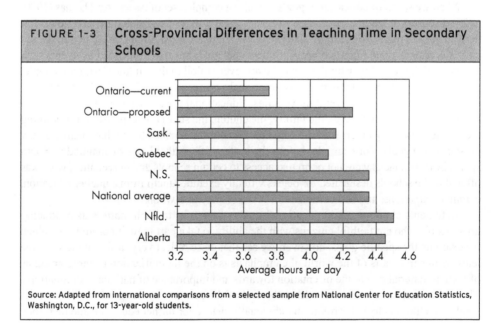

FIGURE 1-3 Cross-Provincial Differences in Teaching Time in Secondary Schools

Source: Adapted from international comparisons from a selected sample from National Center for Education Statistics, Washington, D.C., for 13-year-old students.

aspects are dealt with at the provincial/territorial level. Each province and territory has its own ministry of education, which oversees matters relating to the organization of school boards, parent involvement in school management, curriculum, examinations, teacher education, and teacher certification.

By contrast, in the United States, for example, the role of the federal government in education is being eroded by increasing pressure for local control, driven by an ideology that favours less government interference in the life of the family and the individual. Interestingly, this ideology coexists with a form of nationalism that places much emphasis in the schools on the establishment and perpetuation of national identity and loyalty. In Canada, the promotion of nationalism plays a less obvious—if not inconsequential—part in the schooling process.

Educational Goals

Most industrialized countries today have a national system of education that has been influenced historically by Europe, England, or the United States. In the late eighteenth and the nineteenth centuries, education was seen as a way to ensure politically friendly relations between different countries (i.e., to reduce the risk of war), especially as it was primarily reserved for the political elite. For national development purposes, the state controlled schooling. Control of educating the masses was thus taken away from local elites, from churches, and from families, with the capitalist class creating a system that would serve its need for compliant workers. It was only by the end of the nineteenth century that universal, public systems of education were established in the Western world, while attempts were made to introduce similar systems in the colonies of Africa, Asia, the Middle East, and Latin America. These attempts were more or less successful for the elite of those countries, but less so for the masses, mainly because of the nature of global economic and political relations, persistent poverty, and culturally irrelevant curricula (Thomas, 1990).

When we speak of **educational goals** we raise a complex set of issues. As Thomas (1990, p. 25) discusses at length, societies do not vary greatly in terms of stated general goals, but they do vary in regard to the more specific ones. These are most often closely tied to the society's economic conditions and needs. Educational goals are also influenced by events such as wars and the sequel to natural events; the discovery of oil in the Middle East, for example, led to a rapid expansion of the region's educational system, access to formal schooling for all, and the establishment of several universities. Educational goals vary depending on which institutions in the society (e.g., the family, the church, the state) are responsible for defining them. They also vary in terms of the way that decisions are made about which learners may pursue which goals. For example, before the system of apartheid was dismantled in South Africa in 1995, blacks were not permitted access to certain schools and universities; what was offered in the schools designated for blacks virtually excluded them from a quality education, certain occupations, and full participation in the society as a whole.

Statements about general educational goals often refer to such matters as producing good people who are faithful citizens with the ability to take part in their community. When we examine the specific goals, however, we see that these reflect very different views of the learner. In some parts of the world, the emphasis is on the memorization of large amounts of factual material due to the orientation towards and importance of national examinations. These examinations, normally held at the end of the primary cycle (grade 6, 7, or 8, depending on the country), determine an individual's chance for further education and therefore, his or her lifelong occupational opportunities. In other regions of the world, including most of the West, the emphasis is on teaching children how to learn, how to study, how to judge what they read, and so on.

Closer examination of these differences reveals that they may be related to the number of available spaces at the secondary or university level. When there is a shortage of spaces at the next level of schooling, we often find a national examination system, deemed to be fair and objective, that allows the system to select the number of students for whom there are spaces at the next level. It is important to note that the number of available spaces determines the cut-off point (the failure point) in examination results. The definition of failure has little to do with what the children have learned; it simply identifies the few who can be absorbed into the next level of the system.

One consequence of this situation is that there are huge numbers of people in some countries who must live with an artificially defined and externally imposed sense of failure. In the case of some African countries, where economic conditions created serious shortages of spaces at the secondary level and beyond, there was a need to select about one-third of primary school leavers, for whom there were available spaces at the secondary school level. For the remaining two-thirds, their education ended at the primary level. This situation persists in some countries, is worsening in others (such as Zimbabwe and Zambia), and is improving in South Africa. In Canada, we have no need for such an all-important examination system because there is no shortage of spaces at any level; however, as we shall see later, Canada is still far from providing the same educational opportunities for everyone. The discussion of a seemingly straightforward matter such as educational goals thus quickly raises a number of issues connecting an education system to economics, politics, and the dominant values of the society in which the system is rooted.

RESEARCH IN SOCIOLOGY OF EDUCATION

- Who carries out research in sociology of education?
- What questions are explored, how, and why?
- What are some of the unresolved issues of the field?
- Are there new questions arising with social and technological change?
- Are there new directions in research that could be or need to be taken?
- How are the results of studies analyzed and used?
- Who benefits from the research?

Sociologists of education are interested in exploring questions relating to several main issues. To do so, they draw from existing theory, align themselves with one or another of the ways of looking at social reality (paradigms), and decide on the most appropriate method or set of methods to explore the educational issue or problem. Some of the issues to be explored are located at the **macro** level, where society at large and education connect. For example, researchers want to know why it is that *inequality* in society is perpetuated through the process of schooling, and they want to know as precisely as possible what the mechanisms are for this occurrence. It is only with such understanding that solutions to the perpetuation of inequality, for example, can be proposed. In Canada, the distribution of educational opportunity and the quality of that opportunity from one region to another would be a starting point for a large and interesting study using survey methods. Related to this issue is the matter of the demographics of poverty in Canada. If number of years of schooling is related to upward mobility (and increased income), and if the number of years of schooling is rising in all regions, the research questions to be explored are: why does the regional distribution of poverty persist; what role does the educational process play in this?

Other issues that may be investigated are located **mid** level, at the level of the school and the social relations that occur within it (Martin, 1976). For example, one study was about the nature of the social relations between French- and English-speaking students in Canadian schools where both groups are found, and asked if these relations reflect the long-standing separation between the groups in society at large (Cleghorn & Genesee, 1984). A recent study centred on the development of national/linguistic/ethnic identity amongst students whose home language is neither English nor French ("allophones") who have been taught in French (post- Bill 101) in Quebec schools (Chwojka, 2006). Another such study was carried out on the experience of aboriginal students with the telling of their own history in the curriculum that they were exposed to (David-Cree, 2004).

Although most educational research that is carried out at the **micro** level tends to be psychological in nature, focusing on factors affecting learning in individual students, there is considerable scope for sociological research at this level too. For example, we might ask if teachers interact with and use speech differently with learners from different ethnic, racial, or social class backgrounds. Another set of questions that have in fact been explored relate to possible differences in discourse patterns in Native Canadian classrooms as contrasted with non-Native classrooms (Crago, Annahatak & Ningiuruvik, 1993; Lipka, 1991; 2002). When questions like these are explored using careful, systematic research methods, we add to what is known about the optimal psycho-social learning conditions for different kinds of students. This knowledge enables teacher educators to develop courses for future teachers that will inform them about the particulars of such conditions.

Further to what has just been said, research stands to contribute information about the ways that schools do or do not create equitable conditions for learning. In due course, through educational research we understand better how to maximize the opportunities in schools and classrooms for equality of access to education, equality of treatment within the school and classroom, *and* equality of results. We are not implying here that everyone has a right to the same results, simply that everyone has a right to be schooled in conditions that allow each student to reach his or her own potential.

What methods do educational sociologists use to explore the kinds of questions just mentioned? The answer to this depends on the nature of the problem being explored as well as the way that the researcher conceptualizes the nature of social reality. Stated differently, the researcher's view of social reality (personal theoretical perspective) underlies the ways in which educational problems are formulated as research questions; in turn this determines the methodological choices that the researcher is likely to make for exploring the problem. For example, if under-achievement in school is seen as located entirely within the individual, the causes of under-achievement will be researched very differently than if the problem is considered sociologically, in terms of patterns associated with such matters as social class, race, or ethnicity.

Theoretical and Methodological Perspectives in Educational Research

There are several theoretical perspectives that underlie educational research that is sociological in nature. In this section we briefly introduce you to three, as examples. By the time you have read Chapter 2 and the subsequent chapters of this book, you will understand much more fully that there are many different ways to look at and explore an educational issue or problem.

As indicated above, there are different ways of looking at social reality, or stated differently, different schools of thought. To oversimplify for the moment, educational problems or issues that are unresolved may be seen from a functional point of view. That is, educational problems may be seen as inevitable, or "normal." In this view of social reality, change occurs slowly and without serious disruption. Such a view is bound to affect the kinds of issues that are deemed in need of research. For instance, the underachievement of students belonging to certain racial or ethnic groups may be considered simply "the way things are," and subject to change "naturally" over time.

Alternatively, a researcher might see social reality as inherently unstable, in a perpetual state of conflict and disequilibrium. Then relations between different groups in the school may, for example, be looked at in terms of power. With this view the status quo (e.g., the perpetuation of conflict between different groups in the school), is seen as likely to persist unless there is a concerted effort to bring about change, even at the risk of social upheaval.[3]

In contrast to the quite divergent ways of looking at social reality discussed above, another group of researchers might hold to a view that emphasizes the need to study educational systems in terms of the meaning that events hold for those who participate in the process. This perspective is, therefore, interpretive and subjective. According to the **interpretive perspective**, change is seen as occurring through the actions of individuals, most often acting as members of groups. That is, change is seen as occurring from the grass-roots level rather than imposed from above. The researcher who holds to this perspective would need to explore, through group or individual interviews or through the use of a detailed, in-depth questionnaire, the meaning that different groups of students attach to the same events prior to working with those students to resolve conflicts between them.

While these and additional theories will be discussed in much more detail in Chapter 2, this brief thumbnail sketch lets the reader see that there are several ways of looking at the nature of educational problems and the processes and effects of schooling.

Just as social reality can be looked at from a number of perspectives, educational research can be conducted from one of two major, but divergent, methodological **paradigms** or stances. One is **quantitative**, the other **qualitative**. These two paradigms, which are, in fact, not opposites but mutually supporting, represent long-standing differences in research approaches.

---

[3]From a **functional perspective**, the societal structure may be compared to a living organism that is basically stable. Temporary stresses may move the society away from equilibrium, but this tends to be short term, with stability being returned to quite "naturally." According to this view, social mobility takes place within an established social structure or network of personal and institutional relations where people occupy different statuses and roles. The persistence of inequality, therefore, is considered functional for the society as a whole, though not for individuals. In contrast, from a **conflict perspective**, inequality is considered as dysfunctional for the society as a whole, and as something imposed by those in positions of power through institutional processes that may well be taken for granted by most people as simply the "way things are" (Mifflin & Mifflin, 1982). Functional and conflict theories are much more complex than this brief mention suggests. They will be discussed fully in the next chapter along with critical, feminist, anti-racist, and related theories.

The quantitative approach stems from the positivist tradition of the so-called pure sciences; the qualitative approach stems from the humanistic tradition of the social sciences.

When we identify a research problem, frame research questions, and decide how to carry out a study, we draw upon our way of seeing the world, our theoretical perspective. That is, we use a paradigm. Paradigms represent interconnected ideas or sets of assumptions about the phenomenon to be studied—for example, a set of assumptions about the nature of social reality, what constitutes a legitimate research problem, the purposes of research, the nature of truth, and the relationship between the researcher and the research participants (often referred to as subjects). Researchers sometimes disagree about the validity and reliability of the knowledge that is produced from each perspective. Researchers who adhere to the quantitative paradigm tend to rely for proof on statistical analysis of results, while qualitative researchers consider the subjective interpretations of events offered by both the research participants and the researcher as important, valid data.

Researchers who are quantitatively oriented tend to see the schooling process in terms of inputs and outputs (**independent** and **dependent variables**) that can be quantified. The reasons for variability in examination results, for example, can be determined through statistical analysis and manipulation of the input (independent) variables through **controlled experiments**. The number of hours of instruction, for example, might be correlated with test results in one classroom where the hours of instruction have been experimentally altered. The results would be compared to those of another class (the control group) where no change has been made. Such studies are concerned with correlation as well as with **cause and effect**.

Qualitatively oriented researchers tend to see the schooling process as laden with human values, heavily influenced by the interaction between home, school, and personal variables, and affected by the interplay between the various interpretations of schooling events. In the eyes of the qualitative researcher, to try to determine cause and effect through quantification is to reduce the social reality of schooling to a compilation of numbers. After looking at the differences between these two approaches (see Table 1-3 for a summary), we will look at how they can be integrated.

Since this book provides a sociological perspective on educational issues rather than a psychological perspective, our research bias lies towards the qualitative approach. For this reason we will elaborate now on the fact that the term "qualitative" is actually used as an umbrella word for several different methodologies, depending on the focus of a study's concern, such as language, the discovery of regularities (patterns), the meaning of events, or reflection. Here we will briefly discuss **ethnography**, since it is one of the more frequently encountered methods used in qualitative sociological research in education.

Ethnography

Ethnography is a type of qualitative methodology that uses a cultural lens to explore and understand the patterns of schooling. Stemming from the tradition of anthropology, ethnographic research normally takes many months to carry out, since the researcher usually takes on the role of a participant in the setting being studied in order to understand events from the perspective of the participants. The focus in this kind of study is on what people actually do and say; over time the patterns are identified and then described in writing, interpreted tentatively at first and then with greater assurance as the particular "culture" of the setting becomes clear (Glesne, 1999).

TABLE 1-3	Comparison of Quantitative and Qualitative Research Perspectives	
Quantitative		Qualitative

Quantitative	Qualitative
• assumes social reality is stable	• assumes social reality is dynamic
• seeks facts or causes	• seeks understanding of human behaviour
• is outcome oriented	• is process oriented
• considers viewpoints of subjects irrelevant	• believes viewpoints of subject are relevant
• has results that are de-contextualized; a representative sample of the population is studied	• has results that are context bound (holistic); sample is not necessarily representative of the population
• is objective, the researcher is removed from the data	• is subjective, the researcher is involved and close to the data
• is experimental or quasi-experimental	• is exploratory, descriptive
• uses obtrusive, controlled methods of data collection	• uses naturalistic, unobtrusive methods of data collection
• uses survery techniques with structured (close ended) questions	• uses interviews and open-ended questions
• is deductive: tests hypotheses and makes inferences from data	• is inductive: raises hypotheses for further inquiry
• uses statistical analysis; results are reliable, valid, and can be generalized	• uses many sources of data; totality of situation is reconstructed from perspective of the subjects; findings are particular, cannot be generalized
• uses theory testing	• validity comes from richness and depth of data
	• uses theory building

Source: Adapted from Bogdon & Biklan (1992).

Critical ethnography focuses on how the knowledge that is disseminated in schools is not only political but also representative of the dominant culture of the society and thus powerful in its effect on the experience and lives of minorities and marginalized groups. Critical ethnographers take the position that it is not enough to describe the cultural patterns they observe; rather, their aim is to identify ways the education system can or should be changed in order to bring about more equitable learning conditions. Critical ethnographers are thus informed by the conflict theorists (Carspecken & Walford, 2001).

Mixed-Method Approach

Although many sociological studies in education conform either to a quantitative or a qualitative paradigm, we believe that the most suitable approach to most problems and issues in education is one that combines the two, the **mixed-method** approach, although this strategy may be time consuming and costly (Anderson, 2000). Ideally, the researcher should begin a study with a *tentative* or general set of questions, hunches, or hypotheses about an issue, based on existing knowledge and theory that may, for example, have been generated by surveys. Presuming, for purposes of illustration, that the problem being explored has something to do with what goes on in classrooms, the researcher would then spend several weeks or months carrying out classroom observations to obtain a better understanding of the complexity of the issue. At first, the observations would be broad in scope, and would slowly become more focused and systematic as the researcher gained familiarity with the setting. The researcher would then analyze the observational data for consistent patterns and raise specific hypotheses for focused study. At some point, he or she would raise highly specific hypotheses that would suggest the need for a controlled or experimental study, and the ensuing data would be analyzed statistically. The results would then be interpreted according to statistical conventions *and* in light of the subjective observational data. At this point, it would be appropriate to return to the classroom for further observation, and, possibly, for discussions of the results with the teachers and students. Their views of the situation being studied would then be incorporated into the final interpretation and theory-building stage of the study.

Several theoretical perspectives and their relationship to the kinds of questions that educational researchers ask have been mentioned briefly in the above section of this chapter. In the following chapter, these and other theories and their origins will be discussed in detail so that the reader can more fully understand the prevailing ideas about schooling and society.

SUMMARY/CONCLUSIONS

In sum, the scope of the field of sociology of education is broad. Sociologists of education are concerned with multifaceted issues that may be broken down into a multitude of interrelated parts. We are able to understand the issues and devise solutions to persistent educational problems, both locally and abroad, due to the large amount of research that has been conducted and continues to be conducted in this field.

This chapter has provided the reader with the formal terms and vocabulary that will be needed to discuss and write about topics in sociology of education. We have tried to stay away from jargon and indicate as clearly as possible that some of the terms may have two sets of meaning—an everyday meaning and a more abstract sociological one. We hope that these terms will become useful tools for expressing complex ideas, both inside and outside the university setting.

In this chapter we have also introduced the student to a sociological view of the history of schooling in Canada for a few of its different groups. This is by no means exhaustive. We invite the reader to explore the topic in more detail with regard to Canada's well-established multicultural population and the schooling experiences of students who are more recent arrivals—from the Middle East and Asia, for example.

Although the section on research is brief, it is intended to be comprehensive enough for students to grasp the main idea that there are different ways of looking at and exploring issues and problems in education. An understanding of the different research perspectives is necessary to identify the various components of an education problem and then explore it in detail.

KEY TERMS

aboriginal	centralized system	cultural genocide
acculturation	conflict perspective	cultural production
achieved status	controlled experiments	culture
ascribed status	critical ethnography	culture contact
cause and effect	cultural diffusion	custodial function

decentralized system
dependent variable
diversity
division of labour
dominant group
educational goals
equality of educational
    opportunity
ethnography
First Nations
formal education
functional perspective
functionally literate
governance
ideology

in loco parentis
independent variables
informal education
intended functions
interpretive perspective
involuntary minority
legitimating ideology
    (legitimation)
macro, mid, and micro
    levels of analysis
meritocracy
mixed-method research
    approach
Native peoples
non-formal education

paradigm
qualitative paradigm
quantitative paradigm
selection and allocation
    function
social class
social context
social control
social mobility
social process
social stratification
social structure
unintended functions
voluntary minority

EDUCATIONAL ISSUES AND QUESTIONS FOR DISCUSSION

1. What does this chapter tell you that you did not know before about the educational system that you went through?

2. Using some of the terms from this chapter, explain to a friend or the other members of a class group what you think was unique about your own schooling experience.

3. Select an educational problem that is sociological in nature. List all the aspects of the problem that you can think of. Suggest a feasible plan to explore the problem.

4. The history of Canadian education may be told from the perspective of Canada's different ethnic and language groups. Select a minority/immigrant group that you are familiar with and explore the educational experience over the last 10 to 30 years from that group's perspective.

5. What ways could be devised to ensure that all Canadian children have equal access to educational opportunity, regardless of geographical isolation or the economic status of their community?

RECOMMENDED READINGS/REFERENCES

Anderson, G. (2000). *Fundamentals of educational research*. New York: Falmer Press.

Apple, M. W., & Christian-Smith, L. K. (Eds.). (1991). *The politics of the textbook*. New York: Routledge.

Aronowitz, S., & Giroux, H. (1993). *Education still under siege*. New York: Bergin & Garvey.

Banasik, B. (2002). *Teacher turnover in isolated Native communities: A qualitative reflection*. Unpublished masters thesis, Department of Education, Concordia University, Montreal.

Barman, J. (1987). *Indian education in Canada*. Vancouver: University of British Columbia Press.

Battiste, M., & Barman, J. (Eds.). (1995). *First Nations education in Canada: The circle unfolds*. Vancouver: UBC press.

Bogdon, R. A., & Biklan, S. (1992). *Qualitative research for education: An introduction to theory and methods.* Boston: Allyn and Bacon.

Bowles, S., & Gintis, H. (1976). *Schooling in capitalist America.* New York: Basic Books.

Cardinal, H. (1977). *The rebirth of Canada's indians.* Edmonton: Hurtig.

Carroll, A. (2006, June 7.) Families take on Bill 101 schooling restrictions. *Montreal Gazette*, p. A8.

Carspecken, P., & Walford, G. (2001). (Eds.). *Critical ethnography and education.* Oxford, U.K.: Elsevier.

Chwojka, C. (2006). *Shades of identity: Constructing identities in a multicultural Quebec public school.* Unpublished masters thesis, Concordia University, Montreal.

Cleghorn, A., & Genesee, F. (1984). Languages in contact: An ethnographic study of interaction in an immersion school. *TESOL Quarterly, 18*(4), 595–625.

Crago, M., Annahatak, B., & Ningiuruvik, L. (1993). Changing patterns of language socialization in Inuit homes. *Anthropology and Education Quarterly, 24*(3), 205–223.

Danylewycz, M. (1987). *Taking the veil: An alternative to marriage, motherhood, and spinsterhood in Quebec, 1840–1920.* Toronto: McClelland and Stewart.

David-Cree (Katsitsenhawe), L. (2004). *Would you like to hear a story? Mohawk youth narratives on the role of the history of Quebec and Canada on indigenous identity and marginality.* Unpublished masters thesis, Concordia University, Montreal.

Dei, G. (1996). Black/African-Canadian students' perspectives on school racism. In M. I. Alladin (Ed.), *Racism in Canadian schools* (pp. 42–57). Toronto: Harcourt Brace.

Dickie, D. J., & Palk, H. (1951). *Pages from Canada's story.* Toronto: Dent & Sons.

Dickinson, G. (1995). The legal dimensions of teachers' duties and authority. In R.Ghosh & D. Ray (Eds.), *Social change and education in Canada* (2nd ed., pp. 254–278). Toronto: Harcourt Brace.

Dobyns, H.F. (1983). *Their number become thinned: Native American population dynamics in eastern North America.* Knoxville, TN.: University of Tennessee Press.

Ennamorato, J. (1998). *Sing the brave song.* Schomberg, ON: Raven Press.

Fletcher, C. (1999). Nunavut EMBA information package. Halifax: Department of Anthropology, St. Mary's University.

Glesne, C. (1999). *Becoming qualitative researchers: An introduction.* New York: Longman.

Gordon, R. (1997). Structural adjustment and women in Zimbabwe: Effects and prospects. *Canadian Journal of Development Studies, XVIII*(2), 263–278.

Government of Canada. (1867). The British North America Act. Retrieved from: laws.justice.gc.ca/en/const/index.html

Government of Canada. (1982). The Constitution Act. Retrieved from: www.laws.justice.gc.ca/en/const/index.html

Health Canada. (1998). Ottawa: Government publications. Retrieved from: www.justice.gc.ca/en/ps/fm/childafs.html

Jaenen, C., & Conrad, M. (1993). *History of the Canadian peoples.* Mississauga, ON: Copp, Clark, Pitman.

Levin, B., & Young, J. (1994). *Understanding Canadian schools.* Toronto: Harcourt Brace.

Lindsay, B. (1990). Educational equity in cross-national settings. In M. Thomas (Ed.), *International comparative education: Practices, issues, and prospects* (pp. 197–226). New York: Pergamon.

Lipka, J. (1991). Toward a culturally based pedagogy: A case study of one Yup'ik Eskimo teacher. *Anthropology and Education Quarterly, 22,* 203–223.

Lipka, J. (2002). Schooling for self-determination: Research on the effects of including Native language and culture in the schools. (Report No. EDO-RC-01-12). Indian EduResearch.Net, ERIC Digest, Special Edition.

Magnuson, R. (1980). *A brief history of Quebec education.* Montreal: Harvest House.

Martin, W. B. W. (1976). *The negotiated order of the school.* Toronto: MacMillan.

Medicine, B. (1995). A prologue to a vision of Native education. *Canadian Journal of Native Ediucation 21, supplement,* 42–45.

Mifflen, F. J., & Mifflen, S. C. (1982). *The sociology of education: Canada and beyond.* Calgary: Detselig.

Missionary Register. (June, 1828). A periodical published by the Church Missionary Society, 284–85.

Mohatt, G. V., & Erickson, F. (1981). Cultural differences in teaching styles in an Odawa school. In H.T. Trueba, G.P. Guthrie, and K. Au (Eds.). *Culture and the bilingual classroom: Studies in class-room ethnography* (pp. 105–119). Rowley, MA.: Newbury House.

National Center for Education Statistics, Washington, D.C., 1994.

Norris, S. P., & Phillips, L. M. (1990). *Foundations of literacy policy in Canada.* Calgary: Detselig.

Nunn, E. J, & Boyatzis, C. J. (1998/99). *Child growth and development.* Guilford, CN: McGraw-Hill.

Ogbu, J. U. (1991). Low school performance as an adaptation: The case of Blacks in Stockton, California. In M. A. Gibson & J. U. Ogbu (Eds.), *Minority status and schooling* (pp. 249–286). New York: Garland Publishing.

Organization for Economic Cooperation and Development. (1996). *Education at a glance: OECD Indicators.* Paris: OECD.

Orpwood, G., & Garden, R. A. (Eds.). Assessing mathematics and science literacy. *TIMMS Monograph Series No.4.* Vancouver: Pacific Educational Press.

Porter, J. (1965). *The vertical mosaic.* Toronto: University of Toronto Press.

Royal Commission on Aboriginal Peoples. (1996). Ottawa. Retrieved from: www.inac.gc.ca/ ch/rcap/index e.html

Slavin, R. E. (1991). *Educational psychology: Theory into practice.* Englewood Cliffs, NJ: Prentice Hall.

Stairs, A. (1991). Learning processes and teaching roles in native education: Cultural base and cultural brokerage. *Canadian Modern Language Review, 47(2),* 280–294.

Statistics Canada. (1993). *Aboriginal data.* Document 94-327. Ottawa: Statistics Canada.

Statistics Canada. (1996 & 2001). Retrived from http://www.ainc-inac.gc.ca/nr/prs/ s-d2004/02527bbk_e.html

Stigler, J. W., & Stevenson, H. W. (1998/99). How Asian teachers polish each lesson to perfection. In E. J. Nunn & C. J. Boyatzis (Eds.), *Child growth and development* (pp. 90–101). Guilford, CN: McGraw-Hill.

Thomas, R. M. (Ed.). (1990). *International comparative education: Practices, issues and prospects.* New York: Pergamon.

UNESCO (2000). *Education for all.* Dakar, Senegal.

UNICEF. (1994). *Children and women in Zimbabwe: A situation analysis.* Harare, Zimbabwe.

Werner, W. (1987). Curriculum and socialization. In R. Ghosh & D. Ray (Eds.), *Social change and education in Canada* (pp. 91–101). Toronto: Harcourt Brace.

Wilson, J. D., Stamp, R. M., & Audet, L.-P. (Eds.). (1970). *Canadian education: A history.* Scarborough, ON: Prentice-Hall.

Theories of Schooling and Society

CHAPTER OBJECTIVES

The intent of this chapter is to

• provide an overview of dominant theorists in sociology and briefly summarize the most important perspectives (theories or paradigms) sociologists of education use to explain the relationship between school and society

• draw on these theories to explain various aspects of the schooling process in later chapters

• critique each approach presenting its limitations

WHAT IS THEORY?

Theories are statements about how certain social phenomena are connected or interrelated. Essentially, the purpose of theory in sociology of education is to explain the relationship between school and society. This includes explaining how sets of assumptions and concepts form a view of the schooling process. When we write about the theories of schooling and society, we are referring to the origins of the sociology of education as a field of study. Like most fields of study, sociology of education goes through various stages, embracing theories and then discarding them for new ones as time goes on. Theorists then return to a theory only to understand or show how the theory reflected the thinking of that point in time. Thus, it is important to keep in mind that the process of explaining the relationship between school and society is not static—it is ever changing.

ORIGINS OF PRESENT-DAY THOUGHT IN SOCIOLOGY OF EDUCATION

Present-day thought in sociology of education has been informed by the writings of mid- to late nineteenth-century sociologists and social philosophers. The works of classical sociologists and social philosophers such as Karl Marx, Max Weber, Emile Durkheim, and George Herbert Mead are the most important in understanding schooling and its relationships to other social and economic forces in modern life. Although none of these founding "fathers" of sociology wrote extensively about education, they are important because their political ideologies influenced the development of sociology of education in Europe, and later, in Canada and the United States.

Karl Marx

Karl Marx's (1818–1883) political ideas have shaped history in many ways and persist in doing so. Born near the border between Germany and France, Marx was the son of a Jewish lawyer who converted to Christianity to avoid persecution. In Germany, Marx studied philosophy and German; later, in Paris and Brussels, he studied economics.

Deeply affected by the living conditions of workers in Europe, Marx sought to explain capitalism theoretically and to fight it politically. He wrote important works in London, where he moved to escape hostility due to his political views and activities. Marx believed that the economic organization of a society is central to its class structure, institutions, cultural values, and beliefs. At the core of his theory is the belief that the economic base of a society, that is, the mode of production, determines the "social, political and spiritual processes of life." More specifically, he argues that the way people earn their living profoundly affects how they think, how they relate to others, and, most significantly, to the structure of society and culture. This has come to be known as economic determinism.

For Marx, **socialism** (ownership by workers of their society's factories, land, and other productive assets) would follow **capitalism** (private ownership of the means of production) as the final stage in the evolution of history and politics. This change would occur only after a social revolution. The importance of Marx's thought to the field of education can be seen in present-day theories relating to the question of power and how those who are in important positions in economic and political institutions control the structure of the educational system. For example, in Canada it is the ministry of education of each province that controls the curriculum in elementary and secondary schools, while both provincial and federal governments allocate funding to the schools.

Max Weber

Max Weber (1864–1920) was born in Germany, the son of a wealthy German politician. Weber wrote on many subjects—religion, economics, politics, authority, bureaucracy, class and caste, and the city. Like Marx, he was interested in explaining the rise of capitalism; however, unlike Marx, he believed that systems of ideas, including religions, influence economic behaviour, not the reverse. He also believed that understanding people's actions through the meanings of their own and others' behaviour must be of primary concern for the sociologist. Weber's primary objective was to discover a causal explanation for social action. Questions he posed were derived from broad situations, such as the historical interplay of Protestantism and capitalism. He analyzed historical and comparative data to show that religious or cultural ideas are not only the result of, or solely dependent upon, economic factors. Weber maintained that although materialistic factors played an important role in the rise of capitalism, the ideas and belief systems that make capitalism possible should also be considered. That is, we must consider the "spirit" of capitalism, generated from values of hard work, thrift, and the willingness to use profits for new investments and expansion. Weber argued that Puritan Protestant sects, (the Protestant ethics of Calvinism) are an excellent example of "spirit." His data demonstrates that modern capitalism emerged where these beliefs and ideals were present.

Weber's analysis proceeded from the construction of theoretical **ideal types**, which he used to interpret historical events and actions and create causal explanations. For example, he studied complex formal organizations or bureaucracies in terms of ideal types that are founded on the characteristic institutions in the basic organizations of the society. Another of Weber's major contributions is his analysis of **status groups**. Status group is a term used to describe people who share a social identity based on similar values and lifestyles. For instance, members of the same status group may belong to the same social clubs and participate in similar social activities. We will see later on how theorists use this concept to explain inequality in educational opportunity.

Emile Durkheim

Emile Durkheim (1858–1917) focused his studies on **social order** and used statistics and empirical methods to explain the forces that he believed made social events regular and predictable. Born in Eastern France, Durkheim was the son of a rabbi. His major contribution to social theory was his analysis of social integration, social control, ritual and the moral base underlying society, all of which he said make social order possible. For instance, Durkheim saw schools as key institutions that provide moral unity through forging a sense of nationhood and a commitment to common values and beliefs, creating cohesion or social integration.

Durkheim was interested in the societal mechanisms that account for the maintenance of social order as well as in the deviant aspects of that order. For instance, he focused on what he perceived as the societal causes of suicide, (looking at patterns of suicide among different social classes and groups). He was one of the first to note that personal difficulties, such as depression and school failure can be linked to economic conditions and other societal processes. Durkheim's work has thus helped us to understand how larger (macro) societal processes affect individual learners through school and classroom processes.

In contrast to the social, economic, and political concerns of the European sociologists, North American philosophers and social theorists in the 1920s were beginning to analyze the nature of social reality from the perspective of the individual, the individual being a member of a group, and groups being the constituents of a society.

The Chicago School

In the 1920s, sociologists at the University of Chicago (also known as the Chicago School of Sociology) developed the new perspectives of **symbolic interactionism** and

interpretive phenomenological theory. These sociologists were primarily concerned with the role of perception in the nature of self and social interaction. Among the most prominent in this school of thought were Charles Horton Cooley, W.I. Thomas, and George Herbert Mead.

Charles H. Cooley's (1864–1929) theory of the origin of the self centred on the *looking glass effect*. By way of the looking glass metaphor, Cooley illustrated that individuals, through interaction with parents, peers, and teachers, come to see themselves as they imagine others see them. W.I. Thomas (1863–1945) presented us with the concept of the **definition of the situation**, suggesting that if we define a situation as real, then it becomes real in its consequences. George Herbert Mead (1863–1931) incorporated Cooley's and Thomas' insights but went on to state that self-development and self-awareness require the capacity to use language and to interact symbolically. Symbolic interaction involves individuals responding to objects, situations, and events according to the meanings that these have for them. Mead argued that to interact with others the individual must *take on the role of the other,* that is, to imagine how this other views him or her and to know what this other expects. Mead believed that individuals act and react to one another according to these mental interpretations.

Mead's concept of self includes the me, that is, a part of the self that represents internalized societal attitudes and expectations. The self also contains a unique and emancipated part of the self that produces spontaneity and individuality. These societal and individual aspects of the self collaborate to form an interactive quality he called interactionist. Chicago school theorists will be discussed further in the section on socialization in Chapter 5.

In their search for basic knowledge about schooling and their desire to explain the common assumptions about what schools actually do, various sociologists drew on many of the concepts put forth by the ground-breaking figures presented above. The following section describes the different sociological perspectives that were developed to explain the educational process.

THEORIES OF SCHOOLING AND SOCIETY

Functionalist Theories

Social and historical context is most important to a clear understanding of the various theories in the discipline of sociology and sociology of education in particular. The functionalist perspective was one of the first theories that arose to explain the salient features of a developing industrial society. The 1950s brought immense technological advances in North America, a large influx of immigrants, and a population movement from rural to urban areas. A concern with social order and maintaining **social equilibrium**, ideas grounded in Durkheim's work on social integration and the moral basis of society, became of primary importance.

In the United States in the 1950s the general thinking was that organized, formal schooling would lead to an individual's success in life. We must bear in mind the time, period, and place we are talking about—not Europe during the aftermath of World War II but America, where the post-war boom is well underway. Functionalists theorists viewed dramatic changes due to the industrial revolution as also affecting the occupational structure. From this perspective, the expansion of higher education was important to ensure a literate society that could fill occupational job requirements. This expansion, seen as necessary for the maintenance of social order, was linked to a deep-seated commitment to capitalism.

The functionalist view, then, became a source of explanation and justification for the role of schools in maintaining the organization of society in what was perceived as equilibrium. The role of the school was to teach the necessary skills and norms for the individual to participate in society by sorting, selecting, and training people for jobs at each level.

Functionalist theorists' primary concern was not with inequality in educational opportunity. They turned to Davis and Moore (1945) to explain why this condition is necessary to maintain a stable social order. Davis and Moore compared society to a human organism that consists of many parts. For instance, just as our heart functions for a specific purpose, as do our liver and lungs, so too do the social institutions (educational, religious, political, and familial) serve to make up the organism of society, working together to keep society functioning to maintain itself. Thus these major institutions must work together to maintain social equilibrium. The following is a brief summary of the basic principles Davis and Moore put forward.

- Society is a system consisting of various parts, which together contribute to a balanced social order.
- For a society to remain balanced, the most important positions must be filled by the most qualified, talented people. The number of people with the talent and/or training to fill these roles is limited.
- Thus, society allocates more rewards to those who fill the most important positions that require scarce talent and sacrifice.
- Societies fill the most crucial positions with the most skilled people, thus establishing a system of inequality.
- A degree of inequality is not only inevitable but contributes positively to the functioning of societies.

This functional perspective is perhaps most clearly reflected in the works of Talcott Parsons (1967), James Coleman (1968), and Robert Dreeben (1968). They viewed the classroom as a social system that socializes and allocates individuals on the basis of the criteria, beliefs, and values accepted by the dominant group in society. The school's function was seen as dictated by and central to the economic and occupational structure of a developing modern industrial society. The theorists were concerned with how differentiation of status (social class) occurs on the basis of achievement. They saw the assignment of differential rewards to various positions in the status hierarchy as a necessary technique to motivate talented individuals to achieve high-status positions. From this perspective, education offers greater opportunities for attaining higher social status to those who can master the system.

To summarize, functionalists argue that schools socialize individuals by teaching norms, values, and skills so they can function in society. That is, schools must prepare individuals to meet the needs of the occupational structure. Functionalists are concerned with social stability and do not address the need for social change; they ignore the social class origin of individuals and its effect on school achievement. This then leads to certain questions. Does the educational system serve the democratic and technocratic needs of industrialized society? Does higher education increase equality of opportunity?

Some Canadian Functionalist Sources

The most important work that reflects the functionalist perspective in Canadian educational research is that of Pierre Belanger and Guy Rocher (1975). Their analyses are based on the political situation in Quebec during the 1970s. They were concerned with developing a general theoretical framework for a sociology of education that would explain the educational and cultural revolution in that province. In the early 1960s the role of the Roman Catholic Church in society and in education began to decline, while nationalism among French-speaking Quebecois began to increase. Political tensions rose between French- and English-speaking groups.

Murphy (1979) notes that Belanger and Rocher turned to a systems model of social action based on the works of Talcott Parsons to explain the relationship between school and society. They viewed society as a complex organism that can be analytically divided into separate institutional structures such as the family and education, and into socio-economic, political, and religious divisions. To maintain a state of equilibrium, change in one of these institutions would inevitably create change in the others. For Belanger and Rocher, education was one form of social action; education could transmit symbols, values, and rules of behaviour necessary to the maintenance of a stable social order.

Belanger and Rocher's concept of social action consisted of four systems that were both separate and interconnected. These were the biological, the personality-based, the social, and the cultural systems. Each had its functions (needs or prerequisites of interconnected institutions) that were essential for the system to exist. The school system can be analyzed by these functions. The school is a subsystem of the larger society in relation to other subsystems, such as the economy and political structure.

These are the most basic aspects of Belanger and Rocher's general theory, which they proposed for a sociology of education. Their work contains rich analyses and we urge students to read their writings (please see references at the end of the chapter).

John Porter (1965) is another Canadian sociologist whose work reflects the functionalist perspective. Some argue that his major work, *The Vertical Mosaic*, points to the functionalists' concerns because he, like functionalists, views society as an organism consisting of interrelated subsystems. Unlike most functionalists, however, Porter highlights the importance of power. He points to the tension that exists between the meritocratic and technocratic features of society, tensions which lead to a power struggle among the dominant groups. For Porter, educational institutions exist to meet the needs of technological change and occupational requirements of society. However, he emphasizes how the dominant power groups or the elite who control wealth, power, and prestige monopolize and manipulate higher education.

Wallace Clement (1975) replicates Porter's work on elites and discusses how these groups maintain power through elite education—that is, by teaching the values and beliefs of those who are in power. His primary concern is to show how private schools and elite universities socialize the elite and restrict others through the promotion of dominant class values and beliefs (Mifflen & Mifflen, 1982, p. 73).

Conflict Theory and Neo-Marxist Theory

In the 1970s a controversial debate developed about talent/intelligence and school achievement on the one hand and the relationship between schooling and an individual's future status on the other. Conflict theorists argue against the basic assumptions of the functionalists. Collins (1971), for example, notes that society is not in a balanced state; rather, competition and the struggle between groups for power, wealth, and prestige is the more common situation. According to conflict theorists, functionalists support the status quo by stating that society is fine the way it is. Thus, **conflict theory** is grounded in the assumption that whenever one group gains, another one loses. The question is: who dominates whom?

Collins refutes the functionalists' notion that job skill requirements have increased due to technological advances and that formal education provides the training necessary for upgrading job skills. He states that the main contribution of education to economic productivity occurs at the level of transition to mass literacy; better educated individuals are not necessarily more productive, and furthermore, most skilled manual labourers learn on the job. Collins turns to Weber's concept of status and suggests that schools teach **status culture**, a particular lifestyle of language, dress code, peer association, and interests, that is deemed desirable by the dominant group in society. Students who learn this status culture will be more successful in achieving a higher social status. Collins notes that there are also distinctions among status culture groups based on ethnicity and class. These groups struggle for wealth, power, and prestige. Schools are controlled by powerful groups that provide near-exclusive education for high-status culture groups, and consequently, education becomes a means of cultural selection. Collins notes that a conflict theory of education must focus on two things—the struggle between status culture groups and the way status culture is learned in school.

Pierre Bourdieu (1977), whose work is referred to as the cultural and social reproduction theory, adds another dimension to status culture. He views education as a significant social and political force in reproducing the class structure of society. Bourdieu argues that the language and texts used in schools reflect the interests, values, and tastes of the dominant power groups. Thus he creates a link between class, power, and education. The children of the elite acquire style, tastes, and language through "inheritance"; these higher-status groups transform their **cultural capital** into academic capital. Because children from the lower class do not possess the cultural traits of the elites (they have different linguistic skills than those prescribed by the school, for example) it appears "natural" to sort them into lower streams that offer a different or less demanding curriculum. This streaming has led to the establishment of two different school systems, public and private, distinguished by the type of ability demanded of their students. Bourdieu (1986) explains that acquiring cultural capital in the form of educational (or academic) capital depends on families that possess strong cultural capital transmitting cultural rewards to their children. Thus cultural capital is a key mechanism in the reproduction of the dominant culture through which educational and social inequalities are perpetuated. Bourdieu notes a second form of capital, *social capital,* which is "the aggregate of the actual or potential resources which are linked to possession of . . . institutionalized relationships of mutual acquaintance and recognition" (1986, p. 248). Social capital consists of "connections" that determine the effectiveness of the individual's use of his or her cultural capital.

Basil Bernstein (1973) argues that the explanation of social class differentials in educational achievement lies in the role of language in the primary socialization process. For Bernstein, social class has a great influence on this process. His study of the British working class and middle class indicates that different forms and techniques of socialization effect educational achievement. He notes that in early socialization working-class children's forms of speech (vocabulary, grammatical content) are typified by a "restricted code." For example, when the working-class mother controls her child, she places less emphasis on language and deals with the immediate action in a particular context, rather than relating that action verbally either to general principles or to the consequences of that action.

On the other hand, children of higher status groups are socialized into the "elaborated code," giving them access to knowledge through general principles that orient them towards universalistic orders of meaning. Since the schools operate within the "elaborated code," children from higher social classes have an advantage. Thus Bernstein conceives the working-class child as deprived of something (the "elaborated code") that the middle-class child has as a result of early socialization. However, we can argue that working-class language and culture is as complete and valid as that of middle-class culture. Furthermore, Bernstein speaks of working-class and middle-class groups, each with forms of socialization, language, and class, as if these groups were homogeneous, which is not the case.

As stated previously, in the mid 1970s a controversial debate developed over the links between intelligence, school achievement, and the future status of individuals. Bowles and Gintis (1976), in particular, challenged both the functionalist perspective and some of the concepts put forward by the conflict theorists. They argued that IQ scores, occupational status, and income are positively correlated. However, when socio-economic status is controlled, IQ does not have an extensive effect on either future earnings or occupational status.

Rather than concentrating on how students go about constructing meanings in classroom interactions, Bowles and Gintis focus on the school's role in reproducing the class system and extending the capitalist mode of production. They refer to this process as the **correspondence principle.** They state,

> The hierarchically structured patterns of values, norms, and skills that characterize the work force and the dynamics of class interaction under capitalism are mirrored in the social dynamics of the daily classroom encounters... Schools, through classroom relations, produce students that are docile and complacent—characteristics required in the workplace (Bowles & Gintis, 1976, p. 131).

Bowles and Gintis (1976) argue that the political process, through powerful economic interest groups, determines the role of education in reproducing and legitimizing social and economic inequality. Indeed, for them the root of inequality is the capitalist economy, not education. They claim that schools reproduce and legitimize inequality by

- perpetuating and reinforcing the meritocratic ideology of allocating individuals in the occupational hierarchy;
- rewarding personalities that are compatible with the relationships of dominance and subordination; and
- serving the interests of the dominant groups through the training of an elite group in the skills of domination (pp. 11–13).

Bowles and Gintis' theory has been referred to as **neo-Marxist** because its perspective emphasizes that the values and power of the economic structure determine the nature of the social order and therefore the inequalities therein. The following are some strengths and weaknesses of their correspondence theory that have been noted by several authors. First, their theory shows us how schools cannot be analyzed as institutions removed from the socio-economic context. The correspondence theory posits a class analysis of schooling, one that shifts the blame for educational failure from teachers, students, and school resources to the structural dynamics of the dominant society. Indeed, the theory points to how education contributes to the reproduction of the social order. Second, their theory does not show clearly that the correspondence between school and economic change is determined by capitalism. Third, some authors have questioned their emphasis on capitalist knowledge as being the only knowledge produced in schools. Finally, Bowles and Gintis provide us with a view of students that does not appear to acknowledge the contradictions and tensions that exist between schools and the workplace.

To summarize, conflict theorists focus on competing interest groups, exploitation, and struggle between groups. Some main features of conflict theory and its perspective on inequality include the following:

- Various groups struggle over scarce resources, money, power, and prestige, and compete for social advantages.
- Domination creates inequality. Those with the most resources exploit and control the subordinate groups.
- The most powerful (dominant groups) use their resources to maintain and reproduce their advantageous positions by shaping beliefs to make their positions appear legitimate.

Some Canadian Applications of Conflict Theory and Neo-Marxist Theory in Education

Various articles in books edited by Martell (1974) and Nelsen and Nock (1978) provide us with a critical analysis of how schooling in Canada is integrated into the corporate world under capitalism, and how post-secondary education effects class inequalities by imposing corporate values (for example, by emphasizing profit-making in the curriculum). Studies in works edited by Livingstone (1983, 1985) and Wotherspoon (1987) point to how the Canadian educational system has become ingrained with class-based educational ideologies and practices.

Symbolic Interactionist, Interpretive, and Phenomenological Perspectives

The **symbolic interaction** model, produced by the Chicago School, attempts to link social structural realities such as wealth, power, and status position to patterns of interaction. In other words, the task is to understand how structural variables become incorporated into the individual's perceptions and interpretations of social action and how he or she acts on the basis of these. According to these theorists, the important point is that to understand social differentiation in educational settings we must first understand how teachers categorize and classify various student behaviours. The assumption made is that education is indeed related to social inequality. To understand how schools perpetuate inequality, we must learn more about the basic rules or interpretive procedures teachers use when interacting with students and with each other in an educational setting.

By examining student performance in the context of different types of questioning, researchers have demonstrated that low performance is not necessarily due to a lack of understanding of language and culture; rather, it is the form of interrogation and context within which it occurs in the classroom that affects performance. Accordingly, we cannot assume that meaning is arrived at or transmitted in an obvious process. The interpretation of meaning, definitions, and the recognition of rules are developmentally and situationally constrained. That is, students and teachers, while interacting, respond to each other by reflecting, selecting, and then trying out a response on the basis of their social knowledge and the situation in which they find themselves.

Caroline Persell (1977) links structural variables such as the politics and economic background of students' and teachers' interactions patterns to explain inequality in education. She explains this process by showing how the **dominant ideology** of power groups penetrates four levels—the societal, institutional, interpersonal, and intrapsychic. (A more detailed analysis of dominant ideologies and teachers' differential expectations is provided in Chapter 5.) At the societal level, Persell draws on Marx and Weber to point out how structures of dominance and the ideologies associated with them are interdependent. The institutional level (the structure of the educational system), then, is shaped by the polity and economy. The schooling process—achievement testing, ability grouping, and tracking—reflects the schemes of interpretations structural needs of society.

By drawing on George Herbert Mead's symbolic-interactionist theory, Persell then goes on to describe the interpersonal and intrapsychic levels. Here the focus is on the origins and consequences of teacher expectations. Teachers develop expectations and respond to pupils on the basis of widely accepted criteria of school performance. Teachers' differential expectations tend to limit educational attainment of minority and lower-class students. These expectations have been learned in teacher education programs and reflect the beliefs of the dominant societal ideology.

Some argue that the symbolic interactionist perspective, as well as others previously discussed, tends to make the schools or the teachers morally responsible for the existing inequality in educational opportunity (through expectations of meanings structures). As with previous theories, this approach also over-emphasizes the importance of the socio-economic structure by suggesting that, through societal values, it imposes a particular educational ideology on teachers and schools. Accordingly, since teachers accept the dominant societal ideology, they should be held morally responsible for what goes on in schools.

To explain inequality in educational opportunity, other theorists turn to an interpretive approach that draws on Alfred Schutz's phenomenological sociology. This interpretive and phenomenological approach focuses on the social construction of knowledge and understanding of the common sense world of everyday life, as well as the intersubjective world of common experiences that individuals share and take for granted. The premise is that persons exist in a social world, and as social actors and actresses, they give meaning to actions and situations.

The work of Alfred Schutz has also been influential in sociological theory, particularly in the area of social **phenomenology**. Schutz stresses the importance of examining the interpretive procedures or methods that individuals (including sociologists) draw on to arrive at the use of concepts. Thus, to understand social interaction we must make explicit the obvious but "hidden," or taken-for-granted, facts of interaction. Concepts such as inter-subjectivity, typifications, intentionality, and taken-for-granted social knowledge were first presented by Schutz, and will be discussed in Chapter 5.

Symbolic interactionism and the interpretive and phenomenological perspectives provide us with a better understanding of how meanings are generated in interaction. What is important from this stance is that the content of meanings, relevance of intention, and procedures and practices, which are made to appear real within a situation, must be addressed.

These orientations have been criticized for not clarifying how the leap is made from small group situations to the larger structures of organizations. For instance, if we concentrate on what definitions are important to pupils or teachers, we risk overlooking the broader question of why those definitions are important. That is, we do not come to terms with the economic and political contexts within which these definitions arise. Although symbolic interactionism and the interpretive and phenomenological perspectives focus on how social structure is accomplished through interaction, consideration must be given to the social facts of stratification, political control, and the social distribution of knowledge that affect the practices people use to accomplish or sustain a sense of social structure or social order. Insofar as individuals function within the larger society (macro-structure), they are affected by the distribution of resources and power, which then affects the interactions of individuals at the micro-level, thus setting limits to the choices that they believe are available to them.

Briefly, symbolic interactionists and interpretive phenomenologists believe that we must analyze how people assign meanings to objects, situations, and events. Some of their main arguments are as follows:

- Society consists of individuals who are always in a process of interaction and their actions are based on the meanings that things, objects, situations, or events have for them.
- People act on the basis of their interpretations of inequality, if and when the issue is important to them. Situations of equality or inequality are situationally defined.

A Canadian Application of Symbolic Interactionist Theory

Several Canadian researchers have contributed to interactionist theory in the sociology of education. Wilfred Martin's major work, *The Negotiated Order of the School* (1976), deserves special attention. Martin draws on the symbolic interactionist perspective to analyze teacher-teacher and teacher-student interaction. His concern is with "interactive roles and agenda." Considering these, Martin looks at the process of negotiation, including bargaining and exchange, that occurs when the objectives of either party differ. The important point he makes is that this process of negotiation is truly an attempt to alter or change the way each party (individual) has defined the situation. Again, there is much detail and rich data in Martin's book and we suggest that his work be examined carefully. For an application of Martin's work in a Canadian study of teacher interaction in a French immersion school, please see Cleghorn and Genesee (1984).

Critical Theory

Critical theory refers to both a school of thought and a process of critique. This theory emphasizes

- social class as a unit of analysis and everyday life as a theoretical and political sphere of investigation and struggle;
- the notion of liberation based on a variety of human needs, not just economic ones;
- a conception of society that refutes the dichotomy of subject and object and the distinction between the micro and macro levels of analysis of society;
- a rejection of economic determinism that suggests consciousness is a reflection of social being (human behaviour is more than a reaction to capitalism); and
- social reality and subjectivity (consciousness, needs, intent, interest, motivation) possess a dialectical nature.

From this critical theoretical perspective, the claims of any critique must be questioned and must not hold to their own doctrinal assumptions. Critical theory was developed by what can be described as the Frankfurt School, the members of which responded to orthodox

Marxism. They questioned the notion that class struggle, as well as the mechanisms of domination, takes place primarily within the confines of the labour process. They also questioned the primacy of the mode of production in shaping history. In other words, from a critical theorist's perspective, Marxism is not self-critical and fails to develop a theory of consciousness. Thus the emphasis shifts to issues of how subjectivity (our personal feelings) is constituted and how the spheres of culture and everyday life represent a new terrain of domination. The central focus is to assess the newly emerging forms of capitalism along with the changing forms of domination and to rethink and radically reconstruct the meaning of human emancipation.

Critical theory is dialectical; that is, it recognizes that existing problems in society do not occur in isolation but are a part of the interactive process between individuals and societal structures. Carr and Kemmis (1983) clarify the meaning of the dialectical

> as involving searching out contradictions (like the contradiction of the inadvertent oppression of less able students by a system which aspires to help all students to achieve their "full potential") . . . it is an open and questioning form of thinking which demands reflection back and forth between elements like, part and whole, knowledge and action, process and product, subject and object, being and becoming, rhetoric and reality or structure and function . . . as contradictions are revealed, new constructive thinking and . . . action are required to transcend the contradictory state of affairs (pp. 36–37).

This dialectic view permits us to see both the domination and liberation aspects of schooling. This is contrary to the economic determinism of both conflict theorist and neo-Marxist views of schooling. For example, teachers often recognize that some students are at a disadvantage in the classroom because their values and beliefs are not congruent with that of the school. These teachers would like to change the curriculum to meet student needs, but the ministry of education (or its equivalent) controls the curriculum. Thus, there are opposing forces occurring at the classroom level. A dialectical analysis of such opposing social forces permits insight into objectives, activities and practical interests of individuals in different groups.

Essentially, the orientation of critical theory is derived from the recognition that experience and knowledge are politically charged and interrelated. Thus, knowledge must be used as a practical tool for change; it must be used to transform nature and politics in a way that alleviates oppressive social conditions. For critical theorists, social phenomena must be perceived as made up of dialectical opposing forces. Briefly then, critical theorists provide insights for studying the relationship between theory and society. They have developed a dialectical framework to understand what mediates between institutions and activities of daily life. Habermas (1968), in particular, attempted to develop a conceptual framework in which the connection between theory and practice was stressed at the level of interests, which underlie knowledge formation itself.

It is important to note that, according to Habermas, knowledge has both a political and a practical intent. He argues that neutral or value-free research findings are normally used to reinforce the status quo and maintain the power of those in control. From his perspective society is both exploitative and oppressive, but it is also possible to change it. His emphasis is on individual empowerment, social transformation, and the need to develop critical consciousness in students.

Critical Theory: A Canadian Source

Peter McLaren's book, *Life in Schools* (1998), presents us with a critique of schooling and a detailed account of critical pedagogy based on his work in Canadian schools. McLaren's intent is to direct teachers towards a teaching process that addresses how power and empowerment are played out in the classroom. As he notes, he would like to provide teachers "with a means . . . to critically . . . face our society's complicity in the root structures of inequality" (p. 29).

McLaren also presents us with a journal that he kept while teaching in a Toronto inner-city school in the 1980s. He is aware of his shift in positions. But he argues that

> Some readers may object to my shifting context from a critique of schooling and society in the United States to an inner-city school in Canada. I would argue that the disadvantaged students of whom I speak, and the teachers who work with them, face daily struggles in the classroom that do not recognize the national boundaries between the United States and Canada (p. 33).

While the dimensions of the power structures in Canada and the United States do differ, and are no doubt played out differently in Canadian and U.S. classrooms, we would argue that the principle holds: minorities face struggles that are linked to social structure and power.

Feminist Theory

Liberal Feminism

Previous theories discussed have excluded a feminist perspective on the relation between school and society. In the following section we present feminist theorists who draw on sociological education theory proposed by males.

The analysis of the relationship between women and schooling began with **liberal feminists** and generated from liberal enlightenment thought. Liberal feminists promoted the ideas of rationality, dignity, autonomy, and social justice for members of society. The strength of their perspective was in their documentation of gender discrimination through stereotyping, bias in curricular materials, and school practices. Their aim was to change the biases and distortions of everyday life in textbooks and eliminate the sexism in practices such as course and career counselling for girls and boys.

Although the liberal feminists' works are important, they do not situate the problem of sexism or gender differentiation in a larger sociological context. For example, liberal feminists do not look at power relations in terms of social class and gender. Many argue that we must place schools and schooling in the context of the social, economic, and political structures of our society.

Socialist Feminism

Feminist educational theorists interested in how structures of power and control effect the schooling process turned to **socialist feminism** to explain the relationship between women, education, and their social status position. Much of social feminist research draws on Marxist concepts to explain differential treatment and gender inequality. For instance, Wolpe (1978,1988) and Arnot MacDonald (1980) argue that **patriarchal ideology** is formed and used by the dominant class. Their works focus on the complex relationships between capitalist production, the division of labour, the family, and the educational system. These relationships are all strongly influenced by patriarchal relations and ideology.

(Wolpe and Arnot used the term patriarchy to refer to groups of individuals or groups of organizations in which males hold dominant power over females in terms of access to high-status positions or privileged authority.)

Wolpe (1978) first analyzes the relationship of the educational system to the state and its dominant ideological concerns, and second, the relationship between a sex-segregated labour force and the state. She examines in some detail the processes through which the ideology of gender is constructed through the family unit and the dominant class, and how this construction is mediated by the educational system. From Wolpe's stance, the educational system not only functions to maintain this structure but, at the same time, is the "site of political and ideological struggle" (1978, p. 312).

Wolpe (1978) does not address the question of social transformations through pedagogical practice (i.e., pedagogy as the production of knowledge, identities, and values). In *School Walls* (1988), she argues that, "to overcome the differentials operating on the basis of gender in schools, a breakdown of gender differences must occur at all levels—ideological and practical, both at home and at school" (p.199). Wolpe analyzes non-academic (home economics and craft) and academic (mathematics, science, and humanities) classes and the ideologies expressed by teachers through the classroom practices. But again, her analysis remains at the structural level, focusing on societal ideologies. She writes,

> the practice associated with the integration of subjects for boys and girls appears restricted by a set of ideologies which relate specifically to gender identities in terms of home-centered activities. In other words, it is quite legitimate to integrate all courses provided this does not represent any threat to the status quo of the gender-based division of labor both in the home and place of work (p. 224).

MacDonald (Arnot) (1980) also argues that to more clearly understand women's positions in capitalist society we must reassess existing explanations of schooling, which have not focused on the "sexual division of labor within the school and its impact in determining the relations between the family, schooling and labor processes" (p.13). She discusses two major theories within the sociology of education, the theory of social reproduction (Althusser, 1971; Bowles and Gintis, 1976) and the theory of cultural reproduction of class structure (Bernstein, 1973). Her objective is to use these theories "as the basis for an explanatory model of the forms of women's education within societies which are both capitalist and patriarchal" (p.13).

In particular, MacDonald (1980) uses Bernstein's argument that forms of social organization are reproduced by the school through the "categorization of pupils by age, sex and social class" (p. 22) and reinforced through the classification of knowledge of teacher-student relations, the school structure, and forms of evaluation. An analysis of these factors reveals the operation of gender codes that direct males and females towards the acquisition of particular forms of symbolic property such as ideas, attitudes, and types of certificates and degrees (p.13).

For MacDonald, it is the specific aspects of patriarchal ideology—sexual power relations and gender categorization—that must be researched and explained in a sociological theory of women's education. She accepts the theories of the class structure but argues that these must be modified to include gender differentiation within both schooling and the capitalist work structure.

Arnot (1994) maintains her argument that there is a material base of patriarchy and class structure to gender differentiation, and has given up the concept of "reproduction" in favour of the concept of **male hegemony**. Here she introduces the concept of hegemony to explain how the power structure and the power of the dominant class maintains the status quo. This power goes unquestioned as natural and common sense by those who are subordinated. Hegemony refers to a whole range of structures and activities as well as values, attitudes, beliefs, and morality that in various ways support the established order, including class and male interests (pp. 85–86).

By introducing the concept of male hegemony to analyze class and gender, Arnot (1994) hopes to develop a theory of gender classification that is class-based and will "expose the structural and interactional features of gender reproduction and conflict in families, in schools, and in workplaces" (p. 97). Also, in continuing to believe that Bernstein's theory of classification systems is useful to developing a theory of gender codes that is class-based, Arnot states,

> The idea of gender codes relates well to the concept of hegemony; both refer to the social organization of family and school life where definitions of feminine and masculine are taught in such a way as to accept the natural hierarchy of male over female—the superiority of men in society (p. 97).

For Arnot (1994), the important aspects of any theory of gender are that

- gender categories are arbitrary social constructs carried out by social institutions (schools, churches, mass media);
- gender classifications are not universal or static;
- "gender categories are constructed through a concept of gender differences" (p.101); and
- educational differences are essentially secured via the family, educational system, and structural division of labour.

Her position does not truly shift from her original stance, which is framed by social and cultural reproduction theories. She argues that Marxist feminist accounts of the schooling process do not explain how patriarchal oppression has its own dynamics and concerns in gender struggles because of their main focus on Marxist class categories (p. 93). However, the concept of male hegemony does not account for how patriarchal ideology is sustained through educational practice. That is, Arnot speaks from a Marxist perspective to provide teachers with practical classroom strategies that would demystify the illusion of equal educational opportunity and explicitly address the hierarchical structure and political power that is found within schools.

Another critique of the Marxist feminist focus on patriarchal ideology, which undergirds the economic and political relations that characterize the educational system, is that it leads to fundamental misconceptions about the centrality of subjectivity in the concept of patriarchal ideology. There is also a problem in that the analyses given by Wolpe and Arnot do not provide productive insights into feminists' power relations between men and between women. An understanding of how feminists themselves use power and knowledge to explain subordination is required. This lack of clarification of feminists' use of knowledge and power has serious implications for theorists and pedagogists whose aim is to transform educational practices.

Some feminist educational theorists are presently challenging existing Marxist feminist theory framed by class and class reproduction. The specific interest in these writings is on the oppressive nature of male discourse. That is, knowledge that is controlled by patriarchy ensures the perpetuation of domination. For instance, Diamond and Quimby (1988) note how Foucault's work influenced many feminists' analyses. Foucault analyzed modern discourses on power. His primary concerns were the history of scientific thought, the development of technologies of power and domination, and the arbitrariness of modern social institutions. For feminists, his analysis of power offers a way in which class, race, and gender differences can be taken into account. Both Foucault and the feminists identify the body as the site of power, that is, the locus of domination through which docility is accomplished and subjectivity constituted. They focus on the role of discourse in producing and sustaining hegemonic power. Both criticize the Western masculine elite for producing or proclaiming universal truths about freedom and human nature.

Discourse is a central concept in Foucault's analytical framework. We use the concept discourse, or **discursive practices**, as Gore (1992) does to refer to what can be said and thought, who can speak when, and with what authority. Gore also looks at discursive practices to highlight the ways in which language, subjectivity, social institutions, intellectuals, and power are related (Gore, 1993, p. 159). For a sample of interpretations of Foucault's definition of discourse see Lather, in Luke & Gore, 1992.

Postmodernist Feminism

Some writings show a development of feminist educational theory, that critiques not only the liberal feminist and socialist feminist perspectives, but also the critical educational theory. This literature presents a **postmodern feminist theory** analysis grounded in the work of Foucault.

Postmodernist theory addresses power and knowledge relationships, the negative effects of master-narratives, and the way institutions are not only controlling but also controlled. In the broadest sense, postmodernism challenges the idea of universal truths, or what some refer to as master narratives (Weiler & Mitchell, 1992, p. 5). It is a critique of the dominant forms of analysis or accepted truths (e.g., Marxism, early tradition of critical theory).

Postmodern feminists argue that we must be able to identify the structural contradictions of our differences, which cannot be captured in terms of discursive analysis. It matters who is speaking. Weiler and Mitchell (1992, p. 5) state that postmodernist theory can be seen as a perspective that challenges universal truths. That is, it challenges the idea of universal truths or what some refer to as master narratives. Postmodernist theory is a critique of the dominant forms of analysis or accepted truths that concerns itself with mediation of language in human thought and action. It recognizes the function of discourse in constructing identities and subject positions. The point is to reveal the structuring of one's own discourse (the way we talk and write) in existing disciplines and to bring the reader into the inquiry as an analytic partner in deconstructing and destabilizing theories or texts. This approach contributes to the process of demystification and social change. Its objective is to reveal the structuring of our own text, construction of meaning, and subjectivity.

Essentially, postmodern feminists drawing on postmodern theory call into question the privileged position of white male theorists. They challenge the critical educational theorists, who are predominantly male, to examine how their assumptions and thoughts affect their discursive practices.

Feminist Theory: Some Canadian Sources

Gaskell, McLaren and Novogrodsky, in *Claiming an Education* (1989), and Gaskell (1991), provide us with evidence of women's disadvantages in education in Canada.

Among the important issues they discuss are the problems of inequality in educational opportunity and how women have managed to participate and achieve in the educational system. Dorothy Smith (1987), in *The Everyday World as Problematic*, focuses on various aspects of women's situations in education and societal relations and provides us with research strategies to develop a sociology for women. Marlene Mackie (1987, 1994) gives an excellent account of gender socialization and gender relations in Canada.

Anti-Racist Theory

Academic discourse addressing **anti-racist education** has often been associated with **multicultural education**. In some ways these concepts are seen in terms of a continuum where multiculturalism has evolved over a period of time and taken the shape of the latter (Duarte & Smith, 2000). In another sense, the concepts are used interchangeably (Dei, 2000; Ghosh, 2002). Yet, in another sense, these are looked at as two separate notions that stand in opposition to each other (Grinter, 2000). However much we define and redefine anti-racist and multicultural education, there is no agreement as to how to address these concepts through pedagogical practices within educational settings. For instance, Duarte and Smith (2000) point to the fact that the term multiculturalism is used in many contexts by educators who do not agree on what it means. At a general level, most educators agree that "multiculturalism" has something to do with promoting an understanding and appreciation of cultural diversity" (p. 2).

On the other hand, Dei (Dei, 2000) notes that the task that lies before anti-racist theory is

> to produce new knowledge, to focus attention and efforts on addressing social justice and equity. New knowledge should critically examine the socially constructed ways of making meaning in a racialized, gendered world (p. 25).

Dei recognizes that there has been much controversy over defining the concepts of multiculturalism and anti-racist education. However, he argues that the concepts must be put into a social, historical, ideological, and political context. What is important is to first put forward a working definition of **race**, which he considers as socially constructed in a particular historical context; race is not identified only on the basis of skin colour but also by other social aspects such as language, culture, and religion. That is, race is socially created and is the main force justifying power and maintaining difference. Racism is not simply an ideology supported by the White dominant group; it is an ongoing process incorporating this group's values, norms, and behaviours, which perpetuate systemic racism (p. 44). Dei states that

> Anti-racism deals with representation; that is, the need to have multiple voices and perspectives involved in the production of mainstream social knowledge. Anti-racism also examines institutional practices to see how institutions respond to the challenge of diversity and difference; understood as the intersections of race, gender, class, sexuality, language, culture and religion (p. 34).

Many anti-racist theorists (Frankenberg, 1993; Dyer, 1997; Rodediger, 1994) argue that in order to develop a critical analysis of anti-racism we must critically examine and challenge the unquestioned acceptance of whiteness and white privilege controlled by the white dominant group. A most important point is that whiteness is a social phenomenon of white privilege, power, and cultural and political identity. What is required is to create a school system that disrupts or ruptures the dominance of whiteness.

Frankenberg (1993) provides a three-dimensional definition of whiteness. According to her, whiteness is "first a location of structural advantage of race privilege. Second, it is a 'standpoint,' a place from which white people look at ourselves, at others, and at society. Third, 'whiteness' refers to a set of cultural practices that are unusually unmarked and unnamed" (p. 1). That is, "whiteness refers to set of locations that are historically, socially, politically, and culturally produced and, moreover, are intrinsically linked to unfolding relations of domination" (p. 6).

To summarize, it is important to note that there are many contentious issues regarding the concepts of anti-racism, multiculturalism, racial difference, and whiteness (which are often equated with ethnicity). The lack of consensus as to what constitutes these concepts or how they are defined should not lead to rejection of these terms. For Dei (2000), "what is missing is a theoretical understanding and concrete acknowledgement of race and difference as providing the contexts for power and domination in society" (p. 18). As noted previously, much has been written about these concepts indicating that there is a multiplicity of voices defining them. There are varied definitions of what constitutes racism, anti-racism, multiculturalism, and whiteness. Many authors adapt or conflate the terms using them to mean the same thing while others use the terms in a general or blurred way.

Anti-Racist Theory: Some Canadian Contributions

Recently, several Canadian sociologists have contributed to anti-racist theory of education. Dei and Calliste (2000) examine the concepts of race, knowledge, anti-racist education, and the deconstruction of whiteness, white domination and power. Ng, Staton and Scane (1995) provide an excellent analysis in various articles on anti-aboriginal struggles for social justice in the book they edited called *Anti-Racism, Feminism, and Critical Approaches to Education.* In this book, for example, Rezai-Rashti carefully examines a report on anti-racist and multicultural education written by the Ministry of Education in 1987. She addresses pedagogical issues that will be examined in Chapter 4. Another article, by Regnier, reflects on aboriginal anti-racist pedagogy, which we will also discuss later.

Other interesting discussions on the distinction between the concepts of multiculturalism and anti-racism in the Canadian context are presented by Bedard, in Dei, 2000. See also Gill & Levidow (1987), who make a case for anti-racist education in the broader North-South perspective. Here the argument is that the enlightenment discourses of science and science education are racist and must therefore be challenged. We would also like to refer students to Dei, G., Karumnachery, & al. (2000), who draw on specific examples from Canadian schools to show how anti-racist education can work in a positive and proactive way.

Table 2-1 provides a summary of the main theories, focuses, and concepts presented in this chapter.

TABLE 2-1　Theories of Schooling and Society

Theories of schooling and society	Functionalism	Conflict or Radical (Neo-Marxists)	Symbolic – Interaction, Interpretive, and Phenomenological Perspectives	Critical	Feminist	Anti-racist
DATE	1950s–1960s	1970s	1970s–1980s	1970s	1970s	1990s
Focus	Analysis of social and cultural systems (institutions), which carry certain functions. Each must function to maintain social order.	Emphasis on conflict and social change rather than on social order, equilibrium and maintenance.	Focus is on integration of self and society and the analysis of the social construction of meaning and reality.	This theory is a response to the inadequacy of current social theory to explain social, political, and economic oppression; it suggests ways that the educational system can address social inequality and generate social change.	The focus is on multiple causes of oppression based on class, race, and gender; gender role conditioning; patriarchy and the control over minority groups.	Anti-racism theory focuses on an action-oriented, educational, and political strategy for systemic change in society's institutions. It regards racism in terms of interlocking systems of oppression—sexism, classism, heterosexism, ableism.
Level of Analysis	Macro level – focusing on groups, institutions, and connections between them.	Macro level – same as functionalism.	Micro level – focusing on individuals in interaction with others.	Both micro and macro level – individual interaction with macro level social analysis.	Both micro and macro level – subjective experience embedded in and influenced by institutional structures.	Macro level – focusing on the political, historical, and social processes that maintain unequal power relations.
Concern	How are order and equilibrium maintained through the education system?	How do economic organizations determine the organization of schooling and the organization of the rest of society?	How meaning is the social context constructed through social interaction, how individuals act on the basis of their	To reveal sources of oppression; understand causes and consequences of oppression; understand how schooling can address educational and	Educational reform, inclusive curriculum, challenging all forms of oppression-classis, racism, sexixm.	How to effect change at the societal level while acts of racism and racist attitudes occur at the level of the individual

(Continued)

TABLE 2-1 Theories of Schooling and Society (Continued)

Theories of schooling and society	Functionalism	Conflict or Radical (Neo-Marxists)	Symbolic – Interaction, Interpretive, and Phenomenological Perspectives	Critical	Feminist	Anti-racist
Concern (continued)		What are the contradictions inherent in social organizations, which create conflict and can generate social change? Economic inequality is the major source of contradiction and conflict in education and society.	interpretations of meaning; how these meanings differ.	social inequality through inclusive and liberatory educational practices.		and group. Thus macro level analysis has micro level implications in terms of educational practice.
Major Concepts	Systems, institutions; latent and manifest functions of education, norms, values, rules.	Capitalist ideology, meritocracy, legitimacy, domination, inequality, contradiction, correspondence, social change.	Self, self-concept, language, symbols, meaning, interaction, role, role taking, role-playing, role expectation, construction of reality.	Resistance, human agency, oppression, hegemony, consciousness, dialogue, understanding authority/power.	Patriarchy, oppression, social activism, social change, empowerment, consciousness raising.	Difference, prejudice, discrimination, racism, exclusion, systemic inequality and oppression, group 'membership', identity, group boundaries.
Major Questions	How do schools maintain social order?	What are the sources of inequality and how can the education process contribute to a more equitable society?	What meanings do individuals attach to certain objects situations, or events? How do teachers' expectations, classroom activities, school records, student-teacher or student-student interaction affect school performance?	How do schools contribute to inequality and oppression in society? What pedagogy can address these problems?	What role can schools and classroom activities play in addressing gender inequality? How can an inclusive curriculum be developed to promote challenges to dominant ideological, cultural, and political structures?	What can schools and school administrators do to reduce the tendency of schools to replicate the conflictual and unequal relations between groups in the society at large? How can teachers address societal issues of racism effectively, in the classroom?

Critique	It is a static theory. The focus on order justifies the status quo and social inequality.	Conflict is not clearly defined, nor are the negative and positive aspects of contradictions and conflict clearly explained.	These orientations have been criticized for not clarifying how larger social structural processes such as social class, political processes, social distribution of knowledge affect the interactions of individuals. Also, these approaches tend to make the schools or teachers morally responsible for the existing educational inequality.	Critical theory does not focus on classroom teaching practices. It involves reflective practice, one that critiques the status quo.	There is a constant shift in defining feminism, variations in feminist theory and women's issues, as well as the role of feminist pedagogy in educating oppressed groups.	Humans appear to need a sense of belonging to a group; young people have difficulty identifying with the concerns of humanity at large. Racism is thus very difficult to eradicate given that attitudes are formed early in life and reinforced by societal institutions in society such as the family and local community.

SUMMARY/CONCLUSIONS

We began this chapter with an introduction to the origins of sociology of education. We then presented the major theories—functionalist, conflict/neo-Marxist, critical, feminist, and anti-racist theories, which show us the different ways sociologists explain the relationship between schooling and society.

In the 1950s there was concern for the ways in which the education system related to both divisions of labour and social stratification (the ranking of the individuals on the basis of education, occupation, and income). The major theoretical perspective used to analyze the relationship between schools and society is referred to as functionalism. Functionalists view education in terms of its function to provide a literate and adaptable workforce to meet the needs of an advanced technological society. That is, the education system functions in the interests of society. Functionalists are concerned with reforms that will lead to a stable social order rather than addressing the problem of social inequality. The functionalists emphasize meritocracy, which assumes that each individual has a unique set of abilities and that it is an individual's effort and abilities that will help him or her succeed in school. Thus, according to this view, the number of years spent in school predicts occupational achievement, and therefore social status.

In the 1960s sociologists began to argue that there was a great deal of waste of working-class ability due to streaming and tracking in schools. The extent of inequality in education has been documented, but the causes of inequality remain unexplained. In the late 1960s and 1970s a group of sociologists referred to as conflict, neo-Marxist, or radical theorists focused on the relationship between the political and economic forces and the education system. The education system is viewed as reproducing the class structure of modern industrialist society and functioning in the interest of the dominant group. For example, these theorists believe that education is used to control the patterns of thought, sentiments, and behaviour of the working class. Essentially, education is thought of as authority and social control. The difference between conflict theorists lies not so much in the level of their analyses as in what they consider the implications for social change. Conflict theorists argue that if the education system is to play a part in change, then pupils and teachers need to be radicalized to take part in the class struggle.

The symbolic-interaction, interpretive, and phenomenological theorists focus on classroom dynamics and curricular issues. This approach is anti-functional and anti-deterministic. The central task becomes an examination of the participants in the educational process through an exploration of their perceptions and assumptions as well as their interactions with each other. There is a change in method, most significantly in the exchange of observation for the social survey, and a change in opinion of what are the important problem areas that should be studied. The questions that interest this new generation of researchers are no longer which children fail, or even why they fail, but what is the nature or status of school knowledge, or the nature of failure itself.

Attention then turns to the assumptions held within the school, especially by teachers, on the meaning of success and failure, on definitions of good and bad pupils, and on differences between what teachers said and what they did. Thus, the concept of education as culture becomes important. The management of knowledge becomes a key issue. It is not how we sort and select people on the basis of individual effort and ability that is important; rather, it is how the curriculum is selected and legitimated.

Sociologists critiqued the above approaches, and, in the mid-1980s and 1990s, critical, feminist, and anti-racist theories emerged. Critical theory emerged because some researchers found it unacceptable to focus only on capitalist relations of production and their relations to education—that is, the social and cultural reproduction model was rejected. Thus, theoretical critique and discourse analysis became the primary focus and much of the current research aims at curriculum transformation and the empowerment of teachers and students.

Gendered dimensions have also become a concern in educational research. Feminist researchers look at domination and exclusion in the classroom, as well as subjectivity and identity. While research relating to how class and gender inequalities are reproduced in school cultures has been fruitful, research on racial inequality in this context has not been as productive. Anti-racist research focuses on the ways that curricula and school practices reflect structural realities that devalue the self-image, culture, and identity of visible minority students.

The main difference between the above approaches is their implication for social change. It is important to assess the implications and consequences of the different theoretical perspectives and what each considers to be the solution to educational problems.

The intent of this chapter has been to introduce the major theories in the field of sociology of education. While the contributions of Canadian sociologists have not been numerous, they are important because of what they illuminate—for example, the differences in educational practice in Canada, the United States, or Britain. There is much more to each author's work(s) than what has been presented here. Interested students can note the suggested readings at the end of this chapter.

KEY TERMS

anti-racist education	functionalist theory	postmodern feminist theory
capitalism	ideal types	phenomenology
conflict theory	interpretive phenomeno-	race
correspondence principle	logical theory	social order
critical theory	liberal feminism	socialism
cultural capital	male hegemony	socialist feminism
definition of the situation	multicultural education	status culture
discursive practices	neo-Marxist theory	status groups
dominant ideology	patriarchal ideology	symbolic interactionist theory

EDUCATIONAL ISSUES AND QUESTIONS FOR DISCUSSION

1. Discuss the primary focus and differences between two of the sociological theories presented in this chapter. Which do you think best explains the relationship between school and society?

2. Select a theory that you believe best explains your achievement in school. Support your choice with examples.

3. To what extent do any of the theories "ring true" for other students besides yourself? Explain why.

4. Analyze the contribution made by the functionalist theory to our understanding of the notion of meritocracy in education.

5. Discuss and evaluate the argument that material deprivation is the most important factor influencing educational underachievement.

RECOMMENDED READINGS/REFERENCES

Althuser, L. (1971). Ideology and ideological state apparatuses. In *Lenin and philosophy and other essays*. London: New Left Books.

Arnot, M. (1994). Male hegemony, social class, and women's education. In L. Stone (Ed.), *The education feminist reader* (pp. 84–104). New York: Routledge.

Aronowitz, S., & Giroux, H. (Eds.). (1993). *Education still under siege* (2nd ed.). Westport, CT: Bergin & Garvey.

Bedard, G. (2000). Deconstructing whiteness: Pedagogical implications for anti-racism education. In G. Dei & A. Calliste (Eds.), *Power, knowledge and anti-racism education* (pp. 41–56). Halifax: Fernwood Publishing.

Belanger, P. W., & Rocher, G. (Eds.) (1975). *École et societé au Quebec*. Montreal: Hurtubise HMH.

Bernstein, B. (1973). *Call codes and control*. London: Routledge & Kegan Paul Ltd.

Bourdieu, P. (1986). The forms of capital. In I. C. Richardson (Ed.), R. Nice, (Trans.), *Handbook of theory and research for the sociology of education*. New York: Greenwood Press.

Bourdieu, P., & Passeron, J. C. (1977). *Reproduction in education: Society and culture*. California: Sage.

Bowles, S., & Gintis, H. (1976). *Schooling in capitalist America*. New York: Basic Books.

Calliste, A., & Dei, G. (2000). (Eds.). *Anti-racist feminism*. Halifax, NS: Fernwood Publishing.

Carr, W., & Kemmis, S. 1983). *Becoming critical: Knowing through action research*. Victoria: Dean University.

Cleghorn, A., & Genesee, F. (1984). Language in contact: An ethnographic study of interaction in an immersion school. *TESOL Quarterly, 18*(4), 595–625.

Clement, W. (1975). *The Canadian corporate elite: An analysis of economic power*. Toronto: McClelland & Stewart.

Cohee, G. E., et al. (Eds.). (1998). *The feminist teacher anthology*. New York: Teachers College Press.

Coleman, J. (1968). The concept of equality of opportunity. *Harvard Educational Review, 38,* 7–32.

Collins, R. (1971). Functional and conflict theories of educational stratification. *American Sociological Review, 36*(6), 1002–19.

Cooley, C. H. (1956). *Human nature and the social order*. Glencoe, IL: Free Press.

Davis, K., & Moore, W. (1945). Some principles of stratification. *American Sociological Review, 10,* 242–249.

Dei, G. (2000). Towards an anti-racism discursive framework. In G. Dei & A. Calliste (Eds.), *Power, knowledge and anti-racism education*. Halifax, NS: Fernword Publishing.

Dei, G., James, I. M., Karumnachery, S. J-W., & Zine, S. (2000). *Removing the margins: The challenges and possibilities of inclusive schooling*. Toronto: Canadian Scholars' Press.

Diamond, I., & Quinby, L. (Eds.). (1988). *Feminisms and Foucault: Reflections on resistance*. Boston: Northwestern University Press.

Dreeben, R. (1968). *On what is learned in school.* Reading, MA: Addison-Wesley.

Duarte. E. M., & Smith, S. (2000). *Foundational perspectives in multicultural education.* New York: Longman Inc.

Durkheim, E. (1956). *Education and society.* Glencoe, IL: The Free Press.

Dyer, R. (1997). *White.* New York: Routledge.

Frankenberg, R. (1993). *White women, race matters: The social construction of whiteness.* Minneapolis, MN: University of Minnesota Press.

Freire, P. (1970). *Pedagogy of the oppressed.* New York: Seabury Press.

Gaskell, J. (1992). *Gender matters from school to work.* Toronto: OISE Press.

Gaskell, J., McLaren, A., & Novogrodsky, H. (1989). *Claiming an education: Feminism and Canadian schools.* Toronto: Education Foundation.

Ghosh, R. (2002). *Redefining multicultural education.* Ontario: Thomas Canada Limited.

Gill, D., & Levidow, L. (Eds.). (1987). *Anti-racist science teaching.* London: Free Association Books.

Giroux, H. (1992). *Border crossings.* New York: Routledge.

Gore, J. (1992) Feminist politics in radical pedagogy. In C. Luke & J. Gore (Eds.), *Feminisms and critical pedagogies.* New York: Routledge.

Gore, J. (1993). *The struggle for pedagogies.* New York: Routledge.

Grinter, R. (2000). Multicultural or anti-racist education. In E. M. Duarte & S. Smith (Eds.), *Foundational perspectives in multicultural education.* New York: Longman Inc.

Habermas, J. (1968). *Knowledge and human interests.* Boston: Beacon Press.

Livingstone, D. W. (1983). *Class, ideologies and educational futures.* London: Routledge.

Livingstone, D. W. (1985). *Social crisis and school.* Toronto: Garamond Press.

Livingstone, D. W. (1994). Searching for missing links: Neo-Marxist theories of education. In L. Irwin & D. MacLennan (Eds.), *Sociology of education in Canada: Critical perspectives in theory, research and practice* (pp. 55–82). Toronto: Copp Clark Longman.

Luke, C., & Gore, J. (1992). *Feminisms and critical pedagogies.* New York: Routledge.

MacDonald, M. (1980) Socio-cultural reproduction and women's education. In R. Deem (Ed.), *Schooling for women's work.* Boston: Routledge & Kegan Paul Ltd.

Mackie, M. (1987). *Constructing women and men.* Toronto: Holt, Rinehardt & Winston.

Mackie, M. (1994), Socialization. In R. Haagedorn (Ed.), *Sociology* (5th ed., pp. 89–120). Toronto: Harcourt Brace & Company.

Martell, G. (Ed.). (1974). *The politics of the Canadian public school.* Toronto: James Lorimer & Company.

Martin, W. (1976). *The negotiated order of the school.* Toronto: MacMillan.

McLaren, P. (1995). *Critical pedagogy and predatory culture.* New York: Routledge.

McLaren, P. (1998). *Life in schools: An introduction to critical pedagogy in the foundations of education* (3rd ed.). Don Mills, ON: Longman Publishing Group.

Mead, G. H. (1934). *Mind, self and society*. Chicago: University of Chicago Press.

Mifflen, F., & Mifflen, S. (1982). *The sociology of education*. Calgary: Detselig.

Murphy, R. (1979). *Sociological theories of education*. Toronto: McGraw-Hill Ryerson.

Nelsen, R., & Nock, D. (Eds.). (1978). *Reading, writing and riches: Education and the socio-economic order in North America*. Kitchener, ON: Between the Lines.

Ng, R., Staton, P., & Scane, J. (Eds.). (1995). *Anti-racism, feminism, and critical approaches to education*. Toronto: OISE Press.

Parsons, T. (1959). The school class as a social system: Some of its functions in American society. *Harvard Educational Review, 29,* 297–318.

Persell, C. H. (1977). *Education and inequality*. New York: The Free Press.

Porter, J. (1965). *The vertical mosaic: An analysis of social class and power in Canada*. Toronto: University of Toronto Press.

Regnier, R. (1995). Warrior as pedagogue, pedagogue as warrior: Reflections on aboriginal anti-racist pedagogy. In R. Ng, P. Staton, & J. Scane (Eds.), *Anti-racism, feminism, and critical approaches to education* (pp. 57–86). Toronto: OISE Press.

Rezai-Rashti, G. (1995). Multicultural education, anti-racist education and critical pedagogy: Reflections on everyday life. In R. Ng, P. Staton, & J. Scane (Eds.), *Anti-racism, feminism, and critical approaches to education*. Toronto: OISE Press.

Rodediger, D. (1994). *Towards the abolition of whiteness: Essays on race, politics and working class history*. London: Verso.

Schutz, A. (1973). *Collected papers: The problem of social reality*. The Hague: Martinus Nijhoff.

Simon, R. (1987, April). Empowerment as a pedagogy of possibility. *Language Arts, 64,* 4.

Smith, D. (1987). *The everyday world as problematic: A feminist sociology*. Toronto: University of Toronto Press.

Weber, M. (1947). *The theory of social and economic organization*. New York: The Free Press.

Weiler, K. (1987). *Women teaching for change: Gender, class and power*. Westport, CN: Bergin & Garvey.

Weiler, K. (1991). Freire and a feminist pedagogy of difference. *Harvard Educational Review, 16*(4).

Weiler, K., & Mitchell, C. (Eds.). (1992). *What schools can do: Critical pedagogy and practice*. New York: State University of New York.

Wolpe, A. M. (1978). Education and the sexual division of labour. In A. Kuhn & A. M. Wolpe (Eds.), *Feminism and materialism: Women and modes of production*. Boston: Routledge & Kegan Paul Ltd.

Wolpe, A. M. (1988). *Within school walls: The role of discipline, sexuality and the curriculum*. London: Routledge.

Wotherspoon, T. (Ed.). (1987). *The political economy of Canadian schooling*. Toronto: Methuen.

Wotherspoon, T. (1998). *The sociology of education in Canada: Critical perspectives*. Toronto: Oxford University Press.

chapter three

The Organization of Teaching and Learning

CHAPTER OBJECTIVES

The purpose of this chapter is to

- convey an understanding of schools as formal organizations
- illustrate that the informal interactions between teachers and between students and teachers affect the formal functioning of schools
- provide an overview of the ways in which teaching and learning are organized in school systems and schools
- examine the effect that selected reform movements have or have not had on the organization of schooling in Canada and on society as a whole
- provide information about trends in teacher education and different approaches to teaching

THE SCHOOL AS A FORMAL ORGANIZATION

Much of our knowledge about formal organizations stems from the work of Max Weber (see Chapter 2). A **formal organization** is a type of group or interaction system in which people's behaviour is directed towards specific goals. Unlike family groups, where relations are informal and variable, a formal organization is characterized by a complex division of labour, clearly defined job roles and relationships, hierarchically ranked subdivisions and positions, and a large size. A formal organization exists regardless of the particular individuals who work within it; that is, any individual can be replaced. This implies that formal organizations have established structures with entrenched obligations, rights, privileges, and procedures that its participants agree to and abide by contractually.

Like most formal organizations, schools are also bureaucracies. A **bureaucracy** may be defined as a formal organizational arrangement characterized by a division of labour, specialized functions, a hierarchy of authority, and a system of rules, regulations, and record-keeping. Bureaucracies are characterized by rationality and efficiency, and they coordinate the work of many people in the performance of complex tasks (Blau & Scott, 1962; Mifflen & Mifflen, 1982; Spencer, 1979). The specific goals of schools have to do with the teaching of knowledge, skills, and attitudes as well as the development of healthy "good citizens" who understand the rules of competition and how to behave within a hierarchical structure. Schools are also concerned with other kinds of goals, such as developing in young people an intrinsic satisfaction for learning; thus to some extent the bureaucratic structure of schools and school systems may work against such aims. When personal concerns lie in opposition to the need for efficiency and rationality (when, for example, students complain of being identified by a number), then bureaucracies are looked upon in negative terms.

The goals of formal organizations may be seen as formal, ideological, informal, personal, and inertial (Mifflen & Mifflen, 1982, p. 200–201). The formal goals are those for which the organization was established, often written down in official documents as "mission statements," as in provincial education reforms. Ideological goals are sometimes found within the formal goal statements of an organization and may refer, for example, to the promotion of overarching values such as positive attitudes towards ethnic and racial diversity in Canadian society. Informal goals within an organization arise from the participants' interpretation of or even resistance to the formal goals. People working within an organization tend to interact informally in ways that aim towards the establishment of consensus as to what the actual goals of the organization are. These may well conflict with the formal purposes of the organization and result in personnel management problems. Personal goals refer to the specific reasons an individual may have for working within an organization. Inertial goals refer to the fact that even when the purpose of an organization is to bring about some kind of social or technological change, formal organizations have a tendency to perpetuate themselves, no doubt because the power structure within them has a vested interest in this.

The expected behaviours of individuals who occupy positions in a formal organization are contained within formal, written job descriptions and also governed by shared ideas regarding what constitutes appropriate behaviour. These ideas or rules that define expected behaviour under specific circumstances are called **norms**. Norms may be explicit, as in the case of rules for carrying out particular tasks, or they may be implicit, as in the unwritten rules or expectations governing interaction between people occupying different positions within the hierarchy. Thus, we see the likelihood that every formal organization is inclined to develop a parallel **informal organization** or interaction system. Patterns of informal relations are based on social differences—personal attributes such as race, ethnicity, language, religion, or position and formal status within the organization. Formal divisions within an organization, such as grades and school departments, are a source of subgroups that may contribute further to the informal system of interaction. Informal relations within an organization may or may not be functional as far as they affect the attainment of the formal organization's goals.

Concurrent Trends: Local Control Meets Outcomes-Based Education

There is a trend today, at the beginning of the twenty-first century, not only in Canada but in North America and elsewhere, towards local control or decentralization. This is due to increasing concerns about what is perceived as extreme bureaucratization of the system as well as the ineffectiveness of the traditional model of schooling for large numbers of young people, as evidenced, for example, by high drop-out rates in Canadian secondary schools (Statistics Canada, 2004).[1] This trend may also be evidence of the tension mentioned in Chapter 1 between uniformity and diversity. At the community level there is likely to be more uniformity in the school population in terms of social class and race; in large centralized school systems, especially in urban areas, diversity in the school population is more likely if not inevitable.

Although there is a trend towards decentralization, there is also a concurrent leaning towards more centralization. This is because there is concern everywhere over internal and external efficiency, cost benefits, and school quality (quality of "inputs," quality of results, as well as quality of the instructional process). This is manifested in an increase in bureaucratization with the international spread of policies that promote **outcomes-based education (OBE)**. OBE, while controversial and varied in the form it takes from one country to another, aims to raise standards and increase educational opportunity, especially for disadvantaged minorities, through various measures including school accountability (Jansen & Christie, 1999). Thus the education systems in Canada are increasingly involved in measuring student achievement according to defined competencies, benchmarks of achievement, and public accountability (Council of Ministers of Education, Canada, 2004). One danger of OBE is that there will be a return to "objective" methods of assessing student achievement that will actually result in greater inequality, not less, due to the well-known bias against disadvantaged minorities contained within formal, standardized tests.

The issue of centralized versus decentralized control thus remains unresolved. It is important to ask if the transfer of responsibility for management, control, and the content of schooling to the local level will result in greater equality. What measures will insure that inferior conditions do not simply continue, for example, in Canada's most impoverished Native communities and in many inner city schools? How can we promote more community involvement in the schools without bringing about disorganization with regard to equitable access to resources, leadership, curriculum choices, and the like?

There is evidently a need to take into consideration a diversity of community concerns about schooling while ensuring, in the face of large numbers of school drop-outs, that there are opportunities to re-enter the system at the levels of higher education. For example, many universities in Canada have mature entry programs that give credit for work experience and assess an individual's suitability for post-secondary education on the basis of additional criteria, not simply evidence of a secondary school diploma.

ATTEMPTS TO REFORM THE ORGANIZATION OF TEACHING AND LEARNING

The history of education in the Western world has been marked by a series of reform movements, each of which has had dual objectives. On the one hand, the aim has been to expand and improve the delivery of educational services. On the other hand, there has been

---

[1]The secondary school drop-out rate for Canada is about 12%, with a considerable difference between provinces. The rate for PEI is about 18% and the rate for Saskatchewan about 7%. The drop-out rate for girls, overall, is about 5% lower than for boys.

an attempt to address society's social and economic problems, and in this way to improve society as a whole. That is, change in education has always coincided with a perceived need for social change. What has never been clear is the *direction* of change.

- Does change in society indicate a need for change in schooling practices, or do problems within schools and education systems point to the need for changes within the larger society?
- When secondary school students commit acts of violence, where is the locus of the problem—in the school system, within the family, or in the community?
- It is important to realize that reforms in education are often politically charged: who decides what is to change, why, how, and for whose benefit?

In Canada there have been several attempts to change the organization of teaching and learning and rethink the traditional forms and purposes of schooling in light of their limitations. Few of these reform efforts have taken hold and become institutionalized, at least in part because the correspondence between schooling and the requirements of the workplace, as discussed in Chapter 2, are not easy to dismantle or replace.

Deschooling Revisited

A few educators have put forth a renewed vision of schooling that takes place outside the school and classroom (Henchey, 1987; Hern 1996; Meighan, 1997). We call this **deschooling** revisited because it is reminiscent of the deschooling movement suggested by Ivan Illich (1971), A.S. Neill (1960), John Holt (1964) and others. These theorists began to question what they perceived as the unnecessary bureaucratization and other shortcomings of mass schooling, particularly, but not only, as these relate to the educational outcomes for children from working-class homes as well as immigrant and racial minority backgrounds. Illich, for example, wanted to increase equality by removing the link between schooling and occupational opportunity. He believed that competence acquired outside the system would be fairer. Others, such as the neo-Marxists Bowles and Gintis (1976), also wanted to change the system but understood that schooling was not the only institution to perpetuate inequality.

A. S. Neill's *Summerhill,* Ivan Illich's *Deschooling Society,* and Holt's *How Children Fail* became compulsory reading in education faculties and teacher training programs as well as popular among the public during the 1960s and '70s. These books suggested alternative ways of schooling, which were then put into practice, often with the support of parents who wanted a more egalitarian and humanistic schooling for their children. These authors' vision was of a fully democratic society, free of conflict, organized through goodwill. **Free schools** were established outside the regular school system, usually by parent groups, and organized along democratic lines. Decisions about curriculum, behaviour, dress code, grading, and discipline were decided collectively by students, teachers, parents, and school administrators. Teachers were to guide rather than dictate children's learning. Children were encouraged to explore, work, and study, motivated intrinsically and with a measure of control over what and how they learned.

There are several reasons why the majority of free schools did not survive very long. Like most reform movements, the free schools had built-in contradictions. For example, despite their non-elitist aims, they were essentially private schools, dependent upon tuition, which most parents from the working class could ill afford. Thus the majority of children who attended free schools came from well-educated, middle-class families, that is, from families that already enjoyed the social status that could be passed on to their children through ascription. Another reason for the demise of most free schools was that students, teachers, parents, and administrators had to spend inordinate amounts of time in meetings, trying to come to a consensus about how to run the school. Not only did this often lead to bitter infighting and disagreements, but it took more time than many were willing to commit. Eventually, the organization of free schools became as hierarchical as that of regular schools, with a few people holding positions of power.

Ideas about deschooling continue to be appealing, however. Henchey (1987) argues that if technology is going to be the main transmitter of knowledge then there is no reason for children to be in school. Theoretically, they can be at home (in front of a computer), at the local library (in front of a computer), or anywhere else (at a friend's home, or in another city visiting an absent parent, in front of a computer). While such a vision might be fully supported by parents who are in favour of **home schooling** and are willing to act as teachers or supervisors, it is short on the recognition of all those other things that are taught and learned in school, for better or for worse, through the hidden curriculum, interaction with peers, and the process of becoming familiar with one of society's main bureaucratic institutions. It does not take long to come to the conclusion that such a plan is unworkable on a large scale, especially in today's world, where most parents work. As noted in Chapter 1, the school has an important custodial function to play for society at large. As you will see in Chapter 5, the school plays an important role in the socialization of future citizens.

Open-Structured Schools

In contrast to the free school movement, **open-structured schools** are still found within regular education systems. Instead of each grade with one teacher being confined to a single classroom, space in an open-structured school is organized so that several grades occupy the same large space. This allows for team teaching and flexible, cooperative learning groups. The pace of instruction and learning is determined by student interest and inclination, rather than the sounding of a bell every thirty-five minutes. Interaction between teachers and students and among students is relatively free, with children's behaviour controlled, as much as possible, through cooperation and persuasion. Instruction tends to be based on the constructivist philosophy, which will be discussed later on in this chapter.

Wilfred Martin is one Canadian sociologist who contributes to our understanding of the impact of an open structure on the informal interactions in the school. Martin (1975; 1976) found that the grade level and subject taught and the gender, age, and years of teaching experience all contribute to the informal lines of communication among teachers. Where there is more than one class per grade and where grades form the major structural division within a school, teachers of the same grade tend to form subgroups based on their commonly shared experiences and problems with children of the same age.

In contrast, the norms governing teacher interaction in open-structured schools are different than in regular schools, where teachers work in isolation. Since children are grouped according to achievement level or interest, rather than simply by age and grade, teachers work in teams of two or more. Thus students, space, and materials are shared. Members of the same teaching team must cooperate and agree on the specific instructional goals of their subgroup. Martin found that teachers felt a primary loyalty to their team (subgroup) rather than to the larger teacher group. In contrast, in regularly organized schools, where teachers work in isolation from each other, the entire teacher group is comparable to a single team in which general agreement over program goals is expected.

Unfortunately, advocates of open schools and open classrooms underestimate the effects of noise on the ability to teach and learn, and overestimate the likelihood that children and adolescents will control their own behaviour. In fact, for many children in open classrooms the definition of the situation is ambiguous, since the rules are not clearly stated. More important perhaps is the fact that when the rules governing interaction and other aspects of behaviour are implicit, a shared understanding of those rules requires that the participants share a common culture or social class background. When classes are made up of mostly middle-class students, the students may more easily understand the often unstated rules; however, when students come from diverse ethnic, religious, and language backgrounds they may bring different expectations to school and then behave on the basis of their interpretation of events. Thus there may be many apparent "infractions" of the rules, stemming from cross-cultural misunderstandings, making it seem necessary for the rules to be spelled out and enforced. When this happens, the egalitarian ideals of the open-structured school and open classroom may be quickly abandoned.

Home Schooling

What is home schooling, who does it, and why? Is it effective? Although recent statistics are difficult to locate, a 1993 report showed that about 10 000 children were registered as being home schooled in Canada, while there may be as many as 30 000 children being unofficially home schooled (Smith, 1993).

Parents who choose to home school their children are a diverse lot; however, it is evident that most are fairly well educated. Several reasons are cited for home schooling. First is general dissatisfaction with schools. Schools are perceived as places where creativity and curiosity are squashed rather than nurtured. They are seen as impersonal places where communication tends to be one-way—from teacher to students. Schools are seen as places where groupings by grade and age are unnatural. The belief is that home schooling counters all of these features while promoting self-discipline, self-directed learning, and the personal confidence and self-esteem that comes with a young person's independent mastery of subjects, ideas, skills, and situations.

Home schooling is not for everyone. Although it is an ideal way for parents who are living in isolated communities or foreign countries to ensure that their children keep up with their regularly schooled peers—through correspondence, for example—home schooling is best served by a community that is rich in resources such as libraries, museums, and local businesses that are willing to participate. Since most parents are not sufficiently knowledgeable to teach about every subject, they need to organize themselves to fill the gaps. Home schooling can be hard work, requiring full-time dedication on the part of a parent. On the other hand, neither the parent nor the child is bound to the schedule of a school day, so schooling at home can be flexible.

Questions typically arise among the home schooling skeptics about two matters: the development of home-schooled children's social skills, and the question of whether or not they can compete with regularly schooled students on standardized tests of achievement. In response to this, the advocates of home schooling simply ask if most parents would not prefer to avoid what they refer to as the *tyranny of the peer group*. Although home-schooled children tend to be independent thinkers, there is no evidence to suggest that they become social isolates. And finally, the effectiveness of home schooling is equal to or greater than that of traditional schooling, as measured by standardized achievement tests such as the Scholastic Achievement Test (SAT) (Hern 1996; Meighan, 1997).

Canada's French Immersion Movement

One reform that has taken hold in Canada is the French immersion movement. The movement started as an experiment by a group of monolingual English-speaking parents from the Montreal suburb of St. Lambert. They were determined that in this officially bilingual country their children would become bilingual. In addition, the long-term intention was to improve relations between French and English speakers by improving the ability of children from English-speaking homes to live and work using the French language. The aim was to accomplish this without loss of the children's English-language skills. That is, the total **early French immersion** programs were not intended to be **transitional bilingual programs** that would shift the children to the exclusive use of French, but rather were intended to guarantee **first language maintenance** (English) and develop literacy and other skills in both languages (Lambert & Tucker, 1972).

After consulting with experts in neurology and psychology to reassure themselves that their children would not be damaged by this "experiment," this small group of parents started a school with a kindergarten in a church basement. No local primary school would risk such a novel, untested program in which the language of instruction from kindergarten to grade 3 was French (hence the term early immersion). From the start, this experimental program was carefully evaluated by researchers from McGill University. By the early 1970s, early French-immersion programs had begun in other schools in Montreal; however, they remained officially experimental for 16 years, in part because the ministry of education was not willing to accept the consequences of potentially negative long-term effects. After years of official resistance on the part of the ministry and some parents' fears that children's English-language reading and other skills would be damaged, the program evaluations showed over and over that these fears were unfounded. Evidence of French immersion programs' success brought more and more French immersion schools into existence, first in the Montreal area, and then across Canada. French immersion schools are now found in almost every large community and in some small districts in Canada as well. Today, approximately 350 000 children in Canada are enrolled in French immersion programs (Genesee, 1987, Lambert & Tucker, 1972;).[2] It is estimated that approximately 2 million Canadians have attended French immersion programs of one type or another (early—kindergarten to grade 3; middle—grades 4, 5, and 6; or late—grades 7 and 8) (Genesee, 2004, personal communication).

---

[2]There are several different models of French immersion, too complex and numerous to elaborate on here. Briefly, however, early immersion sees children taught in French from kindergarten through grade 3, with English being introduced for about 40% of the school day from grade 3 or 4 onwards. Middle immersion sees children receiving about 90% of instruction in French in grades 4, 5, and 6, once their reading skills in English have been established. Late immersion takes place at the grade 7 and 8 levels, with most instruction in French and a considerable percentage of classes taught in French after those grades until the end of secondary school. The reader is referred to the websites at the end of this book for additional information.

French immersion schools are often organized with two streams, a regular English-taught stream and a French immersion stream. The two streams do not share the same program objectives; one is concerned with bilingual education, the other has the goals of a regular English school. The French immersion-stream and the English-stream teachers constitute de facto teaching teams that cut across grade levels vertically, reminding us of Martin's discussion of interaction patterns that tend to evolve in differently structured schools. In this instance, English-stream and immersion-stream teachers of the same grade level do not share the same teaching-learning objectives, nor do they share the same problems with learners. Both streams, however, are normally under the direction of one principal and subject to the same policy and curriculum guidelines. Thus on the one hand the teacher group is subject to the regular norms of the teaching profession, while on the other hand the teachers' roles are defined by their membership in the two major linguistic groups—French-speaking and English-speaking—that make up the larger society. This sets the stage for teachers to occupy conflicting roles and for this conflict to further influence their interactions with each other. When the teachers of the two streams are also members of Canada's English-speaking or French-speaking groups, then the stage is also set for interactions within the school to replicate relations between the groups in the society at large, thus inserting a strongly political element into the immersion movement.

Despite some possible negative social effects of bilingual education programs, the French immersion movement has been deemed a success by language-in-education researchers throughout the world, and the model has been borrowed and adapted in the United States and elsewhere. It has been shown over and over that English-speaking children who have been taught in French from kindergarten onwards, with English instruction being introduced in about grade 3, do as well as or better academically and in the long term than their monolingually taught peers. However, it is important to emphasize that the early immersion model cannot easily be transferred to other school settings where the home language not only differs from the language of the school but is also not well supported through its use and through the media in the school community. When the home language is a language at risk, other strategies can be used successfully to develop students' skills in the school's instructional language while also maintaining and developing literacy and other skills in the home language (Benson, 2004; Genesee, 1987; Johnson & Swain, 1997; Stroud, 2002).

Some would argue that French immersion programs have not succeeded in altering the character of French-English relations in Canadian society at large. Others would say they have succeeded at a social if not political level. However, as pointed out earlier, the ability of school reforms to change entire societies is limited due to the multiplicity of factors that cause social discord. Indeed, it would be unrealistic to think that a bilingual education program could influence the several waves of political unrest in Quebec over the past 30 years. Thus we cannot say whether the experiment was successful in improving relations between French and English speakers. We can say, though, that approximately two million Canadians attended French immersion programs over the last 30 years and are now able to work and live in both official languages. Clearly, survey research is needed into the educational background of Canadians who live and work in both languages to provide more definite answers to this question.

To recapitulate this section of the chapter, although some of the reforms discussed above have aimed to affect society as a whole, the parallels between schooling and the

Case Study of One French Immersion School

An ethnographic study was carried out in the early 1980s in one French immersion school located in a Montreal suburb. The school was organized into two streams. There were eight French-speaking teachers and four English-speaking teachers. All classes from kindergarten through grade 2 were taught entirely in French; the upper primary immersion grades were taught a half-day in French and a half-day in English. There were four all-English-taught classes in the English stream in grades 4 though 6. This indicated that the demand for French immersion classes had resulted in a reduction of the English stream in this school.

Social interaction among the teaching staff was observed for one school year, two to three days per week. Observations took place in the staff room, in the hallways, on the playground, and in the classrooms. In addition, a sample of children were asked to guess what language was being used by pairs of individuals who were portrayed in simple drawings depicting the interior of a school, a school playground, and a street scene close to a school.

The study found that there was tension among the staff group that was managed in a variety of ways. French- and English- speaking teachers avoided verbal communication whenever possible. When inter-group communication was necessary, the use of English predominated. These strategies were attributed to now outdated societal norms governing interaction between French and English speakers in Quebec, norms that dictated that English would be used when English and French speakers interacted. The investigation of children's assumptions about the situation use of French or English indicated that they thought more French was spoken in the school community than was the case (it was a predominantly English suburb). This finding seemed to parallel the English-speaking teachers' oft-stated view that "the French are taking over." The study thus concluded that bilingual education programs risk contradicting their stated aims by subtly communicating to learners the long-standing negative perceptions that some members of each group in the larger society hold towards the other.

Source: Cleghorn, 1981; Cleghorn & Genesee, 1984

requirements of the workplace persist. The majority of schools are still organized in traditional ways, where students do not get to choose what or when they learn, nor are they permitted to decide the pace of their work. At the ring of a bell students are expected to turn interest on and off, to make rapid shifts from one subject to another. They are taught in a group, yet they are not permitted to interact with their peers unless directed to do so by the teacher, even though teachers are educated to value the individual and create child-centred classrooms. According to Hurn (1993), in the name of efficiency and profit-making these very characteristics have their parallels in the workplace; however, they are also often associated with job dissatisfaction and low morale. Despite the above-described efforts to reform the nature of schooling, little actual change—within schools or without—has taken place.

THE POLICY CONTEXT OF CANADIAN SCHOOLS

Policies are written statements that are intended as guidelines for making decisions and acting under specific circumstances. In the bureaucratically organized systems of education found in each province and territory in Canada, we find policies that apply to each entire system. Similarly, there are policies at the level of particular school boards and even at the level of individual schools.

Although policies are not laws, they are sometimes transformed into laws or even charters, such as the 1982 Canadian Charter of Rights and Freedoms, which enshrines peoples' rights. A language policy may not be sufficient to guarantee access to French-language schooling in all parts of Canada, but as we saw in Chapter 1, there are laws in Canada guaranteeing children the right to an education in the minority language of each province. The extent to which these rights are realized remains controversial and varies from province to province. Policies, therefore, state who can go to school and where, what is to be taught, who may teach, and how students are to be treated. Unlike laws that can be enforced, policies cannot be enforced except through persuasion or the establishment of consensus.

Policy making always takes place in a context of competing interests. For instance, in education in Canada, there may be tension between those who seek social class or ethnic uniformity in the school and those who value diversity. There is also tension between the need for practices that apply equally to all and the need to respond to exceptional individual circumstances. And although North American culture primarily exhibits an **individualistic orientation** rather than a **communal** one, there is much concern with the topic of equality. In Western culture, educators tend to see such matters as child development, achievement in school, and the development of personal identity as essentially individual concerns (Hatch, 1995). In many other parts of the world, however, the primary focus is on the group or community that the child belongs to, and individual needs and concerns are seen as secondary to the needs of the group (Serpell, 1993).

Policies are made through a political process of negotiating competing interests, thus the influence of politics in education is inevitable. The political process is one in which those who have the most power influence those who have the least. Thus, as suggested above, many changes in education are made in a context of competing values, with one group lobbying for their set of values and another group lobbying for a different set. While this process is democratic, there are indications that policies in education are increasingly influenced by powerful corporate interests, a topic we will return to in Chapter 6. At some point, the key stakeholders in education—teachers, school administrators, parents, and students—appear to have been excluded from the decision-making process. Thus one of the central concerns in education today is to ensure that the voices of those most closely affected by the decisions that are being made have a chance to be heard and to influence the process, too. This explains the pressure towards decentralization and local control mentioned earlier.

Thus we ask the following questions: Who should participate in the policy-making process? Should control over policy be localized at the community level, or centralized at a higher level? These are the key questions regarding education policy. Clearly, there are some decisions that require the advice of highly educated experts, while other issues are more appropriately decided at the level of the community, or by parents. But there are many grey areas, too. For example, during a time of cutbacks in funding to schools, who should decide what is to be cut from the **formal curriculum**? How widely accepted is the position that mathematics and language arts are more important than music and art?

Although the trend in Canada and elsewhere towards increased local control of schools might appear to be a healthy resistance to the concurrent and opposing trend of distant, corporate control, it may not be so.

- Should parents and students decide the content of the curriculum, for example?
- Should parents have the right to decide that the local public school offer instruction in a language other than English or French?
- What are the limits?
- What kind of society do we envision?
- How do we really deal with diversity, in and out of the classroom?

In a diverse, multicultural society such as Canada there are bound to be disagreements and conflicts over what is best for children and young people. One of the ways this inherent conflict is dealt with is to allow a range of different types of schools in any single community. In Vancouver, Toronto, and Montreal we find many private schools, most of which cater to high-income families, and many of which are modeled after the elite "public" (private) schools of Britain, most obviously in their requirement of school uniforms. There are also numerous semi-private religious schools designed to provide education in an environment where parents' religious convictions are not only supported but part of the curriculum as well. The fact that most private schools receive provincial government funding, provided they follow the province's ministry of education regulations in matters of curriculum and examinations, is an indication of the extent to which there is consensus in Canadian society that such schools should exist (McAndrew, 1987).

We cannot leave this section without reminding the reader that from time to time the federal government has played a leading role in establishing policy with regard to what the overriding norms and attitudes ought to be in society at large and within its educational systems. Here we have in mind Canada's policy of multiculturalism, put forth in 1971 by former Prime Minister Pierre Trudeau.

Canada's Policy of Multiculturalism

On October 8, 1971, former Prime Minister Trudeau made the following statement:

> . . . there cannot be one cultural policy for Canadians of British and French origin, another for the original peoples, and yet a third for all the others. For although there are two official languages there is no official culture, nor does any ethnic group take precedence over any other. . . A policy of multiculturalism within a bilingual framework commits itself to the government as the most suitable means of assuring the cultural freedom of Canadians. . . the government will assist members of all cultural groups to overcome cultural barriers to full participation in Canadian society.

House of Commons Debates, October 8, 1971, p. 8545–8548.

The overall intention of this policy was to promote unity in diversity. The policy was a response to the upheaval that Canadian society had experienced in the 1960s with the Quiet Revolution in Quebec, as discussed in Chapter 1. The civil rights movement in the United States had also brought to the fore the rights of minorities, who hitherto had been left out of the mainstream of society. Unfortunately for French-speaking people living in Quebec, multicultural policy did not respond to their needs for recognition. As Chapter 1 pointed out, the situation of French-speaking people in Quebec and in Canada is very different from that of Canada's ethnic minorities, not the least reason for which is that at the federal level English and French have equal status as the languages of the two "founding groups." Perhaps because of the complexity of the Canadian situation, the policy of multiculturalism should be seen as an attempt that has met with both success and failure. The policy was intended to provide a climate in which the Canadian social structure, first described as a "vertical mosaic" in 1965 by John Porter, could be nurtured. To emphasize further, this policy was intended to direct the populace towards tolerance of differences and increase equality. That is, the intention was to confirm an ideology of cultural pluralism as a suitable way for Canadian society to proceed and as an alternative to the tendency towards assimilation that had marked Canada's early history and which remains the prevailing ideology in the United States. Although formal education, as stated earlier, is under provincial jurisdiction, multicultural policy provides a definition of the situation for provincial ministries and local school boards to emulate in their own policies. Although each province has interpreted the policy according to its own priorities and traditions, diversity continues to present a set of complex policy issues to Canada's education systems.

THE TEACHING PROFESSION, TEACHERS' ROLES, AND TEACHER GROUPS

Teaching is a unique profession in many ways. First of all there is debate as to whether or not teaching is a full profession, since the responsibilities, rights, and duties of a teacher are not fully comparable to those of, say, a lawyer or a dentist. While the teacher is obliged to teach children to the best of his or her ability, he or she is not legally responsible for the results; despite an increasing tendency to make teachers and schools accountable, success or failure to learn "belongs" to the child (Levin & Young, 1994).

Second, the teacher-student client relationship is not direct; teachers do not bill students for their services but are paid by the education authorities—the government, the school board, the community—or, in private schools, by the school from tuition paid by parents.

Third, unlike doctors or lawyers, teachers possess a great deal of personal knowledge about their chosen profession from their own past experience as learners prior to embarking on a teaching-education program. That is, before being educated as teachers, most if not all teachers hold distinct images of what constitutes either a good teacher or a poor one (Weber & Mitchell, 1995). It is upon this extensive base of prior knowledge that teachers are socialized into the profession, or quasi-profession (Dickinson, 1995; Goodlad, 1990).

Although teachers are socialized somewhat differently for teaching the elementary and secondary grades, some generalizations can be made. The norms of the teaching profession emphasize the importance of close working relationships and feelings of group cohesion, despite the fact that teachers usually work in isolation from their colleagues and their rewards are classroom centred. Teachers are further governed by norms of harmony and cooperation. They are expected to share common perspectives with regard to program objectives and present a united front to the outside world, including the world of parents. They are expected to share ideas, supplies, and chores.

The allocation of time is an important issue among teachers. Their day is marked by frequent reminders of time, and spare time, in particular, is to be shared equally. Discussions in teacher groups tend to focus on students, taking the form of anecdotal accounts of classroom events. Controversial social or political issues tend to be avoided, except when group action is taken on union-related matters (Canadian Teachers' Federation Report, 1991; Jackson, 1968; Levin & Young, 1994; Lortie, 1975). On this topic, it is of note that teacher associations deal mainly with financial and contractual matters rather than ideological or philosophical issues in education. Yet it is within such organizations that there may be some hope for teachers' voices to be heard; certainly at the level of the school the individual teacher risks being isolated by openly questioning the status quo or trying to bring about change on her/his own.

Friendship patterns among teachers are likely to be based on personal attributes such as age or sex, or, as indicated earlier, to stem from membership in the same formal sub-groups in the school, such as grade level or subject taught, teaching stream, or department affiliation. Older teachers normally enjoy considerable status among their colleagues, with their opinions and advice sought by younger teachers. In the case of immersion schools mentioned earlier, the older teachers were affiliated with the English stream and the younger ones with the more recently implemented immersion stream, thus the advice of the older teachers was perceived as irrelevant to the interests of the younger ones. As Cleghorn and Genesee (1984) reported, this division, among other factors, seriously influenced the otherwise expected harmony of the teacher group. Thus we can say that factors such as gender, language, race, or ethnicity may provide sources of conflict among teachers, again demonstrating the interaction between the formal and informal organization of the school. The manner in which conflict among teachers is managed within diversely populated schools is clearly important, not only for the functioning of the school towards its stated goals, but also for the attitudinal climate the students are exposed to.

Knowing that teacher groups place considerable importance on harmony, it is not surprising then that several researchers have found that teachers use a number of interaction strategies to prevent conflict from coming to a head and recreate an appearance of collegiality when disagreements or inter-group tensions arise. These strategies include bargaining, persuasion, negotiation, impression management, ingratiation, insincere expression of affect, and denial that a problem exists (Corwin, 1965; Goodson, 1992; Martin, 1975).

As suggested earlier, in ethnically or otherwise diverse communities, relations between members of the different groups may be reflected in the interaction patterns in schools. Through the **hidden curriculum**, which will be discussed further in Chapter 5, such patterns contribute to the socialization of children to the norms governing the interactions between members of the same groups in society at large.

In the paragraphs above we have indicated that the norms of the teaching profession contribute to its culture. This is a culture that in regular schools places great emphasis on teacher group harmony, cooperation, and sharing. While these norms may create a pleasant atmosphere to work in, they also lay the basis for considerable resistance to change, since change usually requires debate about choices to be made, disagreements, confrontation with differing personal attitudes, and negotiation. Thus, when individual teachers try to take it upon themselves to implement change within the school or in a classroom, there is bound to be a reaction from other teachers, parents, or the school administration. For example, in a study carried out in a racially mixed inner city school in Montreal, a female science teacher said that her goal was to see "Black girls enter the sciences." However, she reported that her greatest struggle was to get other teachers to take her seriously. Thus it appears that the pressure in this instance was to maintain the status quo.

The Role of the Principal

The foregoing brings us to the topic of the school principal. The principal plays a key role in the development and implementation of school policy, the decision-making process, and the management of the teacher group. The principal also influences the relationship between teachers and the world outside the classroom. He or she is expected to protect teachers and to act as a buffer between them and the outside world—e.g., difficult parents or unwelcome bureaucratic demands from the school board. In return for such protection the principal receives support and respect from the teachers.

Although there are several ways the complex role of the principal could be carried out, most of us tend to see this role as similar to that of a supervisor in a factory. But schools are not factories. The principal is thus normally seen as the leader of a teacher group; however, in a school that is organized into teaching teams, the principal becomes the manager of and the link between the different teams, while also playing a pivotal role in the management of conflict, should it arise, between teacher sub-groups (Lortie, 1975). Leadership style then is an important aspect of the way the role of a principal is played out; it is also affected by the expectations of the teachers. If they are expecting an interventionist style with much authority, they will resist and be unsatisfied with a principal who prefers an egalitarian, democratic, and supportive approach. Although teachers normally enjoy a high degree of privacy and autonomy in the classroom, the classroom, the students, and the supplies belong to others (the school board and parents). Teachers' autonomy is also limited by the principal's authority to enter the classroom at any time; if the principal is perceived as offering help to the teacher, his or her autonomy may be willingly relinquished.

Teachers look to the principal to deal with difficult students and parents as well as teachers who fail to do their share of the school's chores. However, Martin and Macdonell (1978) and Lortie (1975) found that when a principal behaves in an authoritarian manner towards teachers, resistance towards the principal then serves to unify the teacher group. On the other hand, if the principal bypasses a teacher to deal directly with a child's poor academic performance or unacceptable behaviour, the problem is linked to the child rather than to poor teaching. It is by these means that the principal can help teachers. It is also through such mechanisms that the status of the teaching profession remains quasi-professional.

Teachers differ in the amount they want to be involved in the decision-making process, but they are similar in that most want to be consulted. In schools with large staff groups, the principal may meet regularly with representatives of the entire staff. The primary function of this group is to provide the principal with a way of exerting authority in accordance with democratic norms. In staff meetings the principal's wishes are made known, negotiation takes place, agreement is reached, and the rest of the staff is then consulted about the decision.

CANADIAN TRENDS IN TEACHER EDUCATION

The teaching profession and teacher education in Canada have changed dramatically over the last 45 years, as is the case elsewhere. In 1960 a high school graduate (usually a woman) who wished to teach elementary school went directly to a teachers' college, which was usually affiliated with a university. If she wanted to teach the lower primary grades, she spent one year at the college; if she wanted to teach the upper primary grades, she spent two years. Today a primary school teacher must first (in some provinces) obtain a bachelor degree in education; alternatively, she/he must hold a bachelor degree in arts or science, usually followed by a year or two of post-graduate teacher education in a university setting. This pattern of spiralling qualifications required to become a schoolteacher has also occurred in other parts of the world.

We believe that, rather than discuss the mechanical aspects of acquiring a teaching certificate either at the elementary or secondary level, in this section it is more instructive to explore the kind of thinking or philosophy that underlies what it is that teachers are supposed to know and be able to do. In fact, the teacher education programs in Canadian universities differ little from one another, at least at a superficial level; most programs offer a series of courses over a period of years, leading to a bachelor degree in education plus the route to certification. Along with coursework, virtually all programs require a number of internships or periods of supervised practice teaching. The extent to which course-work and practice are blended or sequenced and the order in which these two major components of training take place do vary somewhat from university to university. In addition, several universities offer a one-year teacher education program at the post-bachelor degree level. We believe it is safe to say, however, that there are few truly innovative teacher education programs in Canada; for example, we teach about constructivism, but unlike some of the Scandinavian countries, we tend not to model it systematically for our future teachers (Canada-EU student exchange, Final Report, 2006). We will say more about constructivist principles of teaching and learning later in the chapter, but for now suffice it to say that they refer to teaching and learning as socially situated and developed through social interaction.

Is there a common education philosophy that underlies Canadian teacher education programs? An internet survey of Canada's university-based teacher education programs indicates that they are overwhelmingly rooted in the field of developmental psychology. According to this philosophy or set of theories, the individual child's learning and development is at the heart of the teaching-learning process. The cultural and ecological context in which teaching and learning occurs does not often find a central place in the teacher education curriculum, despite the fact that in some urban schools the majority of children are members of a community or ethnic group whose language, religion, and culture differ markedly from the Canadian middle-class values that are exemplified by the school. Although Uri Bronfenbrenner (1979) and Jerome Bruner (1997) have contributed much to our understanding of the ecology and culture of schooling, the preparation of teachers in Canada remains largely based on the psychology of the developing individual. In the field of early childhood education too there is a lively ongoing discussion in Canada and elsewhere about the dominance and influence of developmental psychology in the education of teachers (Dahlberg, Moss & Pence, 1999; Hatch, 1995; Hatch et al. 2002).

Debates in Teacher Education

There are two main areas of debate in teacher education, and these influence how we think about teaching. The first has to do with the question of what teachers need to know. There are at least four possibilities.

- Do they need to know thoroughly the subject matter that they teach?
- Do they need to know a set of methods for teaching?
- Do they need to know about the learning styles and abilities of the learners?
- Do they need a comprehensive understanding of the social context in which teaching occurs?

Obviously teachers need to know something about all of these things; however, the emphasis in most teacher education programs has been on one or the other of the first three.

The second area of debate relates to the locale and timing of training. Here are two questions to consider.

- Should teachers be fully prepared to teach before they enter the classroom (pre-service)?
- Should the majority of training be provided over the course of the teaching career (in-service)?

While the tendency has been towards pre-service training, there are pressures to increase the amount of in-service teacher education due to the fact that teachers' knowledge of a subject is quickly surpassed by new knowledge, driven mainly by technological developments.

The tendency in Canada is for most teacher education to take place prior to hiring; however, this model is not suitable for all parts of the world. For example, in many still-developing countries the school systems have expanded in the last 15 to 20 years more rapidly than sufficient numbers of qualified teachers could be trained. As a result, untrained or under-trained teachers are hired and then provided with a series of in-service courses, sometimes through distance education, eventually obtaining the necessary education and formal qualifications. Although it may not be ideal to have children taught by inexperienced and under-trained teachers, there is some evidence to suggest that on-the-job teacher training may be as effective as or more effective than pre-service training, especially when the latter involves little classroom practice. This is because practising teachers can bring immediate problems to the courses they take and then try out what they learn in their classrooms. In this way, the oft-perceived gap between theory and practice may be narrowed due to improved understanding of the way theory is situated in practice.

We believe that teachers would benefit greatly by having more courses in their pre-service training that help them to understand gender roles and the social context of teaching. According to Laird (1988) there is a need to reconceptualize teaching because it has long been perceived as a "woman's profession," while at the same time it has not been taken seriously as a profession. Laird notes the supposedly gender-neutral advice of many task forces on teaching that consistently call for reforms that translate into social action while ignoring the contributions of feminist scholars such as Shrewsbury (1987), Martin (1985), Rich (1985) and the Holmes Group (1986). As you read in Chapter 2 and will read more about in Chapter 4, feminist pedagogy alters the basic structure of the entire taken-for-granted patriarchal paradigm of schooling; it is interactive and seeks for women to write their own truths. It suggests that "a community of learners. . . act responsibly toward one another and the subject matter and. . . apply that learning to social action" (Laird, 1988, p. 450, 452). Acker (1988), for example, notes how seldom teachers act decisively to bring about change and how the norms of the teaching profession that promote harmony in teacher groups have been so internalized as to insure that the inclination to resist does not surface. Acker argues that teachers are caught up in "gender regimes," where gender is a major organizing principle in schools, reflected in a sexual division of labour and the distribution of prestige and power that favours males (p. 309–310).

For teachers to resist is to disrupt; to disrupt is to violate the norms of the teaching profession. This has a silencing effect on all concerned, with the result that sex bias in schools is ignored. In the classroom gender differences may be seen as "natural"; social class biases are understood in terms of **cultural deficits** within the learners, and the focus on the individual child in child-centred classrooms provides a neutral, ideological side-stepping of racial, ethnic, religious, and sex differences in schools as well as classrooms (Flores, Cousin & Diaz, 1991).

It is now recognized that educating a teacher is not a relatively simple and formulaic task of imparting a set of methods but rather a very complex process of developing a set of professional attitudes and a variety of strategies for coping with the many difficult encounters and situations they are likely to meet in a classroom. Thus, instead of talking about teacher education or teacher training, it may be more accurate to talk about a process of *socialization* into the teaching profession.

Socialization in adulthood involves change. It involves knowing one's self and confronting perhaps long-held biases and assumptions about others. For teachers, it involves a critical understanding of what is taught, why we teach what we do, how certain subjects are most effectively taught, and alternative ways of teaching. It involves making clear distinctions between classroom management considerations (discipline and order) and teaching-learning considerations. It means being alert to the cultural as well as political aspects of teaching. To paraphrase Bruner, what is taught, the modes of thought, and the forms of language that are promoted in schools cannot be separated from the lives and culture of the students and their teachers (Bruner, 1997, p. 29).

One of the most difficult aspects of organizing education for teachers is fitting their education to the range of situations that they might encounter. For example, how often are teachers truly prepared for the inclusive classroom where learning-disabled and physically disabled children are grouped with students who do not have such difficulties? What preparation do teachers have in some of the still-developing countries for mixed-grade classes numbering 80 or more pupils (and no paper, chalk, or textbooks) (Tabulawa, 1998)? Where are teachers helped to think creatively about the situations they will find themselves in? Where are they given the autonomy to be true professionals, free to implement the creative solutions that they themselves devise? Finally, how can teachers prepare themselves to teach in settings where they are "the other"?

When a teacher has taught in situations where she was the one who was racially, religiously, or otherwise different, it becomes evident how useful **narratives** can be in teacher education for developing a shared consciousness of what it feels like for students who are "other" and what intercultural communication really means (Baverstock-Angelus,1999). In each of the two stories from the field, on pages 74 and 75, the teachers moved from feelings of isolation and powerlessness to new understandings and a personal sense of strength.

Story I from the Field: When the Teacher is "Other" in an Islamic School

For the interview to teach in an Islamic school I donned a long-sleeved dress that fell below my knees. I was greeted by two ladies wearing hijabs (scarves that cover the head) and chadors (floor-length gowns). I was sure I would not be hired because I was not a Muslim. I was shown into the principal's office and interviewed by three men. I could see that the interview went well from the nodding of their heads. They thought I was qualified and liked the fact that I agreed to wear a hijab if I got the job. The following Sunday I received a call telling me that I had the job.

Several new teachers were hired that year so we were given an orientation that included the rules of the school, an introduction to Islam, and assurances that we were all equal under Allah. It did not, however, take me long to realize that women were not equal to men; men made the rules. If a teacher challenged authority she was told that she could leave if she did not like it. This affected the Muslim teachers most, since they did not believe that they could be hired anywhere else. Several of the non-Muslim teachers openly challenged the wearing of the hijab. This brought the matter to the attention of the press and an open debate about religious differences, discrimination, and human rights ensued. While this was healthy in a way, its ugly side was evident when I found an anti-Christian message written in the snow that covered my car. I felt fearful, angry, and powerless. I did not yet have my teaching certification and needed the job—I could not protest too loudly.

Despite other incidents, I stayed at the school for three years. I was often frustrated by the fact that I could not do what I felt was pedagogically good and morally right but in time I gained respect from the staff, the administration, and the students. I learned when to be polite and deferential and when and whom I could push. These were lessons that would serve me well no matter where I taught.

Source: Adapted from Baverstock-Angelus, 1999. Reprinted with permission.

In the second case, the teacher, a young, single mother, found herself the "other" amongst her own people, in part because she tried to conform to the ways of the Cree. Betty had chosen to teach in the North as an ESL (English as a second language) teacher because she wanted to bring up her son in a quiet, unpolluted environment. Her problems were not the Cree but the other non-native teachers, who found living and working in the North very isolating.

Some theorists believe that teacher education should focus more on the education of teachers as critical or transformative intellectuals (Giroux & McLaren, 1989). A **transformative intellectual** is a person who knowingly attempts to bring about social change by acting on the belief that schooling represents both a struggle for meaning and a struggle over power relations. In this regard teachers' intellectual practices are morally and ethically grounded in concern for the educational needs of those who have been disadvantaged and oppressed. Giroux and McLaren also state that if teachers take on the role

Story II from the Field: When the Teacher is "Other" Amongst Her Own People

Before I got to the North I thought that it was cold and snowy there even in the summertime. But when I got there I was amazed to find it was 27 degrees and there was lots of sand. I suddenly realized this was an ideal place to raise a child, mainly because there wasn't any pollution and it was a very small community. It was like a big sandbox for him and he was in heaven. When I first arrived in 1980, all the teachers except the kindergarten teacher were non-natives. Now most of the elementary teachers are native, though it is only recently that whites have been less in charge. I think I was prepared for the experience, not from my degree in TESL but from teaching in other countries. The other teachers were not so prepared; they prejudged the students, didn't think they were bright or talented or even capable of learning in an academic way. So it was the teachers' biases and inexperience that made it difficult for the students. I did not get along well with the other teachers because I did not share their views. They shared their problems with each other and complained a lot about getting fresh groceries and the long waits for the cargo planes to come in.

There was another single mother who lived near me who acted as a liaison between the parents and the teachers. She understood both cultures and could translate from Cree to English

and vice versa. But the other teachers refused to work with her. The animosity went both ways. When I was accepted by some of the natives, the non-natives felt I was snubbing them, so they snubbed me. It was actually a relief not to be invited to their parties, since I did not like going and no longer had to make up excuses.

I tried to incorporate Cree culture into my programs. I was the first person to put their language into the Christmas concert. I created materials that incorporated their language, which helped to draw the "bush kids" back into the school after they had been out on the land hunting or fishing. I knew [that] when they came back they were in culture shock and had lost a lot of their English and fallen behind the others in school. I tried to help the other teachers understand the native way of thinking and get them to realize that their judgments came from their culture, not from the way the native people were. But they resented this.

Even though I have had difficulties in the North, it is still the place I want to go back to more than any other place. There, I feel the satisfaction and challenge as a teacher. I feel the satisfaction in making a difference in a student's life that I can't feel anywhere else.

Source: Adapted from Baverstock-Angelus, 1999. Reprinted with permission.

of transformative intellectual they will then view their students as critical individuals who can question the production of knowledge as well as what knowledge is considered meaningful. Through such an approach they believe that students and teachers become empowered, allowing them to take the first necessary steps in becoming active agents of change. The reader will find more on this topic of **critical pedagogy** in Chapter 4.

Approaches to Teaching: Two Distinct Models

Transmission Model

Ideas about what a teacher needs to know and be able to teach effectively have undergone several revolutions, and so have views about the learner and learning (Alexander, 2000; Bruner, 1997; Giroux & McLaren, 1989; Hatch, 1995; Kessen, 1979). Yet, despite new theories and new ways of looking at the purposes of education as well as the educational process, little has changed at the level of the classroom. For example, as suggested earlier, in many parts of the world, including Canada, teaching used to be seen as a set of methods that could be imparted to the prospective teacher, with minor adjustments for the particular subject being taught. This transmission teaching approach **(transmission model)** of teacher education was premised on a behaviourist view, on the assumption that learning is an objective process, with only minor variations from one student to another, due presumably to differences either in students' intelligence or in their stage of development. Behaviourism in this context emphasizes the accumulation of knowledge and teachers' efforts to transmit it.

According to the transmission model it has been (or is) assumed that an entire class of 25 or 30 students can be taught the same material at the same pace and subsequently tested to determine how much each individual had learned. This view of teaching sees classrooms as uniform places where the teacher possesses the knowledge that is to be deposited into the learner in what has been referred to as the "banking model" (Freire, 1970).

Although classes have, in fact, always been diverse in terms of students' social backgrounds, temperaments, inclination to learn, family support for education, and the like, as long as they were not obviously diverse (multiracial, multicultural) then educators could behave as if the transmission model was appropriate for all learners. Once classrooms became obviously diverse, educators had to change their thinking. Unfortunately, the change was not always for the better, since the presence of "difference" sometimes provides quasi-justification for what amounts to biased treatment in the classroom. As Carrasco (1981) reported from an ethnographic study carried out in a grade 1 classroom in New Mexico, biased treatment in the classroom can be subtle, lying outside the conscious vision of the teacher. When Carrasco shared with the teacher the videotaped evidence of a Spanish-speaking child's actual competence in the classroom, the teacher's assessment of the child's ability changed and her interactions with the child became more inclusive.

Despite considerable change in educators' thinking about teaching and learning, classroom observations both in Canada and elsewhere indicate that the transmission model is alive and well (Cleghorn, Mtetwa, Dube & Munetsi, 1998; Fuller & Snyder, 1991). In addition, as teacher educators, our experience is that undergraduate students in education frequently seek prescriptions for teaching, suggesting that many perceive their future jobs in terms of transmission. One of the main purposes of this book is to dispel such ideas.

Constructivist Model

With the civil rights movement in the United States in the 1960s, the Quiet Revolution in Quebec (Henchey, 1987), the vast increase in numbers of non-English- and non-French-speaking children attending schools in Canadian cities, and an increased awareness among some educators of global issues in education, the importance of diversity and culture in the teaching-learning process came to the fore (Bruner, 1997; Delgado-Gaitan & Trueba, 1991; Ghosh & Abdi, 2004; Grimmett & Wideen, 1995; Levin & Young, 1994).

Theoretically, we have moved far from the transmission model to what is referred to as the **constructivist model** or approach. **Social constructivism** sees teaching and learning as socially situated, child centred, and developed through classroom social interactions. When learning is viewed as socially constructed, the teaching emphasis is on discussion, collaboration, negotiation, and the development of shared meanings. According to this model, teaching is dovetailed to the cultural capital and the prior knowledge of the learners in ways that are in accord with the cultural, linguistic, and other kinds of diversity that prevail in urban Canada and elsewhere. Here we use the term cultural capital in a broader than usual sense to include the home-based ways of perceiving, thinking, speaking, believing, and behaving that all children bring to school. While the term was coined to refer to the advantage that middle-class children experience in school because their cultural capital corresponds to the cultural norms that dominate it, in a multicultural school setting with appropriately trained teachers, the cultural capital of all children should find acknowledgment.

The foregoing suggests that it is not only the student who must adjust to the norms of the school setting, but the school that must respond to the experience and "world view" that students bring to it. It is in this regard that we take exception to the frequency with which children from minority backgrounds are designated as "at risk"; the concept of "at risk" when used this way simply disguises the mistaken (and racist) idea that such children are "culturally deprived."

Where the transmission model emphasizes observable behaviours, constructivism attends to meaning, representation, and thought. The teacher's role is not to dispense knowledge but to provide students with opportunities to build knowledge. Teachers listen and observe in order to determine where a student is in his or her understanding and what is needed next in terms of scaffolding to help the student move to the next step of understanding, seemingly on his or her own. Students' mistakes are thus seen as a means of gaining insight into how they are organizing their knowledge. In this regard, the view of knowledge itself is not static with the "truth" held entirely in textbooks, but problematized, with an eye to how the world could be, not only how it is. Learning thus emphasizes the process and not the product. How one arrives at a particular answer is important. Learning is a process of constructing meaningful representations, of making sense of one's experiential world. Constructivism privileges multiple truths, representations, and realities (von Glasersfeld, 1995).

The teaching approach and teacher education model that is increasingly found in Canadian universities is directed towards teaching in multicultural school settings. **Reflective practice** (Fullan & Stiegelbauer, 1991; 1983), sometimes called the **social reconstructivist model** (Sleeter & Grant, 1993), envisions a new social order that is truly equitable—one that is anti-racist (Dei, 1996), free of social class and gender bias, and preserving of ethnic diversity in and out of the classroom. Unfortunately, and perhaps due to the lack of consensus as to what multicultural education is, the approach to multiculturalism is sometimes superficial and insufficient to effect any real long-term change in the overall structure of society.

Ideally, the multicultural/social reconstructivist model takes into account not only a much more complex view of the learner than before, but a new view of the teacher. The teacher is seen as someone who has been socialized within a particular socio-cultural system, who has a large body of taken-for-granted knowledge, who is likely to be inclined to teach in the manner she herself was taught, hence the need for reflective practice. A great deal of what teachers learn about being a teacher is absorbed throughout years as learners, observing teachers in action. As suggested earlier, there is no other profession in which people observe for several hours on a nearly daily basis for 12 or more years prior to being educated to practice that profession. We believe that the importance of this extensive prior exposure to the teaching profession and the teaching-learning process is still underestimated in its implications for teacher education.

SUMMARY/CONCLUSIONS

Teacher education programs have moved from a direct approach model to an interactive model, and these approaches are reflected in the two main models of teaching we have just discussed. The transmission model is characterized by whole-class, teacher-centred instruction, a subject-oriented curriculum, and a school day that is divided into distinct time units to correspond with the subject approach. The constructivist model sees classrooms organized into small groups, the teaching process as student centred, the organization of time as sufficiently open to allow for a thematic approach in an otherwise integrated curriculum, and learning as socially constructed through interaction.

In this chapter we have tried to show how discussions about the ways that teachers should be educated are closely but not perfectly related to ideas about how children should be taught. Similarly, we see that there are shifting trends in both areas. Despite an abundance of excellent thinking about these matters, the question remains as to why so little change has taken place at the level of the classroom. Indeed, despite all that has been said about change, there is a familiarity that has persisted in schools over the last 50 years or so which still persists in classrooms throughout the world. One can walk past a tin-roofed school in rural Cameroon in West Africa and hear Shakespeare being recited, and a grade 5 mathematics lesson in Zimbabwe sounds almost word for word like a grade 5 mathematics lesson in a suburban Montreal school (Cleghorn, Mtetwa, Dube & Munetsi, 1998). Children may be grouped around rectangular desks rather than seated in rows, but teachers still often stand at the front of the classroom and do most of the talking (Fuller & Snyder, 1991; Prophet & Rowell, 1993). In some classrooms in Canada and elsewhere the power relations have shifted so that children can speak up when they do not fully understand; in others, the teachers and pupils are engaged in an on-going dialogue as they try jointly to solve a problem (to construct knowledge) or devise the appropriate questions for a class research project (Stigler & Stevenson, 1998/99).

The foregoing suggests that the models of teaching which prevail today in our own schools may not really have changed much in the last generation or two. We need to ask, are young people learning more and differently in Canadian classrooms than elsewhere? Are there other effective ways of meeting diverse needs? These are questions that require a much deeper and more critical examination than we have provided here. We hope that by the time you have finished reading this book and reflected on its contents you will be better able to discuss these matters and think about the direction that we might move towards.

KEY TERMS

bureaucracy
communal orientation
constructivist model
critical pedagogy
cultural deficit
deschooling
early French immersion
first language maintenance
formal curriculum
formal organization

free schools
hidden curriculum
home schooling
individualistic orientation
informal organization
narrative
norms
open-structured schools
outcomes-based education
    (OBE)

policy
reflective practice
social constructivism
social reconstructivist
    model
transformative intellectual
transitional bilingual
    programs
transmission model

EDUCATIONAL ISSUES AND QUESTIONS FOR DISCUSSION

1. Policy making tends to be done at the highest levels, for example, the ministry of education. If students or teachers were to be involved in policy making, what would be the priority issues of concern?

2. With the increased reporting of teenage violence, do you think there is a crisis in education? If you agree that there is, what is its nature? If you disagree, can you say why?

3. List all the things that you think should be changed in (a) the ways schools are organized, and (b) the ways teaching occurs. Select one or two things as top priorities from each list and plan a way for the changes to take place.

4. Consider possible alternative roles for a school administrator. What would happen if teachers took turns, say for a year at a time, administering the school, dealing with difficult students and parents, and directing the teacher group?

5. What would teacher education courses contain if the field of education had emerged from anthropology rather than psychology?

RECOMMENDED READINGS/REFERENCES

Acker, S. (1988). Teachers, gender and resistance. *British Journal of Sociology of Education, 9,* 307–322.

Alexander, R. (2000). *Culture and pedagogy.* London: Blackwell.

Baverstock-Angelus, D. (1999). *Using teacher narratives for reflection, representation and reforms in teacher training programs.* Unpublished master's thesis, Concordia University, Montreal.

Benson, C. A. (2004). Bilingual schooling in Mozambique and Bolivia: From experimentation to implementation. *Language Policy, 3,* 47–66.

Blau, P., & Scott, W. R. (1962). *Formal organizations: A comparative approach.* San Francisco: Chandler.

Bowles, S., & Gintis, H. (1976). *Schooling in capitalist America.* New York: Basic Books.

Bronfenbrenner, U. (1979). *The ecology of human development: Experiments by nature and design.* Cambridge, MA: Harvard University Press.

Bruner, J. (1997). *The culture of education.* Cambridge, MA: Harvard University Press.

Canada (1982). The Canadian Charter of Rights and Freedoms. In R. Ghosh & D. Ray (Eds.), *Social change and education in Canada* (pp. 367–372). Toronto: Harcourt Brace Jovanovich.

Canada-EU student exchange (2006). *Education for global competencies.* Final Report to Human Resources Development Canada.

Canadian Teachers Federation Report, 1991.

Carrasco, R. L. (1981). Expanded awareness of student performance: A case study in applied ethnographic monitoring in a bilingual classroom. In H. Trueba, G. P. Guthrie, & K. H-P. Au (Eds.), *Culture and the bilingual classroom* (pp. 153–177). Rowley, MA: Newbury House Publishers.

Cleghorn, A. (1981). Teacher interaction in an immersion school. Unpublished doctoral dissertation, McGill University, Montreal.

Cleghorn, A., & Genesee, F. (1984). Languages in contact: An ethnographic study of interaction in an immersion school. *TESOL Quarterly, 18*(4), 595–625.

Cleghorn, A., Mtetwa, D., Dube, R., & Munetsi, C. (1998). Classroom language use in multilingual settings: Mathematics lessons from Quebec and Zimbabwe. *International Journal of Qualitative Studies in Education, 11*(3), 463–477.

Corwin, R. G. (1965). *A sociology of education.* New York: Appleton-Century Crofts. Council of Ministers of Education, Canada. (2004). Access, inclusion and achievement: Closing the gap. Country Report: Canada. Prepared for the Fifteenth Conference of Commonwealth Ministers, Edinburgh, October 27–30, 2003. Retrieved from www.cmec.ca/international.

Council of Ministers of Education, Canada, 2004. Access, Inclusion and Achievement: Closing the Gap.

Dahlberg, G., Moss, P., & Pence, A. (1999). *Beyond quality in early childhood education and care: Postmodern perspectives.* London: Falmer.

Dei, G. (1996). Black/African-Canadian student's perspectives on school racism. In M. I. Alladin (Ed.), *Racism in Canadian schools* (pp.42–57). Toronto: Harcourt Brace.

Delgado-Gaitan, C., & Trueba, H. (1991). *Crossing cultural borders: Education for immigrant families in America.* New York: Falmer Press.

Dickinson, G. (1995). The legal dimensions of teachers' duties and authority. In R. Ghosh & D. Ray (Eds.), *Social change and education in Canada* (pp. 254-278). Toronto: Harcourt Brace.

Flores, B., Cousin, P., & Dias, E. (1991). Transforming deficit myths about learning language and culture. *Language Arts, 68,* 369–379.

Freire, P. (1970). *Pedagogy of the oppressed.* New York: Seabury Press.

Fullan, M., & Stiegelbauer, S. (1991). *The new meaning of educational change.* Toronto: OISE Press.

Fuller, B., & Snyder, C. W. (1991). Vocal teachers, silent pupils: Life in Botswana classrooms. *Comparative Education Review, 35*(2), 274–294.

Genesee, F. (1987). *Learning through two languages:Studies of immersion and bilingual education.* Cambridge, MA: Newbury House Publishers.

Ghosh, R., & Abdi, A. (2004). *Education and the politics of difference: Canadian perspectives.* Toronto: Canadian Scholars' Press.

Ghosh, R., & Ray, D. (Eds.) (1987). *Social change and education in Canada.* Toronto: Harcourt Brace Jovanovich.

Ghosh, R., & Ray, D. (Eds.). (1995). *Social change and education in Canada.* (3rd ed.). Toronto: Harcourt Brace.

Giroux, H., & McLaren, P. (1989). *Critical pedagogy, the state and cultural struggle.* Albany, NY: State University of New York Press.

Goodlad, J. (1990). *Teachers for our nation's schools.* San Fransisco: Jossey-Bass.

Goodson, I. F. (Ed.) (1992). *Studying teachers' lives.* London: Routledge.

Grimmett, P. P., & Wideen, M. (Eds.). (1995). *Changing times in teacher education.* London: Falmer Press.

Hatch, A. (Ed.). (1995). *Qualitative research in early childhood settings.* Hartford, CN: Praeger

Hatch, A., et al. (2002). Developmentally appropriate practice: Continuing the dialogue. *Contemporary Issues in Early Childhood, 3*(3), 439–452.

Henchey, N. (1987). The new technology and the transformation of learning. In R. Ghosh & D. Ray.(Eds.), *Social change and education in Canada* (pp. 42–56.). Toronto: Harcourt Brace.

Hern, M. (Ed.). (1996). *Deschooling our lives.* Philadelphia: New Society Publishers.

Holmes Group. (1986). *Tomorrow's teachers.* East Lansing: Holmes Group.

Holt, J. (1964). *How children fail.* New York: Dell.

House of Commons Debates, October 8, 1971, pp. 8545–8548.

Hurn, C. J. (1993). *The limits and possibilities of schooling.* Toronto: Allyn and Bacon.

Illich. (1971). *Deschooling society.* New York: Harper & Row.

Jackson, P. (1968). *Life in classrooms.* New York: Holt, Rinehart & Winston.

Jansen, J., & Christie, P. (1999). *The changing curriculum: Studies in outcomes-based education in South Africa.* Cape Town: Juta Academic.

Johnson, R. K., & Swain, M. (1997). *Immersion education: International perspectives.* Cambridge, U.K.: Cambridge University Press.

Kessen, W. (1979). The American child and other cultural inventions. *American Psychologist, 34*, 815–820.

Laird, S. (1988). Reforming "woman's true profession": A case for "feminist pedagogy" in teacher education? *Harvard Educational Review, 58*(4), 449–463.

Lambert, W., & Tucker, G. R. (1972). *The bilingual education of children: The St. Lambert experiment.* Rowley, MA: Newbury House.

Levin, B., & Young, J. (1994). *Understanding Canadian schools: An introduction to educational administration.* Toronto: Harcourt Brace.

Lortie, D. (1975). *Schoolteacher.* Chicago: University of Chicago Press.

Martin, J. R. (1985). *Reclaiming a conversation: The ideal of the educated woman.* New Haven, CN: Yale University Press.

Martin, W. B. W. (1975). The negotiated order of teachers in team teaching situations. *Sociology of Education, 48*, 202–222.

Martin, W. B. W. (1976). *The negotiated order of the school.* Toronto: MacMillan.

Martin, W. B. W., & Macdonell, A. (1978). *Canadian Education.* Toronto: Prentice Hall.

McAndrew, M. (1987). *Le traitement de la diversité raciale, ethnique et culturelle et la valorisation du pluralisme dans le matériel didactique au Québec: rapport de recherche.* Montréal: Conseil des communautés culturelles et de l'immigration du Québec.

Meighan, R. (1997). *The next learning system and why home-schoolers are trailblazers.* Nottingham, U.K.: Educational Heretics Press.

Mifflen, F. J., & Mifflen, S.C. (1982). *The sociology of education: Canada and beyond.* Calgary: Detselig.

Neill, A. S. (1960). *Summerhill: A radical approach to child rearing.* New York: Hart Publishing.

Porter, J. (1965). *The Vertical Mosaic.* Toronto: University of Toronto Press.

Prophet, R. B., & Rowell, P. M. (1993). Coping and control: Science teaching strategies in Botswana. *International Journal of Qualitative Studies in Education, 6*(3), 197–209.

Rich, A. (1985). Taking women students seriously. In M. Culley & C. Portuges (Eds.), *Gendered subjects: The dynamics of feminist teaching.* Boston: Routledge & Kegan Paul.

Schön, D. (1983). *The reflective practitioner.* London: Temple Smith.

Serpell, R. (1993). *The significance of schooling.* Cambridge, U.K.: Cambridge University Press.

Shrewsbury, C. M. (1987). What is feminist pedagogy? *Women's Studies Quarterly, 15*(3–4), 6–14.

Sleeter, C. E., & Grant, C. A. (1993). *Making choices for multicultural education.* Toronto: Maxwell Macmillan Canada.

Smith, D. S. (1993). *Home schooling in Canada.* Francombe Place Research Associates.

Spencer, M. (1979). *The foundations of modern sociology* (2nd ed.). Englewood Cliffs, N.J.: Prentice Hall.

Statistics Canada (2004). Retrieved from http://www.statcan.ca/english/freepub/81-004-XIE/200410/mafe.htm

Stigler, J. W., & Stevenson, H. W. (1998/99). How Asian teachers polish each lesson to perfection. In E. J. Nunn & C. J. Boyatzis (Eds.), *Child growth and development* (pp. 90–101).Guilford, CN: McGraw-Hill.

Stroud, C. (2002). *Towards a policy for bilingual education in developing countries.* Education Division Documents No. 10. Stockholm: Sida.

Tabulawa, R. (1998). Teachers' perspectives on classroom practice in Botswana: Implications for pedagogical change. *International Journal of Qualitative Studies in Education, 11*(2), 249–268.

Trudeau, P. E. (1971). Policy on multiculturalism. House of Commons Debates, October 8, pp. 8545–8548.

Trueba, H., Guthrie, G. P., & Au Hu-Pei, K. (1981). *Culture and the bilingual classroom: Studies in classroom ethnography.* Rowley, MA: Newbury House Publishers.

von Glasersfeld, E. (1995). *Radical constructivism : A way of knowing and learning.* London: Falmer.

Weber, S., & Mitchell, C. (1995). *That's funny, you don't look like a teacher!: Interrogating images and identity in popular cultures.* Washington, D.C.: Falmer Press

chapter four

Critical Perspectives on the Politics of Teaching and Pedagogy

CHAPTER OBJECTIVES

The purpose of this chapter is to

- clarify the distinction between teaching and pedagogy; to do so we build on the theories presented in Chapter 2, providing a detailed account of critical, feminist, and anti-racist pedagogies, which are informed by the work of Paulo Freire

- present a study that illustrates the implementation of critical pedagogy into classroom practice; this stands as an example of what is possible when educators fully understand the political nature of the schooling process

- discuss feminist and anti-racist pedagogies and how these attempt to go beyond critical pedagogy to work towards changing class, race, and gender inequities

THE POLITICS OF TEACHING

Teachers bring to the schooling situation a great deal of both common sense and taken-for-granted knowledge. This knowledge has been acquired not only during their formal teacher education but also during their own socialization within the same socio-cultural system in which they later on teach. For example, the idea that schools, organized in traditional, familiar ways, are appropriate places for students to learn generally goes unquestioned. Similarly, we have all been influenced by the belief that we live in a meritocratic society, where individual effort and ability lead to higher educational achievement. These beliefs are bound up with what we have earlier referred to as society's dominant ideology.

The reader will recall from Chapter 2 that ideology is commonly taken to mean a set of beliefs and values held by a group (or a society), usually based on an interpretation of the past with prescriptions of policy for the future. For Marx, ideology refers to a belief system that legitimates the dominant group. He maintains that this system is generated and controlled by the owners of material production. In other words, the economic dominance of the ruling class controls the world of ideas as well. Marx's conceptualization is of value because it grounds ideology in material experience and observable human behaviour, but it becomes problematic insofar as it implies that societal ideas and beliefs are deliberately manipulated in a calculated way so as to indoctrinate the subordinate class. According to Marx, ideology serves the powerful group by presenting the powerless or subordinate groups with a definition of reality that is false; as this defin-ition becomes part of the shared belief system it provides order to the surrounding world.

Weber (1947) broadens Marx's notion of ideology to include the idea that ideology and control are more powerful and effective when they are cloaked in beliefs that make them appear legitimate through the education system. For Weber, one of the major roles of an education system is to disseminate the dominant ideology through the populace.

Later development of these ideas came from Gramsci's (1971) concept of hegemony, which shows how ideology originates and operates in a subtle fashion as a kind of prepon-derance of influence. The hegemonic aspect of ideology arises from its ability to build social consensus by appealing to a selective interpretation of the past and people's common sense assumptions about the world. For instance, the genesis of the myth of the "American dream" stems from the success stories of a minority of new Americans, with the Puritan ethos of hard work serving as an explanation for their success. After industrialization and the advent of institutionalized education for all in the nineteenth century, this ideology was translated into educational values. The reward for hard work in school was translated into the achievement of a higher social status. Individual success stories, however, such as that of Henry Ford in the U.S. and Samuel Bronfman in Canada, can be cited as evidence of the fact that the accumulation of fortune is not necessarily linked to educational credentials.

Briefly then, ideology is a dynamic rather than a static mechanism; it is a living belief that is bound up with and brought to life in the consciousness of the student. From within the institution of the school, the dominant ideology affects and develops the consciousness of the student, shaping his or her perception of self and society in many significant ways. Education is not merely a distant mechanism for sorting and selecting individuals for the work world; the institution of school operates as such because people have come to believe that this is part of its task. That is, education aids in the reproduction of this ideology; schools reproduce social and economic inequality by perpetuating patterns of success and failure, which, as already stated, go unquestioned since they are considered "normal." When institutionalized ways of doing things become part of the intra-psychic make-up of the individual, the system supports the dominant group. The primary institution where these mechanisms of control are played out, passed on, and perpetuated, then, is the school. This is what is meant by the politics of teaching and education.

TEACHING AND PEDAGOGY

In this section we further examine how the politics of education finds its way into peda-gogical practice. As Roger Simon (1987) notes, **pedagogy** refers to the production of knowledge, identities, and values; it must, therefore, be distinguished from teaching.

> Pedagogy [refers] to the integration in practice of particular curriculum content and design, classroom strategies and techniques, and evaluation, purpose and method. All of these aspects organize a view of how a teacher's work within an institutional context specifies a particular version of what knowledge is most worth, what it means to know

something, and how we might construct representations of ourselves, others, and our physical and social environment. . . (p. 370).

The shift away from teaching, the transmission of knowledge, to pedagogy, the production of knowledge, has led researchers to look on pedagogy as a form of **cultural politics**. By cultural politics we mean that those in positions of power determine such matters as curriculum. That is, those in power determine what others ought to and, perhaps, may learn. If, for example, those who make the decisions consider computers to be more important than, say, art or music, then computers will win out. Simon further states, "In other words, talk about pedagogy is simultaneously talk about the details of what students and others might do together and the cultural politics such practices support. In this perspective, we cannot talk about teaching practices without talking about politics" (p. 370).

Simon (1987) and Giroux (1989), drawing on Freire's work, use a critical perspective to view culture not only as a way of life but as a form of production that involves relations of power and legitimization of certain meanings and experience.

Paulo Freire: Liberation through Education

Freire's primary concern was with social transformation and developing an emancipatory or liberatory education. He explains how this process can occur by focusing on educational practices, the empowerment of teachers, and teachers as agents of empowering students. Much of his work has been regarded as highly political and has become the foundation for the development of a new, more liberating pedagogy.

Since both the critical and feminist pedagogists were greatly influenced by Paulo Freire, it is useful to discuss his views in some detail. First, however, it is important to note that Freire's philosophy reflects the societal conditions in Brazil, the country that he came from and was most familiar with. That is, his first experience was with an impoverished society, where there was a huge gap between a small, wealthy, and educated elite and a large, extremely poor, and uneducated peasant class. Nevertheless, Freire speaks to and is heard by all who have experienced oppression, as well as those who are concerned with increasing equality.

Freire (1970) aimed to develop a **theory of liberation** that could provide a basis for educational theory and practice. For him, it is not only people who are processed in schools; knowledge is selected, organized, and then processed as well. Freire believes that individuals have the power to come to an understanding of their own situation in the world. He refers to this as critical consciousness. It is important to note that Freire believes that both teachers and students are agents engaged in constructing and reconstructing meaning. That is, they are agents who could transform educational practice.

Freire's theory of liberation attempted to provide a basis for educational theory and practice in the radical sense, by focusing on social change and fracturing the status quo, and to bridge these dichotomous strands of pedagogy. Thus, according to Freire, researchers must ask questions about the selection and organization of knowledge. They must treat knowledge, or what counts as knowledge, as socially constructed. That is, researchers need to explore how and why certain dominant categories of knowledge persist, how they link with certain interests and occupational groups, and understand the influence of the elite's traditions. Freire asks whether educators cannot change the criteria of high-class knowledge so that it is concrete rather than abstract, oral rather than literate,

Paulo Freire

Educator Paulo Freire was born September, 1921, in Recife, Brazil. He was brought up in poverty and experienced the consequences of social discrimination, hunger, and lack of freedom of expression. Because he lived among poor rural families and labourers, Freire gained a deep understanding of their life experiences and the effects of socio-economics on education.

In the early 1940s Freire was able to study law at the University of Recife while working part-time as an instructor of Portuguese in a secondary school. Following a short career as a lawyer, he returned to teaching Portuguese; later he worked in adult education. These years of public service were crucial in bringing him closer to the cause of the urban poor. In the 1950s and 1960s Freire began to formulate ways of communicating with the peasants and developed the dialogical method of teaching and learning. In 1964, he was imprisoned for several months in Brazil, accused of being a traitor. After a brief stay in Bolivia he lived in Chile for five years. In 1967 he published his first book, *Education as the Practice of Freedom,* and in 1968 he wrote *Pedagogy of the Oppressed.* Following the publication of these books Freire obtained a position as visiting professor at Harvard University in 1969. In 1979, after 15 years in exile, he was permitted to return to Brazil, where he joined the Workers' Party in São Paulo and supervised its adult literacy project. After his success with this project he was appointed Minister of Education for the city of São Paulo. The Paulo Freire Institute was created in 1991. It attracts scholars and critics of the theorist's pedagogy and maintains the Freire archives.

Paulo Freire died in São Paulo in May, 1997. He made a number of important theoretical innovations that have had a significant impact on the development of educational practice, both in formal and popular education. His pedagogy heightened awareness to the causes and consequences of human suffering and the need to develop a critical, ethical pedagogy for social change. Freire left a legacy of indignation about social injustice as well as a lifetime commitment to the cause of oppressed peoples throughout the world. His work continues to be reinterpreted and re-clarified according to the ongoing changes in political and intellectual thought.

communal rather than individual, therefore seeking ways to make the accepted (upper-class) knowledge accessible to the peasant and working classes.

Freire views education as a radical project for economic, political, and cultural change in which power relations are transformed. Pedagogy (classroom management, teaching style, classroom activities, evaluation) is the means or process by which curriculum (subject content, knowledge) is communicated. All pedagogy, therefore, is essentially political.

Culture and Schooling

In this section, we look at Freire's view of culture and schooling and link it with his theory for achieving social change through education. Freire sees the function of culture as more than passing on a heritage: its function is political. The dominant culture functions to legitimize existing modes of social relations and production. It also functions to provide the motivational structures that link individual needs with social needs. Furthermore, culture provides a society with the symbolic language for interpreting the boundaries of individual and social existence.

Freire is concerned not only with making knowledge accessible to the poor and other oppressed people, but also with transforming pedagogy so that the views of the elite change as well. He thus diverges from the standard, deterministic view of pedagogy to suggest that new understandings can be constructed by the higher classes even though their perceptions of social reality may differ from those who are oppressed. That is, Freire does not see schools in purely mechanistic terms. Schools do not simply process students for the realms of leisure and work.

Freire places ideology within the sphere of individual consciousness. Ideology shapes people's perceptions of reality, which are defined by the dominant classes who control educational access, processes, and content. But there is passivity among the oppressed. Pedagogical practices are thus saturated with mechanisms to maintain the position of the elite, with the result that those who do not have control are robbed of the possibility of developing a critical consciousness. In other words, whatever teaching and knowledge those without control do receive ensures that they remain passive. This Freire refers to as the **culture of silence**.

By suggesting that ideology is part of consciousness, Freire views consciousness as a contradictory force, since it is composed not only of the dominant ideology but also of critical, good sense. In this way, consciousness is characterized by a constant struggle between people's capacity to think critically and the power of hegemonic ideology. This struggle within our consciousness is revealed through **dialogue**. The purpose of dialogue is not only to validate the voices and subjective experiences of the oppressed but also to expose both the subjective and objective nature of ideology, that is, the beliefs and practices that influence our thoughts and actions. By critiquing our thoughts through dialogue, we begin to carve out a path towards becoming critically conscious actors engaged in the construction of a more humane world.

The kind of dialogue that Freire has in mind relates to the concrete situations and lived experiences that inform our daily lives. This kind of dialogue leads to the recognition of one's own cultural capital and how it can be used to reclaim one's own identity. This pedagogy does not teach reading and writing passively. It is a pedagogy that questions. The content of instruction must, then, be rooted in the cultural capital of learners and made problematic through critical dialogue.

Briefly then, students have to learn how culture functions in the interest of the dominant classes. They must examine the form and content of the approved texts to reveal the ideologies, images, and ideas they present. The words, setting, and images contained in school materials have to be examined, their political implications and social consequences noted. Through such analysis, students come to see that they can engage in social and political reconstruction. That is, a means for promoting critical comprehension of contradictory cultural meanings and practices is developed.

Concept of Dialogue

The dialogue form of pedagogy presupposes that the student and teacher are equals; both are subjects in a world characterized by ideological and structural forces that shape and influence thought and action. Therefore, in order for dialogue to be successful in recovering, validating, and critiquing the experiences of students, teachers must not impose knowledge on students in the traditional manner of "banking" education. Banking education occurs when teachers consider students to be empty receptacles, which they are to fill with knowledge. When teachers approach education this way students memorize knowledge yet rarely question or analyze it to reveal its underlying interests.

Pedagogy that takes a dialogical form seeks not only to question the knowledge that students learn in school, but also to validate the knowledge that students already possess, that which they gain from experiencing life as particular individuals in a particular historical and social circumstance. Stated another way, individuals are not merely passive receptors of knowledge and ideology. Rather, they are always mediating these through common sense and their own identities, which are shaped by their class, race, ethnicity, and gender. The exploration of subjective experiences thus also reveals the choices and actions that individuals make to counter or resist the forces that seek to shape and limit them.

Perception of Knowledge

For Freire, liberation means being able to construct your own meanings, frames of reference, and self-determining powers through an ability to understand reality. Knowledge is not neutral; it is generated from human activity situated in norms and interests. The act of knowing is more than a technical issue—it is a political issue. Under the guise of objectivity, knowledge has been used to legitimate belief and value systems. "Objective" knowledge mystifies and turns people into spectators by removing underlying norms, values, and interests from public debate.

We need to do more than demystify knowledge; we also need to question the processes used to constitute and legitimate knowledge and experience. How can this be accomplished? We must transcend the realms of intellectual habit and common sense. Radical educators must learn to highlight and make problematic the knowledge they present to their students, and to question meaning and the nature of knowledge itself. Knowledge, then, must become the mediator of communications and dialogue. For instance, students should be asking:

- Whose reality is being legitimated by this knowledge?
- Whose interest does this knowledge represent?
- Why is this knowledge being taught this way?
- Does this knowledge have meaning for the learner?
- Is this knowledge part of the learners' cultural capital?

Conscientization/Critical Consciousness

Conscientization is the term used by Freire to refer to an awakening process. The path towards critical consciousness or conscientization involves a reinterpretation of what is considered to constitute knowledge. It indicates that individuals exist not only *in* the world but also *with* the world. We cannot separate ourselves from our own personal world, nor can we separate ourselves from the structural and ideological barriers of the external world.

This dialectical view provides a basis by which individuals can become not only conscious, but most importantly, critically conscious, and ultimately, act to create a more humane world. The difference between the two sides of consciousness lies in the ability to decipher how societal forces, both ideological and structural, enable and limit individuals. An inability to analyze these forces and link them to dominating interests means that an individual has not developed a critical consciousness but is still at the stage that Freire refers to as "native consciousness". At this stage, the individual is considered a determined being because, although she or he possesses a consciousness, it is not his or her own but that of his or her oppressor.

As part of the subject-object dialectic, knowledge is crucial to the liberation of oppressed individuals; they will come to know that it is a social construction and that they can participate in its construction. In the classroom, critical consciousness involves not only the validation of the knowledge-based experiences that individuals bring to school with them but also a simultaneous critique of school knowledge. A critique of school knowledge demystifies the supposed objectivity of knowledge and its links to the interests of dominant groups.

An understanding that knowledge is socially constructed and never complete forms part of the process of empowerment of disenfranchised individuals. In other words, knowledge gives people power. When students' subjective experiences are acknowledged and incorporated through dialogue into the learning process, students gain voice.

Schools as Centres of Liberating Praxis

According to Freire, schools are centres of **praxis** (reflection and action), where social change can occur. It is in schools that a multiplicity of personal, subjective experiences come together under conditions of supposed equality. Yet education rarely entails questioning the knowledge that it teaches for its own underlying interests, nor validates the knowledge that students bring into the classroom. In this way, education maintains the status quo and is seen as a profoundly political process.

Inherent in any educational design are value assumptions about the nature of humankind and specific forms of knowledge. These notions, validating certain subjective understandings of experience while devaluing others, are passed down through pedagogy and reinforced in the minds of students.

Defined by ideologies and practices, the politics of education can be as liberating as they can be constraining. Schooling practices that shape the individual and collective consciousness of students can be questioned. Issues of power relations between individuals and society can be addressed. School knowledge can be critiqued. The student's perception of her or his oppression can be validated. Basically, the power of hegemonic ideology can be overcome in schools. Schools can be centres for change because it is there that the individual can begin to learn that he or she can participate in the organization of his or her society.

Critiques of Freire's Work

Some have argued that Freire's work is situation specific. That is, they think that Freire's pedagogy is aimed too much at the liberation of oppressed populations in underdeveloped nations. It is true that oppression of the kind existing in underdeveloped nations may not be as prevalent in the developed ones. This criticism, however, does not dismiss the fact that the more developed countries are also characterized by domination and oppression, albeit of a more subtle variety. So Freire's pedagogy cannot be imposed in a grid-like way, but it can be altered to take into consideration the varying forms of oppression and domination in our unique historical and social context.

Another critique centres on the idea that domination is legitimized through the dominant ideology, which permeates all levels of society. There are different forms of legitimization. We must clarify how the legitimization of domination has been applied in schools so as to obscure political interests. For example, science and technology are used to conceal class-specific interests and values (Aikenhead, 1990). Freire does not account for this. His notion of ideology needs to be developed to address the legitimization and socialization process in schools in modern industrialized countries.

In clarifying Freire's concept of ideology we must also go beyond the material and psychological forces that sustain ideologies to include the historical forms of political and social life that produce them. That is, the social composition of the political forces at work in these dominated societies must be identified. We have to account for the organizational and mobilization capacities of the social groups involved before Freire's vision of social transformation can be considered as viable.

Another concept that needs to be developed further is dialogical communication. We must ask if we can clarify the intended and unintended consequences of the hidden curriculum through dialogical communication. Freire assumes that in battling oppression, the oppressed will move towards humanization. The oppressed, however, can become the oppressor once their oppressive conditions have been overcome. Freire's response to this criticism has been that individuals must engage in self-critique and question their assumptions and practices in order to understand how their actions can also become oppressive.

A final critique of Freire's work is that he appears to create an illusion of equality amongst the oppressed, in terms of their experiences as well as their conception of a more humane society. The oppressed cannot be considered a homogeneous group, even if they are all experiencing one common form of oppression. Individuals who are oppressed may experience within-group forms of oppression, which will alter their vision of how a more humane society ought to be organized.

Despite these critiques, Freire's pedagogy cannot and has not been dismissed. In the following sections we examine the work of a number of critical and feminist pedagogists who were influenced by Freire.

CRITICAL PEDAGOGY

Critical pedagogy is fundamentally concerned with understanding the relationship between power and knowledge. Knowledge is socially constructed and deeply rooted in power relations. Critical pedagogy asks how and why knowledge gets constructed the way it does and how and why some constructions of reality are legitimated by the dominant culture while others are not. It asks, then, what are the social functions of knowledge (McLaren, 1998).

The dominant culture is able to exercise control through the process of hegemony, in which the powerful gain the compliance of the oppressed in perpetuating their own oppression. Hegemony is supported by ideology, whether it be the ideology of communism, socialism, or capitalism, and permeates all of social life. We use ideology to "make sense" of our world. When ideology is queried we come to understand which concepts, values, and meanings obscure, or, alternatively, clarify our understanding of our place within the world.

Resistance

The work of Giroux (1983; 1989; 1996), Weiler (1988; 1991), and Willis (1977) on resistance among youth subcultures illustrates the practical applications of critical pedagogy in educational practice. Youth subcultures infiltrate schools, creating profound effects on student motivation, classroom management, academic standards, school discipline, and safety. That is, they constitute a problem requiring a more concerted response than simple disciplinary measures. The challenge is to find ways to harness the resistance of these groups so that they remain within the system and become more willing participants in it. This is thought to be possible if they share in the power relations and if their experience is given a voice, that is, if they are permitted to contribute to the meaning of the knowledge that they themselves construct. By understanding the reason for the emergence of the structure and the purpose of these subcultures, educators may be able to embrace these youths as allies in the learning process.

One particular explanation for the emergence of youth subcultures has to do with the notion of resistance. Resistance is defined as any behaviour, passive or active, that goes beyond simply opposing one or many elements of the dominant group. To evaluate the degree of resistance, both the quality as well as the consequences of the resistant behaviour must be taken into account (Giroux, 1983). Youth subcultures frequently offer the adolescent the opportunity for resistance against the prevailing power structure, which in schools is clearly demarcated between teachers and administrators, who are in positions of power and control, and students, who form a subordinate group with little actual say in what happens to them for several hours each day. As Weiler (1988) points out, the ideology that supports the system of control over the subordinate group is a system of values, morals, and beliefs, or a structure of thought and consciousness that frames the individual's perception and experience of the world. Giroux's (1983) analysis of resistance includes the individual's needs, history, and subjectivity as well as his or her ability to act, struggle, and critique both self and society on a personal and political level. He notes that an opportunity to resist may lead certain youths to a new consciousness and recognition regarding their place in the social structure. It is this behaviour, which opposes the status quo and is out of reach of those formerly in control, that is deemed to be a problem. Individual members within a resisting youth subculture understand that they are not passive recipients of domination, but rather active agents engaged in negotiation, mediation, and alteration of personal and collective meanings, capable of transforming their environments (Giroux, 1983). Resistance cannot be simply the rejection of a dominant value, nor can it be an acceptance of submission or a partial uncovering of the dominance. It must lead to a change in the hegemonic ideology. Such change may come only with a fully developed critical consciousness, a result of praxis (Freire, 1968), which involves not only the youth, but the teachers and the other adults in their lives. Freire's praxis involves the power of the individual to act as an agent of change and create and recreate meaning.

Praxis allows the individual to understand the limitations of the environment and uncover the means to resist these very limitations. The reflective period leads to some form of action with the intent to transform and change the environment. By "naming, reading and knowing reality" (Weiler, 1988, p. 18), the individual challenges the received vision of reality and appropriates a personal vision. Such a critique of hegemonic ideologies through reflection-action-reflection can lead to social transformation.

By questioning situations, traditions, history, and their own life world (intellectual, emotional, and physical space), students can be taught to think critically and move towards liberation. This type of teaching, known as critical pedagogy, succeeds best when the multiple subjectivities of both teacher and student are included in the classroom and the students themselves present the conflicts and issues that are discussed and explored. The development of a critical consciousness occurs in three stages: intransitive (fatalistic); semitransitive (some hope for change), and critical transitivity, or praxis (dynamic relationship between thought and action). This approach is particularly effective when used by teachers working with resistant youths who feel disempowered. We would suggest, however, that it not be viewed simply as a remedial strategy, but that it belongs in all classrooms; if used more often, it might go a long way towards preventing resistant youth subcultures from forming.

Paul Willis' 1977 study, *Learning to Labour,* carried out in England, is one of the most influential on the topic of resistance. The study showed how class culture is reproduced and how working-class boys resisted the dominant ideology and power that were imposed on them. These working-class boys, or "lads," as they were referred to by Willis, rejected the ideology of the school that is, the class-tainted values and knowledge embedded in the curriculum, which was offered without mediation in respect to the cultural capital that working-class children bring to school. From the boys' perspectives, the school rejected their working-class culture, the characteristics of which they chose to emphasize as a strategy of resistance. They rejected and actively resisted the values and knowledge of the school, which they viewed as imposed on them. Indeed, they saw manual work as productive, and mental work as destructive to maintaining their working-class culture. However, their resistance to schooling and their emphasis on their own class culture did not lead them out of their genuinely oppressive conditions. Rather, the social boundary between their position and the position of those in control was solidified. Thus, in a way, their resistance was an indication of their complicity in remaining where they were. The following case study illustrates the practical application of critical pedagogy in a school where youths have resisted traditional norms and values.

The Alternate School

The Alternate School is an alternative secondary school aimed at helping at-risk and troubled youths in a small setting of 65–75 students. The school is for youths who have dropped out of regular school or are deemed to be dysfunctional or delinquent. These students have experienced social and personal difficulties that have interfered with their academic success (e.g., conduct disorders such as temper control and impulsiveness; sexual crises such as rape, incest, abuse, and teen pregnancy; substance abuse such as alcohol, food, and drugs; and delinquency such as prostitution, gang membership, living on the street, armed robbery, assault, and drug trafficking). The students at The Alternate School are considered troubled adolescents and categorized into various levels of delinquency, which is considered a normal, natural entry requirement of the school. These are youths who have resisted the traditional educational system and are in search of an alternative route.

By existing within the traditional education system of Quebec but practising outside this system, The Alternate School is transformed from an authoritarian, anti-intellectual, passive, teacher-talk model of education to the one proposed by Freire, as described by McLaren and Leonard (1993). This model is democratic, intellectually challenging, student active, and emancipatory. According to the tenets of critical pedagogy, the philosophy of The Alternate School is founded on mutual respect and equality. These are not simply empty words; they are put into

action daily. The traditional approach, where the teacher is the authority, always right, and has certain inalienable rights, does not exist at The Alternate School. From cleaning toilets together to discussing courses of discipline, from structuring examinations to designing curriculum, teachers and students perform the same tasks as a team. Staff and classroom decisions are made after extensive dialogue takes place and a consensus is achieved. This democratic atmosphere encourages these students to see themselves as active agents of change (Giroux, 1983). Through the process of dialogue and consensus, students are encouraged to question the rules, contest the decisions, and redefine their situations. That is, their voices are heard.

When students enter The Alternate School, they have already experienced and resisted certain limitations within their environment. They have understood that simple oppositional behaviours (e.g., skipping classes, verbally assaulting teachers, and avoiding homework) do not change situations; they realize that, if anything, this behaviour makes them worse. Students who demonstrate oppositional behaviour in regular schools contradict the everyday social order for a limited period of time, but eventually, most of them fade back into the mainstream.

Through their problems, students who resist the traditional education system find solutions that require action. Their resistant behaviour offers them a sense of freedom from the dominance of a system that they feel does not work

(Continued)

The Alternate School (*Continued*)

for them. After a period of reflection, when they may view their situation as problematic because it is affecting their lives, students move towards action, either by withdrawing from the system, existing independently in it, or counter-resisting.

The first action officially required of the students is to make the initial contact with The Alternate School. Students must refer themselves to the school by making a telephone call to establish an interview time. This first step is critical, for it indicates that they are attempting to take charge of their situation and make changes. It shows that they have left behind the fatalistic and hopeless voice of intransitive thinking and have moved into a stage of semitransitive thought, as outlined in Giroux's (1983) description of critical consciousness. It is this stage that is the key to success in the students' experience at the school. At this point in their lives, the particular issues related to mainstream schooling have become problematic. Through the process of questioning and evaluating, the students reach the conclusion that change must occur. They redefine their situations and see the possibilities for a new reality. The phone call is the first step for change.

As much as schools make youths feel powerless and submissive, this phone call has the opposite effect. It signals to them that the everyday social order can change. Following the first or second interview, students spend a trial period in the school so that they may determine if it is appropriate for them. This second phase in the entry procedure places the power for change, once again, in the students' hands. After this

trial period, students have the choice of leaving the school and seeking out something elsewhere that benefits them. For those students who choose to stay, the third phase is a probationary period, a period of time when they participate fully in classes and school life. Students who choose to remain at the school are those who have already experienced a discrepancy between "what is and what is supposed to be." A desire to change the self and the system is the common motivation amongst these students. This common perspective instantly unites many of them into the role of human agent of change, capable of transforming their environments. Students spend much of their one-year stay at the school in one of two stages: semi-transitive thought, whereby they demonstrate some hope for change, or critical transitive thought, whereby they demonstrate a strong, positive dynamic between thought and action.

These patterns of thought and action are resistant behaviours because they empower students to understand their place in the hierarchy and transform the existing social structure. For instance, Mary, a 14-year-old female who left an abusive relationship with her 26-year-old boyfriend, volunteers at a battered women's shelter to gain back control and fight against the system. Liz, an 18-year-old female fighting anorexia nervosa, runs seminars in elementary classrooms about the ravaging effects of the disease. Tim, a 19-year-old male, actively speaks out against sexual abuse when he recounts the effects of a male rape he experienced at the age of 14. Adam, a 17-year-old male, resists the

(Continued)

wave of family violence he experienced and donates his time and photographic talent to an urban organization that works to combat youth street violence. All these examples show how students who understand the source of their struggle can see active solutions within their problems and extract meaning from their environments.

Critical Consciousness

The students at The Alternate School share certain values. Because the school's mode of instruction is cooperative and interactive, students immediately begin to talk about their ideas, thoughts, and feelings with their peers and teachers. Because an atmosphere of democracy and equality prevails, students are free to express their opinions. They are challenged to step forward and take responsibility for themselves, the group, and the social conditions at the school. Social problems such as homelessness, the abuse of women, and the use of weapons, become the focus of class discussions in which the students initiate projects that address these problems on both a personal and social level. Projects such as serving meals to the homeless, volunteering time at a women's shelter, and participating in the annual Amnesty Weapons Day help students to assert their leadership skills, activate their compassion (often dormant in troubled adolescents), and distance themselves from their personal crises. Furthermore, when these students are enmeshed in the neighbourhood and bonded to the community, their delinquent acts are reduced; it is difficult for them to perform destructive acts towards people who are known to them, who are not faceless individuals.

As the first step in helping students to develop their thinking processes, teachers are asked to "suspend personal belief biases" (Bibby & Posterski, 1992, p. 16). To understand the student perspective, teachers must first examine their own biases. Teachers at The Alternate School are reminded that, when working with negative youth subcultures, the starting point of learning, discussion, and change may be more important than where the process ends. Activities must originate from the students themselves, who are taught to think about, discuss, and tackle issues using a six-step process that is presented in question format.

1. What is the actual content of the issue?

2. Who is presenting the issue, and how does this impact on its truth?

3. How do I know what I know?

4. How is this issue like/unlike something else I know?

5. To whom would this issue be relevant and why?

6. Why bother looking at the issue in the first place?

Using this approach, students are asked to look past the superficial. They are asked to analyze the deeper meaning of the social issue, understand its context, determine its relevance, and articulate a response in their own voices. Students are taught to understand their actions and to link these to the actions of others. They see that their choices are directly tied to the limitations of others. For example, black students were recently discussing the problems that they face when entering local stores. They expressed anger at immediately being

(Continued)

scrutinized by store owners. Linking this experience to the study of the historical oppression of black Americans and the civil rights struggles of the 1960s, students were shocked to realize that, in their view, very little had changed since then. They understood the effects that affirmative action and gaining the right to vote had, but saw that difficulties still exist on both a personal and a societal level.

Generative Themes

Critical pedagogy requires that students assert themselves, see the inequalities of the social order, tackle the injustices of domination, and uncover the politics of education. Freire (1968) suggests that it is the duty and moral obligation of teachers to become problem posers and present thought-provoking subjects based on social issues relevant to student life. Teachers, by using student vocabulary, lead students to reflect on social issues. **Generative themes** help highlight the dilemma behind many social conditions and can lead to action and change.

At The Alternate School, generative themes appear through innovative curriculum. "Gender Issues," "Great Thinkers," and "Student in Society" are three separate courses that are based on student-generated issues. These courses were created and piloted at The Alternate School and have been approved and accepted by the ministry of education of Quebec as accredited secondary-leaving courses.

Student-Centred Dialogue

Creating a safe environment in the classroom for students to express their concerns about relevant issues is one of the single most important tasks for teachers practising critical pedagogy. Just as generative themes permit students to explore these issues, student-centred dialogue serves as the vehicle for this exploration. Through the development of **voice,** freedom, and **empowerment,** students engage in dialogues that transform their resistance into an acceptance that they can contribute to the teaching/learning process.

Voice, according to Weiler, is a tool that allows the teacher and students to recognize themselves as active agents of change. At The Alternate School, most classrooms have a climate of trust. Students safely discuss their cultural and personal experiences, such as rape, incest, incarceration, discrimination, and sexism. Through this discussion, teachers and students understand how the hegemonic ideology and institutional practices frame experiences, develop cultural meanings, and construct individual identities. The sharing of biographies and multiple subjectivities helps the individual to emerge as a dynamic member of the educational process. A safe atmosphere for voicing subjectivities also helps to develop consciousness.

Voice also allows the meaning of words to be validated. Since words and language do not exist as neutral tools of expression, individuals adopt and appropriate the language, making it their own. Words and language are shared and interpreted within a context. At The Alternate School, in order for teachers to converse and communicate with their students, it is imperative that they develop an understanding of students' argot. Not only does the use of argot in the classroom help teachers with youth subcultures, but it also

(Continued)

shows students the importance of language as a contextual tool.

At The Alternate School, one particular situation points to the change that can occur when a student chooses to voice resistance. Sally, an 18-year-old female, was extremely weak in math. Her confidence was more than doubly shattered when the males in the class openly taunted her with the stereotype of being "blonde, female, and dumb." Regardless of reprimands, their behaviour changed only superficially. Each day, Sally would state that the taunts didn't bother her, since she "was used to guys bugging her." Unable to quickly change the behaviour of the group, the teacher worked on changing the behaviour of the individual instead. Talking with Sally about standing up for herself actually led to change. When she finally saw her situation as problematic, Sally decided to resist the stereotype regarding her skills. One day, while struggling to solve a math problem on the board with the class snickering all around her, Sally finally stated her dissatisfaction with her male counterparts. Silence descended upon the room. She successfully finished the problem, and the class cheered. (Sally still struggles with math, but smiles since she silenced the males.)

When students are allowed to express their voice through a student-centred dialogue, they may often experience the opportunities that freedom of choice may bring. An illustration of how students exercise their freedom lies in the work experience component of the course "Student in Society." Students attend school four days a week with the fifth day serving as an accredited work-experience day. They volunteer with local businesses (e.g., offices, garages, restaurants) or community agencies (e.g., centres for the homeless, hospitals, schools, daycare centres, senior citizen homes). Linking students to local communities helps on many levels. Students are free to make the choice to engage either positively or negatively in the work placement. When they make the choice to immerse themselves in the placement, they are often offered part- or full-time jobs. Respectable employment leads to many opportunities, and students understand how choices affect their lives. They understand the constraints of their actions.

The idea of freedom is closely linked to the idea of empowerment in critical pedagogy. To empower does not imply to give power to students, but rather "to help them exercise power" (Weiler, 1988, p. 59). This orientation removes teachers from the position of authority and benevolent givers of power. Empowerment requires that teachers understand the limits and errors often involved in human judgments as well as the inconsistencies of human action.

At The Alternate School, the philosophy of placing students in situations that challenge their desire to change is witnessed in most actions. For example, it is the responsibility of the student, not the parent, the lawyer, the psychologist, or the social worker to make the initial phone call to establish an interview time. All communication is with the students; parents play a secondary role. At the start of each year, a "parents night" is held to introduce parents and guardians to the school and its philosophy. Following this session, parents are asked not to return until the end-of-year ceremony. All report cards are given to the

(Continued)

students. All disciplinary measures are established with the students, regardless of their age. Any parent-teacher-student conference must be approved by the student, and consequences for actions are determined in a cooperative manner. For example, after lengthy discussions with their core teacher (significant advocate), students who have broken the law will step forward, with their core teacher present, to report the crime to both the legal authorities and their guardians. Teachers help students to analyze the situation and readjust their frame of reference so that they can make respectable, normative choices regarding their future behaviour.

Students, as a group, determine how the day will unfold. There are no bells, no structured periods for instruction, no lunch hours, and no set time to end the day. Teachers and students determine how much time to spend on each subject, based on the interest and motivation of the group as a whole. Students may eat their lunch during teaching time. Students end their school day when their lessons and work for the day are done. In some cases, teachers and students have stayed at school to complete unfinished assignments anywhere from midnight to six o'clock in the morning.

Source: Adapted from an article by Joyce Barakett and Judith Leonard, Resisting Youth Subcultures: Classroom Practice and Critical Pedagogy, *Transformations: The Journal of Curriculum Transformation 10(2)*. Printed with permission, Transformations.

Critique of the Alternate School

In general, the Alternate School demonstrates the key elements of Freire's (1968) critical pedagogy while working with youth subcultures in the secondary school system. This is a school that does not use traditional classroom methods such as tracking (the grouping of students according to academic abilities) or standardized textbooks. It is a school that demonstrates the worth of its troubled students not only by its philosophy and practice but also by its physical location and appearance. Housed in a shopping mall, the school is decorated (by students) with wallpaper, wicker furniture, Monet prints, and plants, and includes a modern kitchen. It has created partnership with parents, community, police, businesses, psychologists, social workers, media, and local universities. Students spend more time reading, thinking, and talking than taking notes and listening to lectures.

Yet the Alternate School is not without its limitations. First, teachers and students alike enter their relationships with ingrained patterns of behaviour and learned beliefs about power. For some teachers and students, it is difficult to disavow authority. For some students, the presence of authority fuels their aggression and resistance, making it very difficult to work with them. Furthermore, teacher interests can either enable or constrain students in the classroom discourse. Teachers are critical players in influencing the climate of their classroom because they are the gatekeepers of the generative themes. In essence, it is the teachers who funnel the discourse. Sometimes, when the climate for discourse is not trustworthy, teachers fall into the trap of defending their own interests rather than exploring that of the students. It is an ongoing process for teachers to release their views of authority and encourage their students to share their values, intuition, insight, and philosophy.

Second, since The Alternate School is recognized by the ministry of education, the mainstream curriculum must still be covered. Students are required to write the standardized provincial examinations in June and compete for entrance into post-secondary programs. These time and curriculum constraints limit the number of generative themes that can be covered. Third, due to budget cuts, certain courses such as art, dance, and music have fallen by the wayside. Such a restriction creates students who, as Shor explains, have "become cultural deficits dependent on the teacher as a delivery system" (1993, p. 31). Fourth, the partnership with business is tenuous, since it requires a delicate balance between accepting their financial support while diverting their philosophical input. Critical pedagogy is a call for The Alternate School to continue being critical and emancipatory rather than a functional thumbprint of the elite. But change is slow. As Shor (1993) states, "the transformation of teachers and students from authoritarian to democratic habits is a long-term project" (p. 29).

We have witnessed the success of critical pedagogy at The Alternate School, both on a personal level, with students, and on a bureaucratic level, with the accreditation of school-generated courses. This success has also carried over to professional development at the school. Over the years, teachers have attended endless workshops, conferences, and seminars on troubled adolescents and youth subcultures. Feeling dissatisfied with the content, they embarked on a plan for their own professional training. They shadowed two youth vice detectives from the anti-gang squad of the Montreal police force on night shift. The teachers literally "walked the streets" to obtain first-hand knowledge of youth subcultures in action. In sum, the teachers recognized their needs, resisted mainstream training, and took action, putting critical pedagogy to work on themselves as well as their students.

FEMINIST PEDAGOGY

As noted in Chapter 2, the orientation of critical and feminist theory is derived from the recognition that experience and knowledge are politically charged and interrelated. Thus knowledge must be used as a practical tool for change, to alleviate oppressive social conditions, question the ideological foundations of society, and bring about greater equality.

Gore (1993) points out the difference between critical and feminist pedagogy as well as the differences within each. She perceives two main strands of discourse within critical pedagogy. One strand "emphasizes the articulation of a broad social and educational vision" (for example, the works of Giroux and McLaren, which aim to politicize teachers and students concerning social injustices and inequities), and the other strand (distinguished by the works of Paulo Freire and Ira Shor) focuses on "developing explicit educational practices to suit specific contexts" (p. 17).

Like critical pedagogy, **feminist pedagogy** also has two strands of discourse. Unlike critical pedagogy, however, these strands are distinguished by their respective communities of writers, rather than by individuals. One strand emphasizes the instructional aspects of pedagogy through women's studies programs, the other emphasizes feminism(s) and theories of schools of education. Feminist pedagogy that is founded in women's studies programs focuses on what constitutes feminist perspectives; feminist pedagogy that is constructed in education departments (or schools of education) focuses on how gendered knowledge and experience are produced and transmitted.

Both critical and feminist pedagogy are concerned with democratizing schools and society. Feminist pedagogy, however, deals specifically with gender oppression, self-reflection, and personal experience. For the most part, the objective is to develop new criteria for what is considered to be knowledge rather than merely adding to the existing knowledge about women. The aim is also to allow for the development of women's abilities through education to increase both their influence on and their control of the representation and distribution of knowledge in academic settings and, ultimately, in society as a whole. For this, a **gender-inclusive curriculum** is essential. A gender-inclusive curriculum includes not only the writings and life experiences of women but also women's accounts and interpretations of history, as well as their analyses of the body of knowledge (produced mainly by men) that has come to be considered the appropriate content of curricula for all (Fox-Genovese, 1986).

Manicom (1992) states that feminist pedagogy's objective is to inform students and teachers about ways of moving towards social justice. The emphasis is on social change, which focuses on feminist pedagogy generated from critical and radical pedagogies, which view education as a mechanism for empowerment and social change. She notes, "Feminist pedagogy is teaching with a political intent and with visions of social change and liberation—not simply with an aim to have (some) women 'make it' in the world of (some) men, but to learn to act in and on the world in order to transform oppressive relations of class, race, and gender (p. 366). As Manicom points outs so succinctly, instead of teaching to change women, we need to change the world to help women to fit into it.

To summarize, feminists point to several tenets as most important in the practice of feminist pedagogy.

- Feminist pedagogy focuses on social transformation, consciousness-raising, and social activism. It is highly committed to improving the lives of women.
- Feminist pedagogy explores issues of class, race, and gender to analyze individual's relations to institutional demands.
- Feminist pedagogy is concerned with whose interests are being served by knowledge and advocates that both learners and "knowers" must understand the uses of knowledge.

Feminist Critique of Critical Pedagogy

Like Freirean pedagogy, feminist pedagogy strives for changes in structures of inequality. According to Shrewsbury (1987), feminist pedagogy

> . . . does not automatically preclude any technique or approach. . . . It is not limited to any specific subject matter but it does include a reflexive element that increases the feminist scholarship component involved in the teaching/learning of any subject matter. It has close ties with other liberatory pedagogies, but it cannot be subsumed under other pedagogical approaches. It is transformative, but it can also be phased into a traditional teaching approach or another alternative pedagogical approach (p. 12).

However, Freire's educational theory does not consider inequalities based on gender. It must be expanded, therefore, to include multiple and sometimes contradictory forms of oppression. That is, theorists must acknowledge the diverse identities and subjectivities produced by different social and historical conditions (Weiler, 1991; Brady, 1994).

A number of transformative possibilities for an educational practice are reflected in the work of various feminist educational theorists. Here we wish to focus on the works of

Weiler (1988, 1991) and articles in Luke and Gore (1992), studies that examine critical pedagogy from various standpoints. These theorists critique the institutional practice of teaching, the discourse of critical pedagogy, and the educational practice resulting from this discourse. And, since critical pedagogy involves a critique and interpretation of pedagogy, feminist theorists and pedagogists challenge other critical theorists and pedagogists to reexamine how their own assumptions and thoughts affect their discursive practices.

Weiler (1988), who confronts the difference between feminist and critical pedagogies, and advocates "teaching for change," points to how some teachers, in their everyday work in schools, can interject feminist theory as a natural part of the teaching process through course content, questions asked, and responses to students' questions. She is concerned with how concepts are used to analyze the schooling process and how critical pedagogy can be used by teachers "teaching for change." She notes that the women in her study described their classrooms as places where consciousness and meanings were questioned, and analysis and criticisms of tests or assignments were encouraged.

However much we would like to think that there are many teachers who are generating change through their classroom practices, the reality is that two major constraints exist: educational emphasis on order and control, and institutional hierarchy. For instance, a few feminist teachers in Weiler's study question ideology, nurture resistance, and encourage change, but there are many who are caught in resistance, which causes greater domination and submission of both themselves and their students (Acker, 1988; Lewis, 1992). On the other hand, Ellsworth (1990), whose concern is with the contradictions of critical pedagogy, interprets her experience of teaching a course, "Media and Anti-racist Pedagogies." An important distinction between Ellsworth and other feminist and critical theorists in education is that her study is based on personal experience. Her main objective is to analyze the discourse in studies of critical pedagogy in relation to her own experiences. She asks: which interpretations do these discourses facilitate, which do they marginalize or silence, and whose interests do they serve?

Ellsworth's (1990) attempts to teach and practice anti-racist pedagogy in the university classroom using critical pedagogy discourse proved to be ineffective. She argues that the discourse of critical pedagogy and the key assumptions, goals, and pedagogical practices that underlie it give rise to repressive myths. Rather than pointing to how the problems she encountered in her practice of critical pedagogy could lead to reformulations of concepts in the field, Ellsworth's essay opposes critical pedagogy. Luke (1992), in her essay "Feminist Politics in Radical Pedagogy," also criticizes critical pedagogical discourse for being masculinist, which "renders its emancipatory agenda for gender theoretically and practically problematic" (p. 25). Thus critical pedagogy reinforces the master patriarchal narratives. Luke notes that "Theorists who do not engage substantively with feminist theory and research, of course cannot be expected to contribute to a feminist reworking of theory or politics, or to renounce the patriarchal signifier in theories and texts. . . " (p. 40). But she goes on to argue for a pedagogy that focuses on the struggle of identities and subjectivity or disclosure of the self, one that accounts for differences.

Weiler, in *Freire and a Feminist Pedagogy of Difference* (1991), supports the notion that

> . . . in action, the goals of liberation or opposition to oppression have not always been easy to understand or achieve. As universal goals, these ideals do not address the specificity of people's lives; they do not directly analyze the contradictions between conflicting oppressed

groups or the ways in which a single individual can experience oppression in one sphere while being privileged or oppressive in another (p. 450).

Rather than dismiss critical pedagogy because it is masculinist, Weiler argues that we need to reexamine the assumptions underlying critical and liberatory classroom practices. She believes that feminist pedagogy can enhance liberatory pedagogy. For instance, in her analysis of the role and authority of the teacher, she notes that "there is an institutionally imposed authority of the teacher" (p. 460). But women asserting this authority in their classroom practices must also strive to empower students by having them question and analyze their own experience and recognize their own power. In other words, feminist pedagogy can address the contradictions between the goals of feminism and the hierarchies of power and knowledge in school settings. She notes that "Recognizing the standpoint of subjects as shaped by their experience of class, race, gender, or other socially defined identities has powerful implications for pedagogy, in that it emphasizes the need to make conscious the subject positions not only of students but of teachers as well"(p. 470).

What is missing in the theoretical writings of many of the critical and feminist pedagogists is a clearly articulated vision of how their ideas translate into actual practice, especially in school settings where established ways of doing things are thoroughly entrenched. Not only would the prescriptions for change insert themselves in the system, but, in so doing, they would cause a reaction at once institutional and individual. As we saw earlier, the norms of the teaching profession promote harmony and thus operate to support the status quo. The challenge, then, is to effect change without bringing about such counter-resistance that the status quo is reinforced.

Weiler (1991) and others such as Giroux (1989) suggest that we develop a pedagogy *of difference, for difference.* Such a pedagogy sheds light on the conflicting ideologies and social experiences of students' lives, allowing students and their teachers to understand the practices that take place in their political, cultural, and social millieux.

ANTI-RACIST PEDAGOGIES

As noted in the anti-racist theory section of Chapter 2, there is a debate as to the important concepts that must be examined and addressed in developing an anti-racist theory. It was emphasized that there are many contentious issues regarding definitions of anti-racism, multiculturalism, racial difference, and whiteness. To add to the complexity of the debate, these concepts are frequently equated with ethnicity. The lack of consensus as to the definitions of these concepts is reflected in the numerous anti-racist pedagogies, which developed from anti-racist theory. Although many anti-racist pedagogists may differ in their approach to anti-racist pedagogical practices in the classroom, for the most part they agree that an analysis of the role race, gender, class, sexual orientation, and ability, and how specific knowledge of these are legitimized in educational institutions is essential.

Each of the anti-racist pedagogies discussed in this section has a particular focus; however, in general they all focus on the powerful impact of social and educational inequalities based on race. In the desire to empower marginalized groups, anti-racist pedagogists acknowledge the economic structures that produce fundamental social inequalities. They turn to educational institutions, curriculum, classroom practices, and the legitimation of different forms of racism. Dei and Calliste (2000) note that anti-racists pedagogies "build on existing scholarship and contribute to the knowledge of the integration of race, class, gender and other aspects of social difference" (p. 13). For Grinter (in Duarte & Smith, 2000), "The anti-racist perspective demands a fundamental rethinking of all teaching, including multicultural teaching, and the nature of educational structures" (p. 136). He argues that racism is not only rooted in a misunderstanding of cultural diversity and the acceptance of negative images of black culture. Anti-racist education must go beyond multicultural education. The most significant component of anti-racist education is that it incorporates an understanding of the ideology that contributes to racism. For instance, the acceptance of negative images of black culture does not expose the historical roots of racism, its class context, or the denial of the political, social, and economic rights of marginalized groups. Indeed, this is what supports and legitimizes the ideology of those in power. However, Grinter does not completely dismiss the validity of multicultural education. What we must do is develop a new vision. According to him,

> This vision must refer to a society in which all people, whatever their difference of "race," culture, gender, physical or intellectual abilities, are valued equally and rewarded appropriately. To achieve this vision, both multicultural and anti-racist education will have to be incorporated in a movement that is greater than both, and in which their present bitter dispute can become part of a wider and still more positive debate, assisted perhaps by the adoption of a new terminology (p. 137).

Giroux, like Grant and Sachs, and McLaren (in Duarte & Smith, 2000), propose that we can develop the concept of multiculturalism to include a more critical perspective, one which encourages students to reflect on an understanding of cultural diversity.

Critical Multicultural Pedagogy

For **critical multicultural pedagogists**, it is essential that classroom practices emphasize the sources of social injustices of racism and economic inequity. For instance, these theorists argue that we must call into question racial privilege and how it is embedded in the schooling process in order to develop a more democratic society. Rezai-Rashti and Regnier in their articles (in Ng, Staton, & Scane, 1995) also argue for a critical multicultural and anti-racist education. Rezai-Rashti, in particular, points to educational policies and practices that attempt to address anti-racism in Ontario school boards. His main concern is with developing concrete school activities that would provide students and teachers with various programs addressing issues concerning different ethnic, cultural, and immigrant groups, as well as aboriginal people, and their human rights. Regnier speaks specifically to the problem of confronting the "racist hegemony of educational institutions" (p. 84) in order to achieve a more liberatory aboriginal pedagogy. He "offers an analysis of political struggle as pedagogical struggle in which 'pedagogue as warrior' is presented as a model of anti-racist teaching" (p. 57). For him, warriors and teachers can uncover the contradictions "between dominant ideologies and aboriginal subjugation" (p. 57). Their task is to establish social justice and the improvement of economic conditions.

Pedagogy of Whiteness

Another anti-racist pedagogy that developed from anti-racist theory and concepts is the **pedagogy of whiteness**. Again, as noted in Chapter 2, to develop a true critical analysis of anti-racism we must critically examine and challenge the unquestioned acceptance of whiteness and white privilege controlled by the white dominant group. The authors of *White Reign* (Kincheloe & Steinberg, 1998) argue that we must interrupt and transform the power of whiteness. To do so we must develop a pedagogy that raises political awareness and teaches students that identities are socially constructed in a historical context. Kincheloe and Steinberg, in particular, write about the "concept of positionality." They argue "Positionality involves the notion that since our understanding of the world and ourselves is socially constructed, we must devote special attention to the differing ways individuals from diverse social backgrounds construct knowledge and make meaning" (p. 3). They agree with critical multiculturalists' claim that whiteness is influenced by demographic changes as well as political and social forces but argue that there are indeed economic implications and financial rewards for whites. Furthermore, the authors note that we cannot clearly state what is whiteness; however, we can make some "generalized statements about the dynamics it signifies" (p. 5). They propose a pedagogy of whiteness and base their construction of this pedagogy on the following questions. "How are students and other individuals to make sense of the assertion that whiteness is a social construction? How does such a concept inform the democratic goals of a critical multiculturalism?" (p. 9).

Kincheloe and Steinberg (1998) also point out that teachers and students must call into question the taken-for-granted assumption and acceptance of whiteness or white supremacy as the norm. We must denormalize this assumption. Teachers ought to present to students concepts that provide an understanding of how social, political, socio-economic, and educational forces influence individual consciousness. An understanding of how these forces influence individual behaviour provides the basis to examine how "racial identity, racial privilege, and racial discomfort" develop (pp. 17–18). Kincheloe and Steinberg note that this is a difficult process and must be done in such a way as to avoid placing blame or guilt on the students.

For Rodriquez (in *White Reign*, 1998), a critical pedagogy of whiteness must emphasize that the notion of whiteness is not static. The concept is socially situated and changes depending on the context in which it is encountered. Rodriguez states that it is for this reason that no operational definition of whiteness is possible (p. 38). He points to the "machinery of whiteness." He argues that rather than ask what whiteness does and how it works, we ought to rearticulate whiteness and ask "what can whiteness do?" (p. 40). The objective of this pedagogy of social transformation involves a rethinking of whiteness. "A critical curriculum would focus on how the production of knowledge takes place within unequal terrains of power struggles to name and represent the word, self, and Other" (p. 35).

Chennault (in *White Reign*, 1998) asked Dyson how he "perceived whiteness to be or what [he] understand[s] whiteness to mean." Dyson's response was the following: "Well I think when we talk about whiteness in the context of race in America, we have to talk about whiteness as *identity,* whiteness as *ideology,* and whiteness as *institution.*" (p. 300). Dyson believes that whiteness as identity refers to "self-understanding, social practices and group beliefs" and how these relate to blackness. He states, "Whiteness is called into existence as a response to the presence of blackness." With the concept of whiteness as ideology he means "the systematic reproduction of conceptions of whiteness as domination" (p. 300). With reference to the institutional aspect of whiteness, Dyson is speaking of institutions such as schools, governments, and the church, which are founded on the dominant ideology of whiteness (p. 302).

Dyson notes that "whiteness has been 'outed,' and as a result of its outing, it has to take into account its origin. He points to "the proliferation of ideas, articles, books, plays, and conferences that question the meanings and significations of whiteness. As part of that process, we've got to understand what whiteness has meant and to specify what it can and should mean in the coming century" (p. 303).

Anti-Racist Black Feminist Pedagogy

Anti-racist black feminist pedagogists, starting with bell hooks, present their views of how a social theory of liberation and pedagogical agents of social change could overcome the oppressions of racism, classism, and sexism. The central feature of black feminist pedagogy is autobiographical writings, which enable students to examine their own internalized racism. In her work, bell hooks (1992) discusses how we can integrate feminist and critical pedagogy. She clearly emphasizes the need for developing a pedagogy that would encourage participation and critical thinking for both teachers and students. For her it is essential that women of colour or any marginalized group be able to express their fears and concerns associated with oppression. They must be able to discuss their personal experiences and share these with other students and teachers. hooks uses the term "**white supremacy**" to refer to the use of power and domination at the structural level of society. She views white people privileged and advantaged within society's institutions excluding people of colour and marginalized groups from economic and political structures. It is essential that we teach black feminism to white students to help them recognize what it means to be *white* in a culture of "white supremacist capitalist patriarchy."

Lemons (in Lea & Helfand, 2004) sheds more light on whiteness when he writes about his experiences as a black, male, feminist professor teaching a course on black feminism to white students. He shows us how certain personal, pedagogical, and political changes can occur if we critically address white privilege in the classroom. His pedagogical approach is to have white students examine readings for the course (primarily the articles in Guy-Sheftall's book *Words of Fire*). Through course readings, group discussions, and written assignments, students are challenged to examine black feminist thought through a black feminist lens. Based on recorded student comments, Lemon points to the underlying current through which the course developed student consciousness and awareness of white privilege. Many of his students wrote about their personal reflection, privilege, and cultural forms of whiteness and insight into whiteness. He notes

> black feminist thought, as a social theory of liberation and pedagogical agent of social change can be a powerful tool toward the development of critical race consciousness in white students; and for black feminists, to overcome the oppressions of racism, classism, sexism. . . we may intellectually come to understand multiple oppression as a distinct feature of black women's history in the United States, but a deeper self-reflective level experience a liberatory understanding of it from within (214).

Joseph (1995) argues against the belief that we need a revolutionary transformation of the economic structure to create a more equal and liberating school system. Her position is very clear. We must include the history of blacks, Latinos, and Native Americans, their values, struggles, exploitations, and oppressions to begin building towards a more equitable schooling process and social change.

> I view the educational system as a system in its own right constituted by intrinsic imperatives, and capable of creating building blocks for radical changes in the structure of

American capitalist society. It is in this spirit that I introduce the black feminist pedagogy that I feel complements and goes beyond the Marxist sociology of education" (p. 464).

Her stance is that Afro-American women have their own way of producing knowledge relevant to them based on their own experience. This differs tremendously from the knowledge and interpretations of their experiences offered by the dominant white male groups. Joseph specifically points to how black feminist pedagogy presents an Afro-centric orientation to reality, that is, real life experiences. This includes an understanding of gender and patriarchy and how these affect social, political, and historical processes. Here Joseph is very much in line with generating a political consciousness supported so strongly by Paulo Freire. ". . . political, social, and economic concepts, from a curriculum planned and taught by teachers possessing a black feminist perspective/consciousness, would introduce a radical education methodological imperative" (p. 465). Central to Joseph's black feminist perspective and feminist pedagogy is making gender and patriarchy the most important concepts in constructing a society, which addresses issues of oppression. She calls for the comparison of two existing conceptual systems, one system that of the oppressed, and the other that of the oppressors. Each has very different values, beliefs, and consequences for those who are committed to their system.

Briefly then, black feminist pedagogy proposes to examine the history and philosophy of each of the conceptual systems and treat students as active participants in evaluating these systems and reformulating new values and beliefs, that is, developing an ideology that is designed to challenge the status quo, one which will provide necessary conditions required for radical social and educational change.

SUMMARY/CONCLUSIONS

Critical, critical multicultural, feminist, anti-racist pedagogists, and anti-racist black feminist pedagogists provide insights for studying the role educational practices play in sustaining an oppressive schooling for marginalized groups. They have developed a dialectical framework to understand what mediates or exists between institutions and activities of everyday life in the schooling process. Freire, in particular, developed a conceptual framework in which the connection between theory and practice illuminates how vested interests underlie knowledge formation itself. Freire helps us see how knowledge has political as well as practical content. When competing interests vie for the legitimacy of particular forms of knowledge, those in positions of power claim that their knowledge has been substantiated scientifically and is, therefore, more valid than other forms of knowledge. Freire's work is without parallel for its recognition of the position of the powerless in society. He illuminates what is needed to break through the practices that portray a false reality. Freire had the courage to add these insights to the tapestry of what we consider knowledge.

Critical educational theorists and pedagogists argue that, although society is both exploitative and oppressive, it can also be changed. They emphasize individual empowerment, social transformation, and the need to develop critical consciousness in students. Various studies illustrate how teachers and school administrators can respect the consciousness, concerns, and culture of their students by creating a pedagogical setting in which they can express their problems and their understanding of the social environment. When teachers reflect on their own assumptions about students' behaviours, they create an environment where dialogue can occur. Critical multicultural pedagogists argue that we must develop a pedagogy focused on the concepts of whiteness and social, cultural, and ethnic differences, while anti-racist pedagogists and anti-racist black feminist pedagogists are more concerned with a pedagogy that addresses gender and race differences.

All pedagogies discussed in this chapter are concerned with the production and reproduction of class, gender, and race inequities. They all share similar perspectives of the ways in which the dominant group's assumptions define both school practices and research in education; the ways in which schools and curricula have reproduced oppressive ideology and assumptions; and the openings that exist for teachers to use students' own cultural worlds as the source for oppositional pedagogy. These pedagogists are all concerned with oppression, difference, multiple perspectives, and voices, and all are informed by the earlier critical educational studies of Paulo Freire. Although some of the analyses presented are situated within an American context, we encourage the reader to consider the manner in which they do or do not apply to the Canadian one.

Whether the pedagogy is critical, critical multicultural, feminist, black feminist or anti-racist, the objective is to emphasize a dismantling of the traditional boundaries between the teacher/education and the student/learner. These pedagogies share an underlying concern with the relationship between the individual subject and an oppressive social structure. All demonstrate the tensions between the production and reproduction of theoretical approaches, and emphasize that social structures and knowledge are socially constructed and therefore open to resistance and change.

However, we believe that it is important to move towards a dialogue that speaks to the multi-dimensional aspects of "communities of teaching/learning in the making." The problem with the pedagogies presented here is that they focus primarily on the theoretical aspects of a liberatory pedagogy rather than providing or suggesting some practical strategies or methods that can facilitate the implementation of such a practice. As hooks (2003) notes

> Certainly as democratic educators we have to work to find ways to teach and share knowledge in a manner that does not reinforce existing structures of domination (those of race, gender, class, and religious hierarchies). Diversity in speech and presence can be fully appreciated as a resource enhancing any learning experience (p. 45).

In the following chapter we focus on the informal socializing features of the school and how these affect students' academic performance. In addition, we examine the influence of peer groups and popular culture on the ability of the school to perform its socialization function.

KEY TERMS

anti-racist black feminist pedagogy	culture of silence	pedagogy
conscientization	dialogue	pedagogy of whiteness
critical multicultural pedagogy	empowerment	praxis
critical pedagogy	feminist pedagogy	resistance
cultural politics	gender-inclusive curriculum	theory of liberation
	generative themes	voice
		white supremacy

EDUCATIONAL ISSUES AND QUESTIONS FOR DISCUSSION

1. What do you think is meant by "internalized racism"?

2. Which pedagogy do you think best addresses the problems of social inequality: feminist, critical, or anti-racist?

3. Discuss what is meant by the politics of education and cultural politics.

4. What does bell hooks mean when she uses the term "white supremacy"?

5. What is the main concern and objective of the anti-racist feminist pedagogies?

RECOMMENDED READINGS/REFERENCES

Acker, S. (1988). Teachers, gender and resistance. *British Journal of Sociology of Education, 9,* 307–322.

Aikenhead, G. S. (1990). Scientific/technological literacy, critical reasoning, and classroom practice. In S. P Norris & L. M. Phillips (Eds.), *Foundations of literacy policy in Canada* (pp. 127–146). Calgary: Detselig.

Aronowitz, S., & Giroux, H. (1993). *Education still under siege.* London: Bergin & Garvey.

Barakett, J., & Leonard, J. (1999). Resisting youth subcultures: Classroom practice and critical pedagogy. *Transformations: The Journal of Curriculum Transformation, 10*(2).

Bibby, R., & Posterski, D. (1992). *Teen trends: A nation in motion.* Toronto: Stoddart.

Brady, J. (1994). Critical literacy, feminism, and politics of representation. In C. Lankshear & P. McLaren (Eds.), *Politics of liberation: Paths from Freire* (pp. 142–153). New York: Routledge.

Chennault, R. (1998). Giving whiteness a black eye: An interview with Eric Dyson. In J. Kincheloe & S. Steinberg (Eds.), *White reign: Deploying whiteness in America* (pp. 299–328). New York: St. Martin's Press.

Dei, G. (1999). The denial of difference: Reframing anti-racist praxis. *Race, Ethnicity and Education, 2*(1), 17–37.

Dei, G., & Calliste, A. (2000). Introduction: Mapping the terrain: Power, knowledge and anti-racist education. In J. Dei & A. Callistte (Eds.), *Power, knowledge and anti-racism education* (pp. 11–22). Halifax: Fernwood Publishing.

Diamond, I., & Quinby, L. (Eds.). (1988). *Feminisms and Foucault: Reflections on resistance.* Boston: Northwestern University Press.

Ellsworth, E. (1990). Why doesn't this feel empowering? Working through repressive myths and critical pedagogy. In. C. Luke & J. Gore (Eds.), *Feminisms and critical pedagogies* (pp. 90–119). New York: Routledge.

Fox-Genovese, E. (1986). Gender, race, class, canon. *Salmagundi: A Quarterly of the Humanities & Social Sciences, 72,* 131–143.

Freire, P. (1970). *Pedagogy of the oppressed*. New York: Seabury Press.

Freire, P. (1973). *Education for critical consciousness*. New York: Seabury Press.

Freire, P. (1985). *The politics of education: Culture, power and liberation*. Boston: Bergin & Garvey.

Giroux, H. (1983). *Theory and resistance in education*. Boston: Bergin & Garvey.

Giroux, H. (1989). Schooling as a form of cultural politics: Towards a pedagogy of and for difference. In H. Giroux & P. McLaren (Eds.), *Critical pedagogy, the state and cultural struggle* (pp. 125–151). New York: State University of New York Press.

Giroux, H. (1996). *Fugitive Cultures: Race, violence and youths*. London: Routledge.

Giroux, H. (2000). Insurgent multiculturalism and the promise of pedagogy. In M. Duarte and S. Smith (Eds.), *Foundational perspectives in multicultural education* (pp. 195–212). Don Mills, ON: Addison Wesley Longman, Inc.

Giroux, H., & McLaren, P. (1989). *Critical pedagogy, the state and cultural struggle*. Albany, NY: State University of New York Press.

Giroux, H., & McLaren, P. (1994). *Between borders*. New York: Routledge.

Gore, J. (1992). Feminist politics in radical pedagogy. In C. Luke & J. Gore (Eds.), *Feminisms and critical pedagogy* (pp. 25–53). New York: Routledge.

Gore, J. (1993). *The struggle for pedagogies*. New York: Routledge.

Gramsci, A. (1971). *Selections from the prison notes* (Q. Horae & G. Nowell-Smith, Eds. & Trans.). New York: International Publishers.

Grant, C. A., & Sachs, J. M. (2000). Multicultural education and postmodernism: Movement toward a dialogue. In M. Duarte & S. Smith (Eds.), *Foundational perspectives in multicultural education* (pp. 173–194). Don Mills, ON: Addison Wesley Longman, Inc.

Grinter, R. (2000). Multicultural or anti-racist education. In. E.M. Duarte & S. Smith (Eds.), *Foundational perspectives in multicultural education* (pp. 135–154). Don Mills, ON: Longman Inc.

Guy-Sheftall, B. (Ed.). (1995). *Words of fire: An anthology of African-American feminist thought*. New York: New Press.

Hill Collins, P. (1995). The social construction of black feminist thought. In B. Guy-Sheftall, (Ed.), *Words of fire: An anthology of African-American feminist thought*. New York: New Press.

hooks, b. (1992). Representation of whiteness in the black imagination. In *Black looks; race and representation* (pp. 165–178). Boston: South End Press.

hooks, b. (2000). *Feminist theory: From margin to center*. Cambridge, MA: South End Press.

hooks, b. (2003). *Teaching community: A pedagogy of hope*. New York: Routledge.

Joseph, G. (1995). Black feminist pedagogy and schooling in capitalist white America. In B. Guy-Sheftall (Ed.), *Words of fire: An anthology of African-American feminist thought* (pp. 462–471). New York: New Press.

Kincheloe, J., & Steinberg, S. (1998). Addressing the crisis of whiteness: Reconfiguring white identity in a pedagogy of whiteness. In J. Kincheloe & S. Steinberg (Eds.), *White reign: Deploying whiteness in America* (pp. 3–29). New York: St. Martin's Press.

Lemons, G. (2004). When white students write about being white: Challenging whiteness in a black feminist classroom. In V. Lea & J. Helfand (Eds.), *Identifying race and transforming whiteness in the classroom* (pp. 213–233). New York: Peter Lang.

Lewis, M. (1992). Interrupting patriarchy: Politics, resistance and transformation in the feminist classroom. In C. Luke & J. Gore (Eds.), *Feminisms and critical pedagogies* (pp. 167–191). New York: Routledge.

Luke, C., & Gore, J. (Eds.). (1992). *Feminisims and critical pedagogies.* New York: Routledge.

Manicom, A. (1992). Feminist pedagogy: Transformations, standpoints, and politics. *Canadian Journal of Education, 17*(3), 365–389.

McLaren, P. (1998). *Life in schools: An introduction to critical pedagogy in the foundations of education* (3rd. ed.). Don Mills, ON: Langerman.

McLaren, P. (2000). White terror and oppositional agency: Towards a critical multiculturalism. In M. Duarte and S. Smith. (Eds.), *Foundational perspectives in multicultural education* (pp. 213–241). Don Mills, ON: Addison Wesley Longman, Inc.

McLaren, P., & Lankshear, C. (Eds.). (1994). *Politics of liberation: Paths from Freire.* New York: Routledge.

McLaren, P., & Leonard, P. (Eds.). (1993). *Paulo Freire: A critical encounter.* New York: Routledge.

Regnier, R. (1995). Warrior as pedagogue, pedagogue as warrior: Reflections on aboriginal anti-racist pedagogy. In R. Ng, P. Staton, & J. Scane (Eds.), *Anti-racism, feminism, and critical approaches to education* (pp. 57–86). Toronto: OISE Press.

Rezak-Rashti, G. (1995). Multicultural education, anti-racist education, and critical pedagogy: Reflections on everyday practice. In R. Ng, P. Staton, & J. Scane (Eds.), *Anti-racism, feminism, and critical approaches to education* (pp. 3–19). Toronto: OISE Press.

Rodriguez, N. (1998). Emptying the content of whiteness: Toward an understanding of the relation between whiteness and pedagogy. In. J. Kincheloe & S. Steinberg (Eds.), *White reign: Deploying whiteness in America* (pp. 31–62). New York: St. Martin's Press.

Shor, I. (1988). *Freire for the classroom: A sourcebook for liberatory teaching.* Portsmouth, ME: Bayton/Cook.

Shor, I. (1992). *Empowering education: Critical teaching for social change.* Chicago: University of Chicago Press.

Shor, I. (1993). Education is politics: Paulo Freire's critical pedagogy. In P. McLaren & P. Leonard (Eds.), *Paulo Freire: A critical encounter* (pp. 25–35). New York: Routledge.

Short, J. (1968). *Gang delinquency and delinquent subcultures.* New York: Harper & Row.

Shrewsbury, C. M. (1987). What is feminist pedagogy? *Women's Studies Quarterly, 15*(3–4), 6–14.

Simon, R. (April, 1987). Empowerment as a pedagogy of possibility. *Language Arts, 64*(4), 370–382.

Weber, M. (1947). *The theory of social and economic organization.* New York: The Free Press.

Weiler, K. (1988). *Women teaching for change: Gender, class and power.* Boston: Bergin & Garvey.

Weiler, K. (1991). Freire and a feminist pedagogy of difference. *Harvard Educational Review, 16*(4), 449–475.

Weiler, K., & Mitchell, C. (1992). *What schools can do: Critical pedagogy and practices.* New York: State University of New York Press.

Willis, P. (1977). *Learning to labour.* New York: Columbia University Press.

chapter five

The School as an Informal System of Socialization

CHAPTER OBJECTIVES

This chapter focuses on

- the socialization process that takes place within the family and compares that process with the socialization that takes place in the school
- how the two domains of socialization come together in the classroom, primarily through the expectations that teachers develop toward students
- how teachers' expectations intersect with organizational features of the school and classroom management considerations, which in turn affect the child's academic opportunities as well as identity
- how teachers' expectations are based on schemes of interpretations of students' behaviour
- the role of the school in both moral and political socialization
- the socializing influence of peer groups, the hidden curriculum, the media, and popular culture on the lives and education of young people today

In this chapter we will see how subtly these processes produce and reproduce an achievement history at both the individual and the group level, with further ramifications for patterns of inequality in society at large.

THEORIES OF SOCIALIZATION

Socialization refers to the complex, life-long learning process through which individuals develop a sense of self and acquire the knowledge, skills, values, norms, and dispositions required to fulfill social roles. Stated differently, socialization refers to the process through which the individual takes on the ways of thinking, seeing, believing, and behaving that prevail in the society that he or she was born into.

Within a complex society, social roles and obligations vary; they reflect differences in social class, ethnicity, race, and gender as well as the constant changes within the society. There are several agents of socialization—family, school, peer groups, and the media.

Primary socialization occurs in the micro world of the family, which is a primary group. The process involves the development of language and individual identity as well as identity relating to the particular ethnic or religious subgroup that the family may belong to. It involves learning cognitive skills and self-control as well as the internalization of moral standards. It also involves the development of appropriate attitudes and behaviours for social interactions, and an understanding of social roles. Gender identity and an understanding of masculinity and femininity are also learned during primary socialization. The process is most influential in the years before a child goes to school; however, the influence of the family persists after that, along with influence of the school. The school is the main agent of secondary socialization.

Originally, the concept of socialization was used to refer to the process of eliminating children's inherent unruly behaviours. Over time, as educators and psychologists learned more about childhood and child development, socialization came to be seen as a process of **internalization**, in which the individual incorporates the appropriate social norms, roles, and values into his or her own mind.

The functionalist view of socialization perceives the individual as reacting and responding to people and situations in her or his world according to sets of more or less structured situational responses. This perspective is perhaps most clearly stated by Parsons (1967), who viewed the school classroom as a system that socializes and allocates individuals on the basis of the criteria assigned by the larger society. According to Parsons, differentiation of status occurs on the basis of achievement, not ascription. He summarizes his views in the following way:

> The essential points seem to be that the elementary school, regarded in the light of its socialization function, is an agency which differentiates the school class broadly along a single continuum of achievement, the content of which is relative excellence in living up to the expectations imposed by the teacher as an agent of the adult society. The criteria of this achievement are, generally speaking, differentiated into the cognitive or technical component and the moral or "social" component (p. 653).

Thus social reality is viewed as objective, external to, and independent of the individual. Socialized people know what is expected of them because they are introduced to a culturally specific but generally shared system of symbols, meanings, and values. Socialization is considered necessary to ensure the stability and functioning of the social system.

The theoretical perspectives that we emphasize to explain the process of socialization are symbolic interaction, phenomenology, and interpretive sociology. Symbolic interaction (Mead, 1934) stresses the ongoing process of interpreting and defining actions in order to construct meanings for various situations. Phenomenologists and interpretive sociologists (Schutz, 1973) are concerned with the knowledge and assumptions that individuals need to make sense of and assign meaning to the world.

Mead's Theory

Mead explains that socialization of individuals occurs through the development of a self, which depends on language and social interaction. As noted in Chapter 2, Mead's concept of *self* includes the *me,* which represents internalized societal attitudes and expectations, and the *I,* which represents the spontaneity and individuality of the person. Mead defined the self as that which is an object to oneself. That is, the self is reflexive. The individual becomes an object to herself or himself by taking into account the attitude of **significant others**, those with whom he or she has the most frequent and consistent interaction. These people are primary socialization agents. In this reflexive process, the individual notes, selects, and determines the responses and actions he or she will take. Thus the individual is not merely reacting but interpreting, selecting, and then acting. He or she is an active agent.

The ability to look objectively at oneself depends on the acquisition of language. The acquisition of language and the development of a self require role taking and role-playing. The child is able to play the role of the other by imitating the behaviour of the significant other, but does not understand this behaviour. Role-playing involves the child playing at being a mother, father, teacher, or other adult. That is, the child *plays* at taking different roles and acts out the same responses that these roles call out in others. This is different from role taking, where the child not only imitates the behaviours of others, but also understands the responsibilities attached to the role.

Eventually, the child is able to take the role of the **generalized other**, which consists of the attitudes of the community or society as a whole. At this point, the child has learned to compare and hold different judgments or impressions. He or she has learned the *rules of the game.*

The self develops as a result of social interaction with others who provide meaning of the self through their responses. Cooley (1956) called this the looking-glass self. In other words, responses are taken as representations of what the self must be. Through language, the individual has the ability for symbolic representation and observes the world through a defining and labelling process. What the individual takes into account in this process depends on the existing needs, feelings, purpose, expectations, and rules of the group.

The theoretical concepts above emphasize that situations are created, sustained, and "made to happen" by individuals; that is, they are socially constructed. Children do not behave in certain ways simply due to the internalization of norms; rather, they actively construct situations by negotiating with themselves and others the norms and meanings they will use in a particular situation. There is a negotiated character to norms, and they are interpreted in relation to interests. These interpretations are guided by the socialization process. From this perspective, the child's own thoughts and evaluations are not based simply on instinct or the objective reality of the situation.

Family background, which includes social class, ethnicity, language, cultural practices, and religion, influences the primary socialization process. As indicated above, when the child enters the school system, the **secondary socialization** process begins. Secondary socialization refers to the social learning that occurs in institutions such as schools. The extent of socialization in the school depends on the child's family background. Teachers and peers join family members as authorities as well as significant others. In this context, a teacher may affect the student in a manner that is comparable to a parent or other close relatives. While friends and other adults, such as athletic coaches, may also become significant others, it is important to point out that the significance lies more in the mind and interpretations of the child than in the shared and conscious part of the relationship itself. A more conscious relationship is referred to as **mentoring**.

Schutz's Theory

Following Mead's tradition, Alfred Schutz further explains what occurs in the social inter-action process. He emphasizes the importance of examining the interpretive principles and methods that individuals use to make sense of a situation, and stresses that to understand social interaction we must uncover or make explicit the hidden facts of the interaction process. For Schutz this means we must understand how individuals act in the context of an intersubjective reality. **Intersubjectivity** refers to the knowledge we have accumulated through our experiences, including the knowledge about others that has been transmitted to us by parents and teachers. Schutz refers to this knowledge as common sense knowl-edge since it is knowledge that individuals have at hand, which they can draw on for the practical purpose of defining an object, situation, or event. This knowledge serves as a scheme of interpretation for the individual's past and current experiences.

Schutz then goes on to note that common sense knowledge or schemes of interpreta-tion consist of institutionalized beliefs or constructs of typifications (social types) that help individuals understand the actions of others in similar situations. By taking the subjective position, Schutz attempts to interpret the larger contexts of interactional situations. That is, he tries to explain how individuals construct social types by drawing on larger social con-texts and then behave on the basis of them. For Schutz, the self, language, and interpreta-tions of objects and situations emerge through the typification process (copying of social types) rather than through the internalization of Mead's generalized other (Schutz, 1973).

Other Socialization Theories

There are a number of other theoretical perspectives used to explore and explain the social-ization process. Freud's psychoanalytic theory, for instance, relies heavily on biological factors to explain the development of identity, personality, and behaviour. According to Freud, the mind's irrational and subconscious features are at the base of human behaviour, and early childhood experiences in the family determine adult socialization. He states that the child is born with an **id** but must progress through developmental changes in order to develop an **ego** and a **superego**. The id refers to the individual's biological or unconscious instincts that seek immediate gratification. The ego controls and checks the id. It deals with the world in terms of what is possible, providing the id with limits and direction. In turn, the id and the ego must recognize the limits imposed on them by the superego. The superego, which is the individual's conscience, strives to regulate behaviour within accept-able societal norms.

Piaget, who is best known for developing the **cognitive theory of socialization,** empha-sizes the development of perceptions and thought processes. Behavioural standards are the result of the child's identification with her or his parents, who have communicated society's rules through a system of reward, punishment, and example (Mackie, 1994). Piaget explains children's behaviour in terms of their mental efforts to organize their social environment. In a way similar to Freud's, Piaget explains human behaviour as the collaboration of bio-logical and environmental factors. At the centre of his theory is the development of moral thought. Children are perceived as active learners, attempting to develop a sense of right and wrong. Changes to the child's thought processes are demonstrated through the devel-opment of two levels of morality. *Moral realism,* which is generally attained between the ages of four and seven, judges misbehaviour in terms of the consequences of the act, and *moral autonomy,* generally achieved between the ages of seven and nine, concerns itself with the reasons for misbehaving. The moral realists are not concerned with extenuating circumstances or the intentions of the one misbehaving. They believe that rules are sacred and deviations should not be tolerated. On the other hand, moral autonomists view rules as "arbitrary social conventions" that could be adapted to particular situations. For Piaget, the development of morality is made possible through the maturation of cognitive ability, which evolves from the interaction between genetic capacities and social experiences (Mackie, 1994).

In contrast to Freud's and Piaget's theories, the **social learning theory** focuses exclusively on the environmental factors that surround the child. One principle of this theoretical approach is the notion of reinforcement and how it shapes behaviour to conform to the expectations of socialization agents such as parents and teachers. The child is perceived as a passive learner influenced by the rewards and punishment for appropriate and inappropriate behaviours. Social learning theory also states that children learn vicariously by observing and imitating the behaviour, beliefs, and norms held by those closest to them. From this stance, observational learning also appears to be mainly responsible for the acquisition of language. Children imitate language and learn the meaning of words in the same way they learn other forms of behaviour.

TEACHER EXPECTATIONS

Schools teach selected ideas, values, skills, and kinds of knowledge that have been deemed important. To understand how the educational process affects an individual's academic performance as well as his or her status position, we must analyze interaction patterns in the school setting. Inequality in educational settings, or in society in general, is not merely a question of differing values, social positions, or social and cultural backgrounds. To more clearly understand how social inequality is perpetuated in the classroom, we will examine how teachers use unquestioned, common sense knowledge to interpret and respond to their pupils' behaviours.

Teacher Typifications of Students

Teachers' expectations of students have been internalized through teacher education programs and through their own experiences with teachers. Student teachers are taught how to evaluate, classify, and place pupils into high-, middle-, or low-ability groups. They are taught that this is a good way to dovetail instruction to the learners' needs and facilitate the management of their classes. Sometimes this process results in two or more streams and separate classes at the same grade level; at other times it results in the formation of different ability groups within a single class. This is referred to as **tracking**. Tracking is supported through the use of standardized tests, the results of which are believed to be objective and unbiased. As students accumulate achievement records, they will come to think of themselves in terms of the grade or value that they are accustomed to receiving. Thus a child who is consistently placed in the lower-level reading group may come to think of himself or herself as slow. Even though the initial criteria for such a placement may have been faulty, the child internalizes the effects of the placement. Tracking is important because the social meanings attached to these groupings find their equivalence in the social groups of society at large.

Although there is much discussion among teachers about the importance of encouraging children who are having difficulties to perform better in school, there are serious classroom management considerations that militate against this actually occurring. For example, during the first week of school, children in grade 1(most of whom may not be able to read at all) may be placed into high-, medium-, or low-level reading groups, simply to give the class a structure, making it easier for the teacher to manage in the difficult early days of the school year. Once the groups are formed, however, the boundaries tend to become rigid. Children quickly understand that they have been placed in the "smart" group or the "slow" group and may report the fact to parents. If, for example, the teacher should then decide that a child has mistakenly been placed in the high-level reading group, he or she will then have to find a satisfactory explanation for what may seem like a demotion to the child and the parents. Teachers sometimes use demotions as threats for behaviour management purposes, so it is not difficult to see that the social meaning attached to ability-group placement can be quite complex. In addition, it is easier to manage a class if the size and composition of the groups remain fairly constant. To move one or more children up and out of the low-level group may result in an unmanageable middle-level group, necessitating the movement of another child from the middle-level group to the high-level group, even if the demands at that level are seen as too difficult. Once formed, ability groups tend to remain as they are, contributing (rightly or wrongly) over time to the child's definition of his or her own ability and sense of self.

Indeed, one of the teacher's major dilemmas is how to go about assessing the pupil. Hargreaves et al. (1975) state that over time teachers develop elaborate **typifications** of individual pupils. These typifications become part of teachers' common sense knowledge about students in the classroom. The teacher speculates on the sort of character the pupil has. Generally, the constructs used to assess a student's character are appearance, language ability, conformity to discipline, acceptance of his or her academic role, general likableness, and relations with peers. The teacher may also have knowledge of the pupil's social class background and records from previous schooling as well as information from informal discussions with other teachers. As the teacher accumulates more information about the student, and behaviours and interactions are repeated over time, this knowledge becomes "evidence" to confirm her or his impressions.

As Figure 5–1 shows, standards that are operative in the social organization of the teacher's daily activities are essentially situational and practical. From the teacher's stance, reasons for typifying and categorizing students are justified if they permit a measure of order, or if they follow the organization's logic. They are developed out of a practical necessity to deal with classroom activities, that is, practical circumstances and interests. Thus, ability grouping is not only the consequence of teacher expectations, dominant ideologies, and educational structures, but is also a function of organizing routine classroom activities. Teachers are concerned with interpreting, defining, and managing their pupils' classroom behaviours for the practical purpose of teaching prescribed content to a variety of students.

It is true that teachers are largely bound by the world they live in and by their knowledge of that world. Differentiating their student population helps them to define the characteristics and expectations of performance. Since intelligence and competence are highly valued in our society, teachers are obviously concerned with identifying these characteristics among their students. Typifying, comparing, and classifying student ability helps teachers operate with minimal conflict in a bureaucratic organization.

FIGURE 5-1	The Dialectics of Teachers' Interpretive Processes

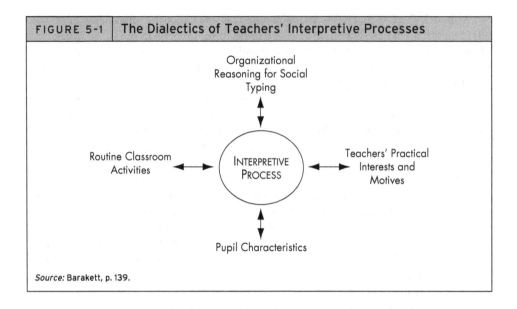

Source: Barakett, p. 139.

Apple (1979) states that the differentiation of students through grading also helps to establish the occupational division of labour. The procedures that stratify students culturally and economically through the application of values and categories are part of the larger political and economic context within which schools are located. It is, however, important to examine these common sense social principles and values. As Apple notes,

> . . . certain types of cultural capital—types of performance, knowledge, dispositions, achievements, and propensities—are not necessarily good in and of themselves. They are often historically and ideologically "conditioned." The categories that we employ to think through what we are doing with students, their and our success and failure, are involved in a process of social valuing. The guiding principles that we use to plan, order, and evaluate our activity, conceptions of achievement, of success and failure, of good and bad students are *social and economic* constructs . . . the very ways we talk about students provide excellent instances of the mechanisms through which dominant ideologies operate (p. 130).

The concept of purpose is important in the analysis of how social inequality is perpetuated in the classroom. First, purposes can operate as masked reasons for actions. That is, some teachers are not reflexive about their purposes or interests, nor about the actions they take based on these. Teachers may not be aware that their purposes produce political, moral, and social consequences. Second, teachers' purposes generate general interests. For instance, actions are rationalized to accomplish specific tasks, but, at the same time, these serve general social interests. Finally, the concept helps us understand how teachers inadvertently reproduce existing structures.

The above educational practices perform a dual role in serving the dominant ideology by using purposeful definitions of the situation and by serving the interests of those who already possess economic and cultural capital. These practices are also linked to our conceptual understanding of education, and form part of a larger **taken-for-granted perspective** that dominates education. If we are to question teachers' management procedures, then we must also raise questions about how hegemony affects categorization. That is, the ways that classrooms are organized and students are categorized both stem from the dominant culture via the teacher's taken-for granted knowledge.

Phenomenologists and interpretive sociologists argue that our taken-for-granted perspectives and common sense assumptions should be examined when analyzing how the schooling process affects educational and social inequality. The ideologies, structures, and attitudes experienced by students influence their attitudes towards their schooling process, their teachers, and themselves. These attitudes dictate student behaviours and beliefs about themselves and their world, and influence their decisions about their future. Student perceptions of self are essentially influenced by typifications, which teachers draw on for the purpose of classroom organization. Indeed, many teachers unknowingly participate in determining students' educational achievements and future positions in the social structure.

MORAL AND POLITICAL SOCIALIZATION

The French sociologist Emile Durkeim also considers that schooling passes on a society's normative system, including the organization of injustice and inequality. As agents of **moral socialization**, schools instill an idealized version of society's values. Further, the knowledge and values passed on by the school become internalized as part of the individual's common sense understandings of the world (Durkheim, 1961). **Political socialization** refers to the role the school plays in inculcating the values and norms that support the prevailing structure of society, including the dominant political ideology (Mifflen and Mifflen, 1982).

A historical look at the development of education in Canada will quickly indicate how thoroughly (and how early) both moral and political considerations were deemed to be the proper concerns of the educational system. With Anglicans, Presbyterians, and Roman Catholics all vying for control, schooling was a key player in, and agent of, political socialization. According to Lazerson, as quoted by Mifflen and Mifflen (1982),

> The content of that socialization included a commitment to a Christianity that could accommodate most Protestants, to Canadians as loyal subjects of the Queen, and to social class harmony within an hierarchically ordered society (p. 20).

What is not so obvious today is how deeply influenced the system in Canada was by the British class model, which upheld one system for the elite and another for the working class. The elite system provided nearly automatic access to higher education and to leadership positions as well as careers in the professions, while children from the working class were provided with the essentials of reading and writing, but little, if any, instruction that could eventually lead to questioning the status quo. Thus, as suggested in Chapter 1, schooling was about maintaining the power structure and social status quo through social control. Although this system has supposedly disappeared with the expansion of near-universal access to post-secondary education, as indicated earlier, the most powerful positions in Canadian society are still occupied mostly by English-speaking people of Anglo-Saxon origin. As educators, we must ask what the present-day mechanisms are for this continued occurrence.

Earlier we spoke about the role of the family in the development of personal and subgroup identity. Here we suggest that it is through the school, as well as through the media, that a sense of national identity may be formed. In Canada, this sometimes takes the form of regional rather than national allegiance (at least until later on in an individual's higher education), possibly because of the Canadian tendency to believe in the value and promotion of **pluralism**. Thus, we see people from British Columbia and Alberta identifying themselves as *Westerners;* people from Ontario, *central Canadians;* French-speaking people from Quebec, *Québécois;* and people from the eastern provinces, *Maritimers.* That this description of regional affiliations and identities does not strike us as particularly threatening or unusual is testimony to the fact that we have come to see the way our society is organized as "normal." Canada is not the **melting pot** that the United States is generally accepted to be. Still, Canadian schools do appear to succeed in helping children from immigrant families become bicultural, at least through the second generation, and often well beyond that. While this may be viewed as a type of partial assimilation, a more accurate term may be integration.

THE HIDDEN CURRICULUM

The fundamental patterns in any society are held together by tacit ideological assumptions. In schools, some rules are not overt, but still serve to organize and legitimate the activities of teachers and students. Much of what the school teaches and the students learn does not appear in the formal curriculum. Successful school performance requires that the student learn what are considered important and useful skills and knowledge. But students must also have the skills to uncover the hidden rules and expectations that affect their dispositions, identities, and personalities. For example, schools emphasize conformity, deferred gratification, achievement, competitiveness, and obedience to authority. Students must understand the social and other dimensions of this hidden curriculum. The hidden curriculum refers to the tacit teaching of norms, values, and dispositions that occur through students' participation in social experiences in routine school activities.

Functionalist writers such as Jackson (1968) and Dreeben (1968) show that the hidden curriculum is part of the regular features of the informal schooling process. They argue that, while the explicit goals of the school, which are reflected in the school curriculum, are an important part of the socialization process, students' social experiences in educational settings are also crucial factors to consider when analyzing the learning process. There are important lessons derived from the hidden curriculum that appear not to be related to the acquisition of knowledge, but that nevertheless contribute to the student's development of an identity and personality.

Another view of the hidden curriculum is presented by Apple and Smith (1991), who point to the importance of textbooks that teach culture. They note that, ". . . texts are not simply 'delivery' systems of 'facts.' They are at once the result of political, economic, and cultural activities, battles, and compromises" (p. 1). Apple and Smith stress that texts reflect the interests of those who write them, but also that texts are published in the context of "market, resources, and power." For instance, if history, sociology, or political science courses do not use texts that address how government policies eliminated traditional aboriginal cultures, how certain policies are biased against some immigrant groups, or how women have been excluded from positions of power, then students do not learn about or develop an understanding of the experiences of different people. The point is that the school's formal curriculum cannot be seen as transmitting neutral knowledge. The knowledge transmitted depends on what is included in texts as much as what is excluded from them.

Likewise, there is not only one interpretive procedure used to understand the text. Apple and Smith state, "From all we have said . . . it should be clear that we oppose the idea that there can be one textual authority, one definitive set of 'facts' divorced from their context of power relations" (p. 15). Finally, they argue that, as teachers, we must create the conditions necessary to enable individuals to participate in creating and, perhaps, changing meanings and values.

THE PEER GROUP AND POPULAR CULTURE

At this point we would like to turn to a discussion of peer groups and popular culture and their effects on student learning. Besides learning role models from the significant and generalized other, students are also influenced by their peer groups, especially during adolescence when individuals begin to explore various possible identities and affiliations. These affiliations and the relationships that develop from them are part of the informal process of schooling, since they occur largely within the school or in association with school-related activities and may have a significant effect on students' attitudes, beliefs, and behaviour.

Many sociologists have argued that peer group values and behaviours may be more important in students' behaviours than school or parental values (Coleman, 1961; Clark & Trow, 1966; Ballantine, 1983). Adolescents develop relationships that often lead to the development of youth or student subcultures. These subcultures constitute participation in sets of norms and values that play an important role in controlling the behaviour of peer group members. For example, for boys, popularity among peers may depend on athletic skills; for girls, it may depend on appearance or personality. Thus the student subculture may be at odds with teachers' expectations and what schools are trying to do. We need only witness conformity in dress, gestures, language, and slang to understand what is deemed acceptable among students in any particular school. Indeed, fads and crazes are important aspects of student subculture: They hold the group together. All of these aspects set the student world apart from the adult world.

Thus the norms and values of the schools and the larger society, with teachers representing the culture of the dominant group, distance the students from their teachers. Popular culture, as reflected in TV shows, films, magazines, and technological artifacts, such as Nintendo games and the internet, which students and youth groups draw on for their general entertainment, represents another dimension that contributes to this distance between teachers and students and may affect school performance.

Students bring their knowledge of popular culture to the classroom, but this is commonly considered to be a less significant aspect of the socialization process than, say, the transmission of cultural capital (language, codes, and values of the dominant culture). But the importance of popular culture in shaping students', teachers', administrators', and others' views of themselves, and, subsequently, their views of different forms of pedagogy, should not be underestimated. Students and teachers alike appropriate popular culture and incorporate this into their educational experiences.

Although schooling, classroom pedagogy, and popular culture do not appear to be related, Giroux and Simon (1989) state that popular culture is part of the student's everyday social life and, therefore, part of the cultural politics of the school,

> . . . it is precisely in the relationship between pedagogy and popular culture that the important understanding arises of making the pedagogical more political and the political more pedagogical. Popular culture and pedagogy represent important terrains of cultural struggle which

offer both subversive discourse and important theoretical elements through which it becomes possible to rethink schooling as a viable and important form of cultural politics (p. 238).

Teachers, then, must become aware of how popular culture can and does affect their pedagogical practices. Students appropriate popular culture and incorporate it into their educational experiences. It gives authority to their voices and experiences. Thus it is appropriate to examine how popular culture affects the informal process of schooling. Indeed, Aronowitz and Giroux (1985) speak to the issue of mass culture and critical pedagogy by stating the following about writing:

> If writing is to become part of the critical process, deconstruction of mass culture . . . is the first priority. We mean that writing could consist in the first place in analysis of TV shows, critical interrogation of popular music, and close scrutiny of film genres that approximate mass culture, such as disaster films, and adventures. In other words, the job of the teacher is to legitimate mass audience culture in order to criticize and transcend it, or to discover whether genuine expressive forms are repressed within it (p. 52).

Briefly, the important point is that knowledge cannot be perceived as a "neutral artifact," learned through either the formal or informal curriculum. We must ask whose culture is being transmitted and in whose interest. Are there certain social subgroups that are related to particular knowledge and power? The debate on the formal curriculum and subject matter for appropriate schooling outcomes should shift to include the significance of texts, peer groups, youth and student subcultures, and popular culture on the informal socialization process of schooling and pedagogical practices.

Dolby (2003) also encourages educational researchers and educators to examine popular culture and its relationship to education. She argues that "The importance of popular culture and its connection to education lies in the role it plays as a site for engaging in the process of democratic practice" (p. 258). She clearly states that it is most important to teach students to analyze and critique media messages. She quotes Willis (1990), who notes,

> The field of education is likely to come under even more intense pressure. It will be further marginalized in most people's experience by common [read "popular" or "everyday"] culture. Insofar as educational practices are still predicated on traditional liberal humanist lines and on the assumed superiority of high art, they will become almost totally irrelevant to the real energies and interests of most young people and have no part in their identity formation. Common culture will, increasingly, undertake, in its own ways, the roles that education has vacated (147).

IMPLICATIONS FOR TEACHER EDUCATION

We have already discussed the two main debates in teacher education programs as well as some approaches to thinking about teaching in Chapter 3. What is left to discuss is the importance of teacher education when addressing educational and social inequality generated through the hidden curriculum.

According to Tom (1987, 1995) and Liston and Zeichner (1987), pedagogical practices within teacher education programs have been influenced by dominant ideological discourses. We believe that, although many researchers argue for or against particular pedagogical practices, teacher education programs essentially fail at educational reform because the programs focus almost exclusively on technical forms of knowledge (Beyer, 1987; Smyth, 1989; Sheehan & Fullan, 1995). Similarly, the teacher's role is presumed to be one that transforms knowledge in a non-critical manner. Efficiency, classroom management and control, and getting something effectively taught, are of primary concern to many teachers. Education of this kind tends to depoliticize rather than politicize both educators and students. In particular, it disempowers rather than empowers learners, and it does not demystify hegemonic, controlling ideologies.

Fortunately, alternative discourses to traditional pedagogical approaches have gained some attention within teacher education programs. Some education reformers suggest that teacher education should prepare student teachers to question taken-for-granted practices that are considered politically neutral. Furthermore, as we have noted throughout this text, critical, critical multicultural, feminist, and anti-racist theories and pedagogies can contribute to teacher education generally, and to teaching methods courses. If we adopt these, we will more easily foster a questioning attitude towards teaching, learning, knowledge, formal and hidden curricula, and the relationship between school and society.

Aronowitz and Giroux (1985) argue that teacher education must contribute to the development of a schooling process that works in the interests of a democratic society by viewing teacher education as a form of cultural politics. Such a program would include the study of various themes, such as language, history, culture, and power. Giroux (1989) notes, ". . . it is important that educators come to understand theoretically how difference is constructed through various representations and practices that name, legitimate, marginalize, and exclude the cultural capital and voices of various groups" (p. 142). It is only through an understanding of how these can be challenged and transformed that teachers can develop a pedagogy *for* difference, one which addresses how differences are constructed in the curriculum, student voices, and conflicting ideologies. These are only some of the issues to be engaged in this approach.

A recent reform movement in teacher education, which Liston and Zeichner (1991) refer to as the social-reconstructionist tradition, aims at preparing future teachers for a diverse student population. Reforms in teacher training programs must be developed to lead to critical consciousness and create a more democratic and just society. Liston and Zeichner argue, however, that criticism of the social-reconstructionist approach has pointed to its marginal status and is merely "an academic discussion that has had very little influence outside its own inner circle" (p. 34). Furthermore, the authors note that studies show that many universities do not support social-reconstructionist-oriented reforms because they do not want to alienate those students who support the status quo in the schooling process. And, perhaps, universities do not want to risk opposing the existing institutional and societal structures (p. 155).

Liston and Zeichner further note that ". . . most accounts of teachers' practical knowledge seem to give little emphasis to . . . cultural, social or political [experiences]" (p. 67). However, the authors believe the social-reconstructionist tradition can contribute to the development of teacher education programs that would emphasize the notion of teachers reflecting on their social and political beliefs, and challenge the reality of classroom practices. That is, teachers ought to be trained to reflect on what kind of teachers they are, (their values and beliefs) and how they became that way.

SUMMARY/CONCLUSIONS

This chapter has focused on the role that the school plays in the process of socialization. We have discussed the way socialization takes place within the family from various perspectives, including the functionalist perspective and various other social psychological theories, such as the psychoanalytic, cognitive, and social learning theories. The theoretical perspectives we have drawn from to explain the informal process of socialization are that of symbolic interaction, phenomenology, and interpretive sociology.

Following the discussion on the process of socialization, we have explained how teachers' expectations affect students' school performance. We have discussed how teachers use unquestioned, common sense knowledge about effective teaching to interpret and respond to their pupils' behaviours, and how teacher typifications of these behaviours play an important role in categorizing pupils for the purpose of classroom organization.

The school as an agent of moral and political socialization was also discussed. Here we saw how national identity and social control are part of the informal process of socialization. Again, the emphasis is on the importance of how educators question this process. The discussion on the hidden curriculum, peer groups, and popular culture points to the significance of these factors on students' social experiences and learning achievements in educational settings.

As we have seen from the description of the Alternate School in Chapter 4, what educators decide about education is important, but what students decide is even more so. A discussion of the problems facing young people today can be incorporated into classroom practice, curriculum design, the structure of the educational system, and teacher education programs.

KEY TERMS

cognitive theory of
   socialization
generalized other
id, ego, and superego
internalization
intersubjectivity
melting pot

mentoring
moral socialization
pluralism
political socialization
primary socialization
secondary socialization

significant other
social learning theory
socialization
taken-for-granted perspective
tracking
typification

EDUCATIONAL ISSUES AND QUESTIONS FOR DISCUSSION

1. What do you believe is the role of the hidden curriculum in producing social class differences in school achievement?

2. How have peer groups and popular culture affected your social and academic experiences in school?

3. As a teacher, what measures would you take to insure that you are not negatively categorizing or typifying the students in your class?

4. Explain the role of teachers' expectations and discuss how these have affected your own social and academic experiences.

5. Why do you think teachers typify students? How do you typify and categorize your peers?

RECOMMENDED READINGS/REFERENCES

Apple, M. W. (1979). *Ideology and curriculum.* Boston: Routledge & Kegan Paul.

Apple, M. W., & Christian-Smith, L. K. (Eds.). (1991). *The politics of the textbook.* New York: Routledge.

Aronowitz, S., & Giroux, H. (1985). *Education under siege.* New York: Bergin & Garvey.

Aronowitz, S., & Giroux, H. (1993). *Education still under siege.* New York: Bergin & Garvey.

Ballantine, J. (1983). *The sociology of education: A systematic analysis.* Englewood Cliffs, NJ: Prentice Hall.

Barakett, J. (1979). *Teacher's theories and methods in structuring routine activities.* Unpublished doctoral dissertation, Université de Montréal.

Beyer, L. (1987). What knowledge is of most worth in teacher education? In J. Smyth (Ed.), *Educating teachers: changing the nature of pedagogical knowledge* (pp. 14–19). New York: Falmer Press.

Clarke, B., & Trow, M. (1966). The organization context. In T. Newcomb & E. Wilson (Eds.), *College peer groups: Problems and prospects for research* (pp. 17–70). Chicago: Aldine

Coleman, J. (1961). *The adolescent society.* New York: The Free Press.

Cooley, C. H. (1956). *Human nature and the social order.* Glencoe, IL: Free Press.

Dolby, N. (2003). Popular culture and democratic practice. *Harvard Educational Review, 73*(3), 258–284.

Dreeben, R. (1968). *On what is learned in school.* Reading, MA: Addison-Wesley.

Durkheim, E. (1961). *Moral education.* New York: The Free Press.Giroux, H. (1989). Schooling as a form of cultural politics: Towards a pedagogy of and for difference. In H. Giroux & P. McLaren (Eds.), *Critical pedagogy, the state and cultural struggle* (pp.125–151). Albany, NY: State University of New York Press.

Giroux, H., & Simon, R. (1989). Popular culture and critical pedagogy. In H. Giroux & P. McLaren (Eds.), *Critical pedagogy, the state and cultural struggle* (pp. 236–251). Albany, NY: State University of New York Press.

Gore, J. (1993). *The struggle for pedagogies.* New York: Routledge.

Hargreaves, D. H., Hester, S. K., & Mellor, F. J. (1975). *Deviance in classrooms.* London: Routledge & Keegan Paul.

Jackson, P. (1968). *Life in classrooms.* New York: Holt, Rinehart & Wilson.

Liston, D., & Zeichner, K. (1987). Critical pedagogy and teacher education. *Journal of Education, 169*(3), 117–137.

Liston, D., & Zeichner, K. (1991). *Teacher education and the social conditions of schooling.* New York: Routledge.

Mackie, M. (1994). Socialization. In R. Hagedorn (Ed.), *Sociology* (5th ed., pp. 89–120). Toronto: Harcourt Brace & Company.

Mead, G. (1934). *Mind, self and society.* Chicago: University of Chicago Press.

Mifflen, F. J., & Mifflen, S. C. (1982). *The sociology of education: Canada and beyond.* Calgary: Detselig.

Nathanson, M. (1970). Phenomenology and typification: A study in the philosophy of Alfred Schutz. *Social Research, 37,* 3–4, 6–8.

Parsons, T. (1967). The school class as a social system. In P. Roge (Ed.), *The study of society* (pp. 647–665). New York: Random House.

Schutz, A. (1973). *Collected papers: The problem of social reality* (Vol. 1). The Hague: Martinus Nijhoff.

Sheehan, N., & Fullan, M. (1995). Teacher education in Canada: A case study of British Columbia and Ontario. In M. Wideen & P. Grimmett (Eds.), *Changing times in teacher education* (pp. 89–101). Bristol: Falmer Press.

Smyth, J. (1989). A critical pedagogy of classroom practice. *Journal of Curriculum Studies, 21*(6), 483–502.

Tom, A. (1987). Replacing pedagogical knowledge with pedagogical questions. In J. Smyth (Ed.), *Educating teachers: Changing the nature of pedagogical knowledge* (pp. 9–17). Philadelphia: Falmer Press.

Tom, A. (1995). Stirring the embers: Reconsidering the structure of teacher education programs. In M. Wideen & P. Grimmet (Eds.), *Changing times in teacher education* (pp. 117–131). Bristol: Falmer Press.

Wagner, H. (Ed.). (1970). *Alfred Schutz on phenomenology and social relations.* Chicago: University of Chicago Press.

Weaver, J. (2005). *Popular culture.* New York: Peter Lang.

Willis, P. (1990). *Common culture.* London: Open University Press.

chapter six

Globalization, Schooling, Technology, and the Curriculum

CHAPTER OBJECTIVES

In this chapter we explore the ways in which globalization, schooling, technology, and the curriculum are increasingly interconnected. The aims of this chapter are

- to define globalization, especially with regard to its meaning for education
- to illustrate briefly but concretely how globalization touches the lives of individuals
- to show how globalization and technology are changing curriculum content and the practice of teaching
- to point to the ways that globalization tends to perpetuate global and local social class distinctions and the inequitable conditions of disadvantaged minorities
- to provide future teachers and other educators with an understanding of the implications for teaching and learning of the connections between globalization, technology, and the curriculum

GLOBALIZATION

We begin this chapter by clarifying the meaning of **globalization**, since it is in the context of globalization that the subsequent discussion of schooling, technology, and the curriculum will make the most sense. There are many aspects to globalization; therefore it can be a vague and confusing concept, even though it is a term we hear and use regularly. Globalization is a favourite catchword of journalists and politicians, used as a shorthand way of describing the spread and connectedness of production (Smith & Smith, 2002). Nevertheless, globalization is not a new phenomenon; rather, it has been increasing for centuries, linked to industrialization, migration, and urbanization; and advances in technology and communication, all of which are trends that are continuing across the world. The situation today is significantly changed, however, due to the volume of international trade and the speed of communication and technological developments, particularly those associated with transportation and the media. Globalization is promoted and stimulated by these trends and, in turn, reinforces and has an impact on them.

As this chapter will show, globalization touches the educational domain in Canada and elsewhere in many ways; these include educational policies, the influence of technology in the classroom, teaching practices, the content of the curriculum, and the development, selection, and use of print and non-print teaching materials. The influence of globalization thus creates considerable grounds for debate about what the priorities should be, and serious implications for the education of teachers. To ask if globalization is a good thing or not is not the point; globalization is here to stay and certain to continue to influence the experience of students in schools and universities in unpredictable ways. Therefore teachers and other educators as well as our students need to be informed about it.

Anthony Giddens (1990) defines globalization as "the intensification of worldwide social relations which link distant localities in such a way that local happenings are shaped by events occurring many miles away and vice versa" (p. 64). Stated differently, globalization refers to a process in which "events, decisions, and activities in one part of the world can come to have significant consequences for individuals and communities in quite distant parts of the globe" (McGrew & Lewis, 1992, cited by Myers, 2001, p. 3). Globalization thus involves a change in the way we understand geography and experience localness. Many of the activities that previously involved face-to-face interaction at the local level are now conducted across great distances due to the ease of telecommunications. Globalization thus has integrative as well as divisive dimensions; on the one hand there is the possibility of the emergence of larger, collective identities and shared meanings, on the other hand there is bound to be persistence of local identities and meanings, due to the apparent human need for face-to-face interaction in familiar situations.

Globalization can be seen in terms of internationalization, liberalization, universalization, deterritorialization, and, in a somewhat different vein, Westernization ("modernization") (Smith & Smith, 2002). That is, globalization has economic, social, cultural, and political elements. In terms of economics, **internationalization** refers to cross-border relations between countries in which national economies are overtaken by international economic exchange and interdependence, while **liberalization** refers to "a process of removing government-imposed restrictions on the movement of goods between countries in order to create an 'open,' 'borderless' world economy" (Scholte, 2000, p. 16, quoted by Smith & Smith, 2002). Socio-economically and culturally, **universalization** has to do with the process of spreading various objects and experiences worldwide. **Deterritorialization** points to the political aspect of globalization in that it refers to the transformation of the meaning of national boundaries (and hence political allegiances) in terms of economic and social relations (Held, McGrew, Goldblatt & Perraton, 1999, p 16). Because of this, there may be a shift in power away from the nation state towards multinational corporations, thus even the so-called central nations may actually be losing political power internationally (McGrew, 2000).

Globalization is often understood as Westernization or modernization (especially in an "Americanized" form—e.g., Disneyfication, McDonaldization), where values and attitudes associated with capitalism and free enterprise, competition and individualism, are spread the world over, undermining pre-existing cultures and local self-determination in the process in a kind of neo-colonialization. With increased economic interconnection the poorer, "peripheral" countries of the South (the majority world) have become even more dependent on "central" economies such as the United States (the minority world), where capital and technical expertise tend to be concentrated. This is but one way in which globalization can be seen to increase the gap between the world's rich and poor (Apple, 2003).

Globalization Affects Individual Lives

Before proceeding to discuss the linkages between globalization, schooling, technology, and the curriculum, we must emphasize that it is important for the reader to see that globalization affects people's lives in very concrete ways.

One feature of globalization that is familiar to most readers involves the spread of the "brand" across the world so that products are developed and then marketed in Toronto, Seoul, Washington, and Johannesburg, as well as in small Inuit communities in Canada's North. Brands like Coca-Cola, Nike, Sony, Nestlé, and a host of others have become part of the fabric of people's lives almost everywhere, sometimes with seemingly benign results and sometimes with disastrous ones (Klein, 2003). It was not long ago, for instance, in several parts of the still-developing world and Africa especially, that Nestlé marketed its baby formula so "successfully" that mothers abandoned breastfeeding in favour of bottle-feeding. But often the only water that was available to mix with the bottled formula was contaminated, so the infant death rate rose dramatically. Another example is found in Canada's aboriginal communities, where the incidence of child diabetes has skyrocketed along with the consumption of soft drinks such as Coca-Cola. Furthermore, with the influence of pop culture and the rise of the brand, there has been an increased commercial effort to condition children and young people to construct their identities around brands.

Globalization also directly affects the lives of families with young children. For example, programs for child care are nested in local, community, national, and cultural environments that affect the way children are cared for through various policies and laws as well as sets of beliefs about the ways children are to be raised. National and cultural contexts are in turn immersed in and influenced by globalization, through aid programs in still developing countries, from international organizations such as UNICEF, the World Bank, and the Canadian International Development Agency (CIDA). Globalization thus stands to have an impact at the local level on families and organizations that are established for the care and early education of children (Myers, 2001).

Globalization also affects the organization of social space. As Henry Giroux points out, there has been an erosion of public space, and this is affecting people's day-to-day social interactions.

> [Y]oung people are increasingly excluded from public spaces outside of schools that once offered them the opportunity to hang out with relative security, work with mentors, and develop their own talents and sense of self-worth. . . recreational space is now privatized as commercial profit-making venture. Gone are the youth centers, city public parks, outdoor basketball courts or empty lots where kids play stickball. Play areas are now rented out to the highest bidder. . .

Giroux, 2000, p. 10

Globalization and Schooling

Globalization directly affects the organization, content, and process of schooling, through the new technologies, curricular choices, and new ways in which curricula are implemented. The forces associated with globalization have conditioned the context in which educators operate, and profoundly altered people's experience of both formal and informal education. Schools and universities have, for example, become sites for branding and the targets of corporate expansion. Many administrators and policymakers now look to market solutions to educational problems and to deal with financial constraints. The "needs" of business and industry are now defining the goals of schooling.

The impact and pervasiveness of globalization means that it should be a central topic in the curriculum for educating teachers and others. The concerns include

- the corporate takeover of schools and curricula
- the threat to the autonomy of provincial educational systems in Canada and national education systems elsewhere
- the impact of changing technologies on the definition of "useful" knowledge and on the content and process of delivering the curriculum
- the conception of the learner as a consumer rather than as a participant
- the differential access to the new technologies because of cost

Due to an increasing tendency towards corporate takeover, we can observe a shift in many universities from a service ethic to a profit ethic, to an instrumental view of what education is all about. *Real education for the real world* says the slogan of one university. In Canada and elsewhere we find economic growth and talk of "international competitiveness on the world stage" at the heart of the restructuring of courses and programs so that they can be marketed, along with an increase in courses offered by distance to achieve economies of scale, and the privatization of M.B.A. (Masters of Business Administration) programs. The pressure to increase student loans and course fees has raised the direct cost placed on students (especially working-class students), while they are now deemed to be consumers rather than participants in the educational process. From our experience as instructors, especially of undergraduate courses in education, the students' view of the process in terms of being a consumer has a serious impact on instructor-student relations. Students increasingly seem concerned with questions of "how to" rather than "why," with technique rather than substance. For some students participation is a waste of time; their motivation is instrumental and focused on how to obtain an "A" in the course.

From the side of policy makers there is a world-wide increase in pressure on all spheres of education, starting at the pre-school level with "efficiency," delivering specified "outcomes," and "accountability." Further to what was discussed in Chapter 3 about outcomes-based education (OBE), in the name of the effort to increase equality of opportunity and to raise standards, there is a trend towards more centralization of curricula, with less and less room for local, community-oriented explorations and student projects, and for what goes on in classrooms to be dovetailed to the cultural, linguistic, and other particular characteristics of the learners. Along with the OBE definition of specified competencies to be achieved by all comes increased formal testing to determine if those competencies have been achieved. According to Apple (2003), Jansen and Christie (1999), and others, this is likely to result in greater inequality because of the insidious way that formal, standardized tests have long been shown to be subtly biased against disadvantaged minorities, and thus discriminatory.

> The language of efficiency, production, standards, cost-effectiveness, job skills, work discipline. . . all defined by powerful groups and always threatening to become the dominant way we think about schooling. . . has begun to push aside concerns for a democratic curriculum, teacher autonomy, and class, gender, and race equality (Apple, 2003, p. 442).

Apple points out that these pressures actually result in de-skilling of the teaching profession, since what is to be taught, and how, is increasingly taken out of teachers' hands. "Even though a number of teachers may support computer-oriented curricula, an emphasis on the new technology needs to be seen in this context of the rationalization of teaching and curricula in general" (p. 448).

The main forces framing newly centralized curricula are economic and directly linked to globalization. Thus we need to ask, to what extent is the process of globalization undermining the long-established value on the autonomy of public educational systems in their aim to promote gender, racial, religious, and other forms of equity in democratic societies? To what extent is the global taking over the local in a process of de-localization of schooling? (Burbules & Torres 2000). However, as we saw in Chapter 1, there has also been a counter trend towards decentralization. For example, since the 1980s there has been an increase in discussion about parental choice and community or local control of schooling. While much primary schooling remains local, a significant proportion of secondary schooling does not. This has both severed the link between locality and schooling, and undermined the idea of community schooling. Following on Giroux's comments cited earlier about the reduction of informal play space, we find—in the United States especially, but increasingly in Canada as well—security gates that mark the boundaries of schools, separating them from the communities in which they are located, as if there is no connection between the two.

Technology and the Curriculum

By **technology** we are referring to the technology of teaching, which, apart from blackboards, chalk, pens, and pencils, brings to mind print (textbooks) and non-print (computerized, Web-based) text materials (Peacock & Cleghorn, 2004). **Curriculum** refers to the subject content of schooling, the process of implementing the curriculum in the classroom as well as the set of beliefs or ideology that underlie what is to be taught, to whom, and why. Thus the curriculum includes the subject matter that is officially sanctioned by an education ministry to be taught at each grade level as well as the amount of time to be devoted to each subject. In Canada, curriculum matters are decided by each province and territory's ministry of education. Along with the set curriculum, text materials may be mandated or a limited choice offered to school boards and teachers. Procedures for implementing the curriculum most often are stated in curriculum documents in terms of recommendations. It is important to note, however, that when we speak of curriculum as a process, this refers to the fact that the curriculum goes through many filters by the time it is delivered in the classroom. In fact, the curriculum that is followed in the classroom may bear little resemblance to that which is set out in curriculum policy documents. This is due to the relative autonomy that teachers have, if not in the selection of texts to be used, at least in the emphasis that they choose to place on one topic or another (Werner, 1991). However, when the curriculum is linked to set objectives as defined by outcomes-based education (OBE), there may be an inclination for teachers to stick closer in their teaching to the objectives and competencies that they know will be examined rather than rely on their good teaching instincts to modify and dovetail the curriculum to their students' specific needs, interests, and prior experience. Again, we see the potential for the effects of globalization to be discriminatory and to perpetuate gender, race, ethnic, and social class-based inequitable learning situations.

Globalization has meant that the curriculum of one country can easily find its way to another through a process of borrowing and adapting policies (such as outcomes-based education), via the content of textbooks and the content of teacher education programs (Steiner-Khamsi, 2004). This is because education systems everywhere are attempting to become competitive on the "world stage" by upgrading the training of teachers. Thus, in addition to the borrowing and adapting of education policies from the more industrialized countries such as the United States and Canada, there is also a borrowing of teaching education models, textbooks, and teachers' manuals. Some of this occurs through student and faculty exchanges between universities in the still-developing countries and the so-called developed countries. This borrowing is also promoted by the conglomerate of the textbook industry, about which you will read more later on in this chapter.

Thus it is difficult, if not impossible, to discuss the role of technology in education without also talking about curriculum and the text materials that embody it. Due to technological developments in the computer industry, there is a proliferation of non-print text materials in schools, in distance learning, and in non-formal learning throughout the world. These include an array of computer and internet-generated materials, CD-ROMs, and web-based programs. Developments in educational technology, especially the use of the internet, multimedia courses, and the growth of distance learning, are thus changing the face of education. At one level these changes can be seen as an instrument of localization; they allow people to study or access information from the internet while at home, if they own a computer, or at an internet café or a university computer lab, if they do not. However, distance education usually involves highly individualized forms of learning and may thwart the possibility of interaction with fellow students. At the same time people from very different parts of the world are able to engage in the same program, and student contact can be across great physical distance rather than face to face. Although this may sound like an efficient way to deliver knowledge simultaneously to a diverse group of students located in many different parts of the world, there are in fact well-identified problems with such courses: cultural differences in students' experience with on-line environments; lack of face-to-face support or tutoring; and misunderstandings between students in course "chat rooms" due to the varied ability of students to communicate via English or other international languages (Bates & Poole, 2003).[1]

---

[1]Student use of the computer lab at a university in one African country was observed on several occasions by A.C. during a visit in 2006. By 7:00 in the morning, the lab, with 100 up-to-date computers donated by an international organization in the United States, was filled to capacity with students trying to finish assignments for that day. Unfortunately, due to technical problems, the connection to the internet was frequently down and students could not access the library and other sites that they needed. These observations bring home to students in Canada that computer access is not only relatively affordable here, but also that the telecommunications and internet services are quite reliable.

The Global Meets the Local

The manner in which globalization affects local curricula and text materials in a process referred to as "**glocalization**" is discussed by Elizabeth McEneaney (2004), using the example of primary science teaching in Canada. McEneaney shows how international organizations such as UNESCO and international achievement tests such as the TIMMS (Third International Mathematics and Science Study) promote global standards in subjects such as mathematics and science, while at the same time elements of the local culture, in this case Canada's, may (still) be found within the content of the curriculum and in textbooks.

McEneaney refers to the latent and manifest functions of text materials, bringing us back to the discussion in Chapter 1 about the latent and manifest functions of schooling. One of the manifest functions of print and non-print text materials is to provide students with effective access to the subject knowledge that a country's curriculum experts and policy makers have decided is essential. Text materials also have latent functions that are connected to the hidden curriculum, such as socializing children into "unequal social hierarchies, usually mirroring discriminatory practices and structures in the classroom and school" (McEneaney, 2004, p. 22). Although the situation appears to be changing, in the past primary school textbooks suggested to students that people of colour and white women had no serious place in the world of science. In some countries, however, it is still the case that the scenarios in which men and women are portrayed in text materials contain explicit messages about sex roles and gender relations.

McEneaney also cites these interesting facts about the power of the textbook industry to affect what is taught at all levels of education. In doing so she points to an area that is in need of more research.

> In the early '90s foreign publishers controlled 85 percent of the postsecondary textbook market in Canada and Canadian-based branches of international companies such as McGraw-Hill Ryerson and Pearson controlled the approved learning resources for elementary and secondary mathematics and science in provinces across the country.
>
> McEneaney, 2004, p. 36

How is the Local Portrayed in Canadian Textbooks?

The reader is reminded that, although curricular and textbook decisions are made at the provincial level in Canada, one can detect a degree of consensus about curriculum content from one side of the country to the other. Canadian mathematics textbooks tend to differentiate themselves from US textbooks by the use of the metric system, for example. In an analysis of 25 grade 4 to 7 science textbooks published in Canada since 1950, McEneaney (2004) found that specific Canadian content comes through in mention of such matters as multiculturalism, Canadian flora and geography, the national health care system, and Canadian scientists. Canadian science textbooks now regularly show people of different races and ethnicities and are beginning to include references to Aboriginal peoples as well as Aboriginal knowledge of natural phenomena. Despite these references to the local, Canadian textbooks also point out clearly that Canada is very much part of the international scientific community (the global). In terms of content, we see the global coming together with the local; in Canadian texts and elsewhere, children and ordinary adults are now being considered their own experts, and the emphasis is not simply on famous (male) scientists. Children's lives and their own multicultural and racial characteristics are now treated as legitimate objects for understanding abstract principles. For example, in a primary science textbook in England, teachers are encouraged to combine anti-racist pedagogy with teaching the concept of continuous variation by drawing on the array of skin tones amongst the multicultural group of children in the classroom (Wynne, 1992). Thus we see how science education moves from a set of abstract principles to something that young children can observe and understand. Science education is no longer reserved solely for a high priesthood of university-trained practitioners. The classical questions are replaced in centrality by a child's everyday questions about their own lives: how bicycles work, whether it will rain tomorrow, why spread salt on an icy road (McEneaney, 2004).

While Canadian texts have changed to become more inclusive and less biased, there is also evidence from other countries (as we saw in the example from England cited above) that this change may be a global trend. Thus, there are local as well as transnational influences on the construction of school curricula. Interestingly, local examples do not appear to contradict the transnational elements, suggesting that the potential for learning to be relevant and meaningful by including familiar examples is enormous. However, in the absence of directives from Canada's provincial ministries of education that texts should contain a Canadian orientation, McEneaney notes that,

> . . . it is difficult to imagine why the handful of multinational publishing conglomerates that increasingly dominate the industry would bother to sustain these nuanced local aspects of school science in Canada. Furthermore, the homogeneity inherent in emerging world culture[2] could prove to be very good for business (McEneaney, 2004, p.46–47).

Along with Brian Street (2001) and other experts in the field of critical literacy studies, we do not agree that literacy is simply a skill acquired by individuals. Street terms that as the "autonomous" view of literacy—that is, literacy is seen as something that exists on its own, disconnected from cultural context. In contrast, Street's "ideological" model of literacy sees literacy as always embedded in cultural activity. Apple (2003) points out that a similar autonomous conceptualization of technology prevails. "It is set apart and viewed as if it had a life of its own, independent of social intentions, power, and privilege" (p. 440).

PROBLEMS WITH TEXT MATERIALS

With the globalization of the textbook industry and the significant amount of policy and program borrowing between one country and another, it is becoming ever more urgent for teachers to be critically aware of the changes that are affecting education and for them to be very knowledgeable when it comes to understanding the many ways in which text materials can pose problems for learners. Text materials have been shown to pose many different kinds of problems because of a number of well-identified faulty assumptions

---

[2]The concept of a **world culture** is widely debated. Boli and Thomas (1997, as quoted by McEneaney, 2004, p. 26) say that a world culture reflects dominant Western values, constructed by and maintained through the sharing of such values by experts working within international organizations. McEneaney also uses the term to refer to the ways in which the rational, the universal, and the individual are portrayed in curricula and texts. For example, and again with regard to science education, rationalism is assumed to have a role in a nation's progress and development. In advocating literacy for all by the year 2015, UNESCO's mandate points to universalism. And literacy is conceived most often as a set of skills acquired by individuals—hence individualism.

that underlie their development—assumptions about learners, learning, and the ways in which the materials will be used by teachers and learners. These difficulties include the following:

- the assumption by the developers of English language text materials that all learners are first language speakers of English
- the way information is linked from one idea to another
- the need for the reader to make inferences rather than having facts stated directly
- textual passages that include new ideas too numerous for the age of the learner
- the use of examples that are culturally unfamiliar to particular groups of learners.

Such difficulties can result in an excessive demand or **cognitive load** for the learner. Briefly, cognitive load theory is concerned with the ways in which the mind is focused and used during the learning process. If there is a mismatch between the abstract level of the content of a text and the age of the learner, high levels of cognitive load may result due to the unnecessary burden on the learner's ability to make the required connections via his or her working memory resources (Leahy, Cooper & Sweller, 2004). The same principle applies if there is a mismatch between the cultural content of the text and the ethnic background of the student, making it difficult, if not impossible, for the student to draw on his or her prior experience to make sense of what is being taught.

It has been shown that the same kinds of problems as those just described are found as well in non-print materials (Peacock & Cleghorn, 2004). With school systems everywhere looking to web-based sources of learning because of the belief that they will assist teachers and improve learning, it is important for future teachers to be aware of the problems that are embedded in the way learning materials are developed, in order to guide them when they must select new materials or when they adapt non-print as well as print text materials to the needs of their learners. Following are but a few of the ways in which teachers can differentiate useful text materials from problematic ones.

- Teachers need to be alert to the seductive quality of eye-catching materials (print and non-print) and to the promise that non-print, web-based learning materials are going to make teaching and learning easier.
- When selecting materials, teachers need to ask if glossy, colourful materials can really be assumed to teach better.
- Teachers need to examine the language used in the materials for its appropriateness to the age of the target group of learners and for the needs of second-language learners—the majority of children in today's multicultural classrooms and in the still-developing world.
- Teachers need to examine web-based materials to see if they properly cue the reader about the order or format that the information is provided in—in effect, how to "read the page."

With regard to teaching young learners to "read the page," Walpole and Smolkin (2004) explain that with the proliferation of eye-catching images, both within print as well as non-print texts, has come a shift in the location of information. Images are no longer subordinate to text but have become the core text. "... these more complex visual environments... present new challenges for young readers and the teachers who work with them" (p 197).

Teachers need to know how to help learners to negotiate these pages by themselves, to know where and how to locate information. To this we would add that similar issues apply in the field of adult basic education.

As just indicated, it is important for teachers to be able to distinguish between glossy, eye-catching text materials, some of which are known to pose difficulties for students to access information, and so-called "friendly" text materials that guide the reader effectively. Following on the preceding discussion, it would be good to include reference to this distinction in teacher education programs, as follows.

A **friendly webpage** is one that contains "considerate prose, page layout and design, user interactivity and/or navigation, and instructional devices" (Barba, 2004, p. 139). These elements take into account that many second-language learners and students from culturally diverse backgrounds often have difficulty comprehending text that has been written as if all learners are first-language speakers of English. Barba's review of the research on this topic covers problems relating to such matters as cohesion (the way information is linked from one sentence to another), explication (facts are stated directly rather than requiring the reader to infer), conceptual density (the number of new ideas and vocabulary contained in a textual passage), and page layout. These are but a few of the issues that teachers need to be aware of when selecting what they believe are appropriate text materials and especially websites for their students. They must go below the glossy and fun surface. This being said, as Barba points out, a poorly designed webpage can also be a valuable teaching tool.

The Teacher-Learner-Text Relationship

Because of the role of the global textbook industry in education, there is another link to schooling, in this case to changes in the teacher-learner-text (T-L-T) relationship that are taking place in classrooms. Thus teachers also need to be aware of the ways in which the T-L-T relationship has been observed to change with the ongoing shift from print to non-print materials (Peacock & Miller, 2004).

The T-L-T triangle illustrates the three key relationships in a classroom and the aspect of text use that each implies. For example, the Teacher-Text relationship is governed by the teacher's knowledge of different text styles, their availability, and the consequent choices of texts the teachers can make. The Learner-Text relationship, on the other hand,

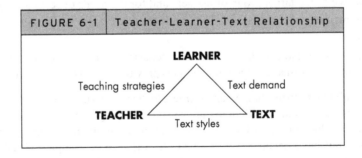

| FIGURE 6-1 | Teacher-Learner-Text Relationship |

is dominated by the "match" between the demands made by a text and the capacity of the learner to manage this level of demand. The role of the teacher in the classroom has been found to shift dramatically when students are "interacting" with computers. On the one hand, this may foster valuable interaction between students if they are collaborating on a project. On the other hand, much of what is being learned (or not) may be out of the teacher's line of vision, making it more difficult for him or her to know when to intervene and provide direction.

The major shift in the learning environment in recent years has been in the Teacher-Learner dimension, i.e., that of teaching strategies. There has been a global move towards less dependence on teachers using text to "tell" students, and a concomitant expectation that learners will engage in practical group enquiry, supported by social constructivist theories of learning that were discussed in Chapter 3. At the same time, web-based material and computers in classrooms have given pupils themselves (in theory, if not in practice) access to a huge range of potentially useful text. Hence the teacher's "knowledge-based" text may now be replaced by the learner's activity-based text and on-line interactive materials.

The main concern is where this shift has proved successful and where it has hit problems; for example, if the texts are not matched to the students' needs (e.g., culture, language, prior knowledge), the Learner-Text relationship may break down. The implications for teacher education are summarized in Table 6.1.

Do Virtual Environments Lead to Virtual Learning?

Another issue that educators need to address in light of the increasing global influence of technological developments on the curriculum has to do with what is actually learned in school via the "new media," or virtual environments. **Virtual learning** refers to learning

TABLE 6.1	Implications of Shifts in the T-L-T for Teacher Education
Text Dimension	Teachers need to know....
The teacher-text dimension	how to analyze text demand and select appropriate texts, where a choice is available
The teacher-learner dimension	how to identify a wider range of ways in which text might be used in the classroom
	how to match their teaching styles with those of the text being used
The learner-text dimension	how to "write" or adapt text material that does not make inappropriate or excessive demands on their pupils
	how to give more attention in all subject areas to language and literacy learning
	how to develop children's visual literacy
	how to teach learners to "read" a page of text

that results from students' interactions with or in virtual environments, including every-thing from pre-school children's interactive computer games and stories to situations where university students receive all of their instruction in or through an online environ-ment. Little is actually known about the effects of learning in such environments and whether learning is actually enhanced by computer technology. As Murphy and Holleran (2004) point out, the primary reason for using computerized text materials lies in the belief that they will enhance learning. Do they?

> . . . on the surface, it would appear that technology is a blessing to educators and to students because it affords almost instantaneous and seemingly limitless access to a universe of infor-mation on any conceivable topic. With the click of a few keys. . . students can explore Pompeii, walk the Great Wall of China, watch the weather unfold in their own neighbor-hoods, or investigate Elizabethan England (Murphy & Holleran, 2004, p. 227).

Again, on the surface, computerized texts would seem to far outweigh traditional text materials in their ability to provide access to knowledge. This is due to the interac-tive quality of some programs, the provision of immediate feedback to the learner, the inclusion of sound and visual images, and the accessibility of the texts from the stu-dent's home at any time of the day (very much the local) or from a library. A study to explore this matter was carried out by Murphy and Holleran, an adapted summary of which appears below.

> Two articles that appeared in a news magazine were read by 131 male and female under-graduate students who were randomly assigned to three groups. One group read the articles in print form. The second group read the same articles in a computerized format from a web-page designed by the researchers. Both of these groups then responded to identical ques-tionnaires on paper. The third group read the articles and answered the same questionnaire in a computerized online format. The wording of the print and the computerized text were the same, the latter simply scanned into a webpage. The questionnaire asked students about their knowledge and perceptions of the articles (Murphy and Holleran, 2004).

There were few differences between the groups, all of which increased their knowl-edge about the topics of the articles. However, students in the print text group found the texts to be much more interesting and understandable than those who read the texts in the non-print format. The researchers had expected students to transfer their reading com-prehension skills, established long ago in primary school, to the non-print format, but this did not appear to happen. The two non-print groups in fact found the articles less inter-esting than the print-format group. This suggests that the computerized format was less accessible to the students than the print format, and that the students who used the com-puterized format were less able to link what they were reading to their prior knowledge in order to make sense of it. As a result of these findings, some tentative conclusions may be drawn.

- Students in this study found print texts easier to understand and somewhat more con-vincing than computerized texts.
- As computerized texts become more enhanced by innovative web design, they may pose additional hurdles for less competent readers, causing them to have more difficulty understanding what they read than they would have from regular, print text.
- The demands of print and non-print texts differ. It is possible that non-print texts increase the cognitive load for the learner.

In line with the encouragement we gave you in Chapter 1 to think like researchers, you may be asking if it is possible that Murphy and Holleran's findings might have been different if a younger group of students had taken part in the study. University students no doubt were taught to "read the page" from standard print text, but younger students may well have been introduced to both forms of text at the time they were learning to read. It is important to find out what, if any, difference such experience would make if the study were repeated with younger students.

To Murphy and Holleran's conclusions we would nevertheless add an observation from the research on **visual literacy** (Gates, 2004; Kress & Van Leeuwen, 1996; Tufte, 1997; Wileman, 1993). Visual literacy refers to the ability to derive meaning by connecting an illustration with the text (print or non-print). Visual literacy needs to be taught explicitly. This is the case for traditional textbooks, in which it is assumed that the reader will "automatically" connect an illustration with the printed text; it is even more the case when students are expected to glean understanding from computerized text and webpages. The information in this section of the chapter on computerized learning environments and the kinds of difficulties that unfriendly webpages in particular may pose for learners thus suggests that the time has come to give visual literacy more serious consideration and a place in the teacher education curriculum.

To recapitulate, vast developments in technology have brought worldwide changes in the teaching-learning process. In particular, non-print computerized texts are taking the place of traditional textbooks in many classrooms. The global textbook industry, in competition with the computer industry, is increasingly producing textbooks with pages designed like web pages. In turn, these changes have affected the role of the teacher in the classroom and changes in the teacher-learner-text (T-L-T) relationship, as discussed earlier. Thus, globalization has affected the content and process of schooling, and teacher education programs need to address the issue so that teachers are better prepared for the realities of the classroom today. As we saw in previous chapters, teacher education programs have been slow to pick up on the need to prepare teachers for the effects of globalization in the classroom, whether in terms of the influence of pop culture, technological changes, or the need for teachers to know how to help learners take a critical stance towards events and developments in and out of school.

> What may happen to teaching and curriculum if we do not think carefully about the new technology's place in the classroom? Will the growing focus on technological expertise, particularly computer literacy, equalize or further exacerbate the lack of social opportunities for our most disadvantaged students? (Apple, 2003, p. 442)

Is there a need for **global** and **technological literacy**? What about **social literacy**? As much as new technology might appear to offer solutions to many of the problems in society and our systems of education, we suggest that never before has there been a time when a more humane, non-technological approach to the effects of globalization on education has *also* been needed. Never before has it been so necessary to incorporate a critical and reflective stance into everything that educators do—the policies that are developed, the way teachers are educated, and the way teachers interact with students. As this chapter has suggested, as the world becomes globalized, there is a risk that no one will be in charge, that decisions will be driven by capitalistic considerations, and the multinational corporate world will, in effect, make decisions for us. In our view, this is the antithesis of democracy. Recent public controversy over media corporations donating computer equipment to schools in exchange for a few minutes of televised current events (accompanied by commercial advertisements) suggests that we may already have reached this stage. We hope that this section will cause the reader to think about some possible alternatives to this bleak scenario.

In the twenty-first century the kind of change that most educators are grappling with has to do with advances in technology and its influence on the educational process at all levels of the system. Although the situation applies in every industrialized country, it is at the forefront of recommendations for reforms in Canadian classrooms. According to Henchey (1987)

> . . . modern technology is changing how and where we work, what work we do, how we communicate with others, how we play, and, at a deeper level, how we think, how we see ourselves, and what we value. It is also changing how, where, and when we learn, as well as why and what we need to learn (p. 37).

A proposal to introduce the use of computers during 25% of class time in one school board in Montreal—a sixty-thousand dollar initiative backed by one of the major computer software corporations was described as an exciting project by a senior officer of the school board; others thought that the money would be better spent on badly needed textbooks (Seidman, 1999). While this account demonstrates the fact that decisions tend to be made without proper needs assessment or public debate, it also underlines the fact that the opinions of those who will be required to implement the change—the teachers—tend not to be sought. We might then ask: Who will be blamed if the outcomes do not match the investment? Are the expected learning outcomes based on well-conducted research or are they driven by international competitiveness and other non-academic considerations?

Technology, in the context of globalization, has thus become an issue in education. Understanding this issue requires that educators be aware of worldwide trends and that they be technologically literate. This goes far beyond the implementation and use of computers in classrooms; it involves teaching students to become socially literate. Social literacy involves "teaching students to think about their education, their future roles in society, and the place of technology in that society" (Apple, 2003, p. 254). It involves being able to "read" one's environment and its plethora of technological hardware and software. As Apple points out, it is rare that the serious issues relating to the new technology are explored in depth in classrooms. Rather, the emphasis is placed on the (questionable) need for "computer literacy" in a number of careers and on a rosy future. Job loss and de-skilling is rarely talked about. According to Apple (2003, p. 455), a curriculum that includes social literacy would have students asking:

- Where are computers used?
- What are they used for?
- What do people *actually* need to know in order to use them?
- Do computers enhance anyone's life? Whose?
- Do computers hurt anyone's life? Whose?
- Who decides when and where computers will be used?

Fleming takes a somewhat different angle to this topic with his reference to technological artifacts. ". . . studying technological artifacts is studying the mind and culture of the mind that produced the artifact. The artifact is a text, allowing for a critical 'reading' of the culture that produced it" (Fleming, 1990, p. 54). Fleming goes on to point out that it is important for educators to understand the many dimensions of technology. For example, most of us think of the hardware when we think of computers in classrooms. Some might also consider the process of manufacturing the hardware, or the cost associated with the development of software. But hardware and software are developed within a socio-technical system, which includes people, a power structure, machines, and other resources. There is also a socio-technical system of use. To be fully literate, then, in a technological, globalized society, a person needs to be aware of the nature of technological knowledge, the nature of the decisions that are being considered, particularly by those in positions of power, and the range of possible consequences (Freebody & Welch, 1993). We believe that this kind of social-technological literacy is particularly important for teachers.

> A technologically literate person must. . . understand the relationship between technology and social change. . . must "read" the artifact to find within it the set of societal assumptions that may cause the artifact to effect change in the society. To do this, one must conceptualize technology as a social organization (Wynne, 1988, pp. 147–167).

Finally, global change is driven by those who have access to economic and political resources. When a new technology causes social strain at the local level, for example, by depleting resources for something else that is also valued (such as textbooks, or art and music being included in the curriculum), then the issue becomes politically and socially charged. If educators are not socially, globally, and technologically literate, they will not have a say in the decisions that affect their lives in the classroom. Furthermore, their jobs are to provide skills, not to de-skill their students. "Unless students are able to deal honestly and critically with these complex ethical and social issues, only those now with the power to control technology's uses will have the capacity to act. . . .As educators, we need to be clear that the future promised to our students is real and not fictitious, that it is a world that all students can share in, not just the select few from well-to-do families" (Apple, 2003, p. 455).

SUMMARY/CONCLUSIONS

This chapter has raised many issues that are interconnected in complex ways. The nature and complexity of the forces involved in globalization are such that any discussion of its impact upon education raises fundamental issues and debate over whose values will prevail. For example, globalization affects the decisions of policy makers regarding curriculum priorities, and with regard to the importance of science, technology, and computer literacy (Aikenhead, 1990: Cobern, 1998; McEneaney, 2004; Murphy & Holleran, 2004).

Globalization has brought extensive corporate involvement in education; it is our position that this will result in more inequality, not less. For example, in the above-mentioned proposal for the extensive use of computers in elementary classrooms in a large Canadian city, parents were willing to pay a $15 per month rental fee. What about the parents who cannot afford this? The newspaper article (The Montreal Gazette, May 12, 1999) also reports that hundreds of schools worldwide have implemented such a computer program. We ask, in which part of the world are these schools located? Surely not in the still-developing world. It is important for educators to realize that inequality is a global as well as a local problem, one that involves us all.

The new linkages between corporations and universities pose an additional concern. We ask how these changes are being implemented and what effect they have on the traditional value of academic work. To what extent is academic freedom relinquished when research is funded by the private sector? To what extent does the knowledge created within universities remain a universally available resource, or does it become available only to those with high-tech access or those who are in a position to purchase it? (Buchbinder & Newson, 1994)

While the publishing industry (print and non-print) has something of a life of its own (extra-national or supra-national) and may be aiming via developments in technology and communications to make text materials "culture-free" and thus universally marketable[3], it is ever more important for educators to be alert to the relevance and user-friendly features of text materials, for in effect, these features structure and present the knowledge that is contained in the curriculum. Although some nations use textbooks written and published by their ministries of education, most nations rely, at least in part, on commercial publishers to produce texts in accord with curricular guidelines. There are, however, global pressures via the international textbook publishing industry on the structure and content of text materials, with subtle but real discouragement of local adaptations and translations into local languages because these are not seen as commercially viable.

The foregoing suggests that globalization and technology present unpredictable implications for the organization of schooling as well as for the curriculum—what is learned in school and how teaching will continue to be carried out. Although there are bound to be changes, especially in the technical means of delivering the curriculum, we remind our readers that schooling is essentially a conservative institution in society, an institution marked more by what are sometimes called "cultural lags" than by innovations. Thus, it remains to be seen how deep into the structures of schooling the connection between globalization, technology, and the curriculum will penetrate.

KEY TERMS

cognitive load	glocalization	technology
curriculum	internationalization	universalization
deterritorialization	liberalization	virtual learning
friendly webpage	social literacy	visual literacy
global literacy	socio-technical system	world culture
globalization	technological literacy	

---

[3]We do not believe it is possible to create "culture-free" texts any more than it has been possible to create culture-free standardized examinations.

EDUCATIONAL ISSUES AND QUESTIONS FOR DISCUSSION

1. Use Norman Henchey's argument regarding schooling in a technologically advanced society as the basis for a class debate. Defend your support for or your opposition to his argument.

2. What might be some alternatives to the corporate takeover of schools and universities?

3. Do you agree or disagree that university students are now consumers rather than participants in their education?

4. Suggest a few ways to research the effectiveness of different kinds of text materials for learning.

5. Debate the issue of globalization and its impact on schooling in terms of its being a positive or a negative influence in today's world.

RECOMMENDED READINGS/REFERENCES

Aikenhead, G. S. (1990). Scientific/technological literacy, critical reasoning, and classroom practice. In S. P. Norris & L. M. Phillips (Eds.), *Foundations of literacy policy in Canada* (pp. 127–146). Calgary: Detselig.

Apple, M. (2003). Is the new technology part of the solution or part of the problem in education? In A. Darder, M. Baltodano, & R. Torres, *The critical pedagogy reader* (pp. 440–457). New York: Routledge.

Barba, R. (2004). Friendly webpages: Their development and use. In A. Peacock & A. Cleghorn, *Missing the meaning: The development and use of print and non-print text materials in diverse school settings* (pp. 239–252). New York: Palgrave.

Bates, A. W., & Poole, G. (2003). *Effective teaching with technology in higher education: Foundations for success.* San Francisco: Jossey-Bass.

Boli, J., & Thomas, G. (1997). World culture in the world polity. *American Sociological Review, 62,* 171–190.

Buchbinder, H., & Newson, J. (1994). Corporate-university linkages in Canada: Transforming a public institution. In L. Erwin & D. MacLennan (Eds.), *Sociology of education in Canada* (pp. 473–498). Toronto: Copp Clark Longman.

Burbules, N. C., & Torres, C. A. (2000). *Globalization and education: Critical perspectives.* London: Routledge.

Cobern, W. W. (1998) (Ed.). *Socio-cultural perspectives on science education: An international dialogue.* Dordrecht, Netherlands: Kluwer Academic Publishers.

Fleming, R. W. (1990). The artifact as text: Being literate in a technological society. In S. Norris & L. M. Phillips (Eds.), *Foundations of literacy policy in Canada* (pp. 53–68). Calgary: Detselig.

Freebody, P., & Welch, A. R. (Eds.). (1993). *Knowledge, culture & power: International perspectives on literacy as policy and practice.* Pittsburgh, PA: University of Pittsburgh Press.

Gates, S. (2004). Visual literacy in science and its importance to pupils and teachers. In A. Peacock and A. Cleghorn, *Missing the meaning: The development and use of print and non-print text materials in diverse school settings* (pp. 223–238). New York: Palgrave.

Giddens, A. (1990). *Consequences of modernity.* Cambridge: Polity.

Giroux, H. A. (2000). *Stealing innocence: Corporate culture's war on children.* New York: Palgrave.

Held, D., McGrew, A., Goldblatt, D., & Perraton, J. (1999). *Global transformations—politics, economics and culture.* Cambridge: Polity Press.

Henchey, N. (1987). Communication technology and the transformation of learning. In R. Ghosh & D. Ray (Eds.), *Social change and education in Canada.* Toronto: Harcourt Brace Jovanovich.

Jansen, J., & Christie, P. (1999). *The changing curriculum: Studies in outcomes-based education in South Africa.* Cape Town: Juta Academic.

Klein, N. (2003). *No logo: Taking aim at brand bullies.* Toronto: Vintage Canada.

Kress, G., & Van Leeuwen, T. (1996). *Reading images: The grammar of visual design.* London: Routledge.

Laptops or textbooks? (1999, May 12). *The Montreal Gazette.*

Leahy, W., Cooper, G., & Sweller, J. (2004). Interactivity and the constraints of cognitive load theory. In A. Peacock and A. Cleghorn, *Missing the meaning: The development and use of print and non-print text materials in diverse school settings* (pp. 89–104). New York: Palgrave.

McEneaney, E. H. (2004). The global and the local in the construction of school science: The case of Canada. In A. Peacock and A. Cleghorn, *Missing the meaning: The development and use of print and non-print text materials in diverse school settings* (pp. 13–32). New York: Palgrave.

McGrew, A. G. (2000). *Global transformation reader: An introduction to the globalization debate.* Oxford: Polity Press.

McGrew, A. G., & Lewis, P. G. (1992). *Global politics: Globalization and the nation state.* Cambridge: Polity Press.

Murphy, P. K., & Holleran, T. (2004). Do virtual environments lead to virtual learning? In A. Peacock and A. Cleghorn, *Missing the meaning: The development and use of print and non-print text materials in diverse school settings* (pp. 133–144). New York: Palgrave.

Myers, R. G. (2001). Globalization, care and educational services for children under six in urban areas. In N. del (Coordinator), *La infancia vulnerable de México en un mundo globalizado* (pp. 169–193). México, D.F.: Universidad Metropolitana.

Norris, S. P., & Phillips, L. M. (1990). *Foundations of literacy policy in Canada.* Calgary: Detselig.

Peacock, A. (1992). *Science in primary schools: The multicultural dimension.* London: Routledge.

Peacock, A., & Cleghorn, A. (2004). *Missing the meaning: The development and use of print and non-print text materials in diverse school settings.* New York: Palgrave.

Peacock, A., & Miller, K. (2004). What changes need to be made in teacher education programs so that teachers can use text materials effectively? In A. Peacock and A. Cleghorn, *Missing the meaning: The development and use of print and non-print text materials in diverse school settings* (pp. 213–222). New York: Palgrave.

Scholte, J. A. (2000). *Globalization. A critical introduction.* London: Palgrave.

Seidman, K. (1999, May 12.) Laptops or textbooks? *Montreal Gazette,* p. A7.

Smith, M. K., & Smith, M. (2002). "Globalization"—*The encyclopedia of informal education.* Retrieved from **www.infed.org/biblio/globalization.htm.**

Steiner-Khamsi, G. (Ed.). (2004). *The global politics of educational borrowing and lending.* New York: Teachers' College Press.

Street, B. (2001). *Literacy and development: Ethnographic perspectives.* London: Routledge.

Tufte, E. R. (1997). *Visual explanations, images and quantities: Evidence and narrative.* Cheshire, CT: Graphics Press.

Walpole, S., & Smolkin, L. (2004) Teaching the page: Teaching learners to read complex science text. In A. Peacock and A. Cleghorn, *Missing the meaning: The development and use of print and non-print text materials in diverse school settings* (pp. 197–212). New York: Palgrave.

Werner, W. (1991). Curriculum and uncertainty. In R. Ghosh & D. Ray, *Social change and education in Canada* (pp. 105–115). Toronto: Harcourt Brace Jovanovich.

Wileman, R. (1993). *Visual communicating.* Englewood Cliffs, NJ: Educational Technology Publications.

Wynne, B. (1988). Unruly technology: Practical rules, impractical discourses and public understanding. *Social Studies of Science, 18*(1), 147–167.

Wynne, B. (1992). Classroom ideas for antiracism through science in primary education. In A. Peacock (Ed.), *Science in primary schools: The multicultural dimension* (pp. 11–27). London: Routledge.

Glossary

A

Aboriginal   Canada's First Nations, Native peoples.

Acculturation   The changes that occur in values, attitudes, and ways of behaving within a group through first-hand cultural contact. Socialization into a new culture.

Achieved status   Social position (status) gained largely through one's own efforts.

Anti-racism   Opposition to discrimination based on race.

Anti-racist black feminist pedagogy   The central feature of this pedagogy is autobiographical writings that enable students to examine their own internalized racism.

Anti-racist education   An active and consistent process of change through an inclusive curriculum to eliminate individual, institutional, and systemic racism.

Ascribed status   Social position based on characteristics that are present from birth, such as race and sex.

B

Bureaucracy   An organization that is set up to achieve specific goals with maximum efficiency.

C

Capitalism   Private ownership of the means of production.

Cause and effect   A linear relationship in which one variable determines the other.

Centralized education system   Control of the education system by the state.

Cognitive load   The burden on the learner's ability to make the required connections when there is a mismatch between the abstract level of the content and the age or stage of development of the learner.

Cognitive theory of socialization   A theory of learning and development that emphasizes perceptions and thought.

Communal orientation   A shared view in which the needs of the group or community are given priority over those of the individual.

Conflict theory   A perspective that characterizes formal education as a system that contributes to social inequality. This approach emphasizes dominant class interests and how these are imposed on the lower and middle classes.

Conscientization (critical consciousness)   Described by Freire as an awakening process that involves a reinterpretation of what is considered to constitute knowledge.

Constructivist model of teaching   A child-centred view of learning that holds that all children construct knowledge within themselves.

Controlled experiment   Testing for the influence of particular factors on specific results.

Correspondence principle (theory)   The role of the school in reproducing the class system.

Critical ethnography   Knowledge disseminated in schools is not only political but representative of the dominant culture of the society and thus powerful in its effect on the experience and lives of minorities and marginalized groups.

Critical multicultural pedagogy   Pedagogy that encourages students to reflect on an understanding of diversity. Classroom practices emphasize the sources of social injustices of racism and economic inequity.

Critical pedagogy   The study of the relationship between power and knowledge. Critical pedagogy asks how and why knowledge gets constructed, and what the social functions of knowledge are.

Critical theory   A school of thought and a process of critique that claim that any critique must not hold to its own doctrinal assumptions but be self-critical.

Cultural capital   The inherited values of one's group and/or social class (economic, cultural, social, and symbolic), reinforced in schools through curriculum and pedagogy.

Cultural deficit   The perception that a student is disadvantaged due to his or her social status or cultural background.

Cultural diffusion   The dissemination of a society's knowledge and culture.

Cultural genocide   When a group loses its ability through oppression to pass on its language and culture to the next generation.

Cultural politics   Those in positions of power determine such matters as curriculum.

Cultural production   The role that higher education institutions play in producing new knowledge in technology, science, the social sciences, the humanities, business, art, and other areas.

Culture   The ways of perceiving, thinking, believing, and behaving that characterize the members of a particular social group.

Culture contact   The contact that occurs when members of one cultural group live in close proximity to members of another cultural group.

Culture of silence   A culture of passivity that is created in the classroom by teaching practices and curricula that stem from the power of the dominant class.

Curriculum   The subject content of schooling, including the beliefs or ideology that underlie what is to be taught, to whom, how, and why.

Custodial function   The role of the school in looking after children during school hours.

D

Decentralized system (of education)   A system that is controlled by local authorities, the community, or parents.

Definition of the situation   When a situation is defined as real it becomes real in its consequences.

Dependent variable   The factor measured in an experiment that may change because of manipulation of the independent variable.

Deschooling   The removal of education from schools into the community.

Deterritorialization   The political aspect of globalization; the transformation of the meaning of national boundaries (hence political allegiances) in terms of economic relations.

Dialogue   An approach to teaching that is characterized by cooperation and acceptance of interchange ability in the roles of teacher and learner.

Discursive practices   What can be said and thought, by whom, when, and with what authority.

Diversity   A society in which the members are of different ethnic backgrounds, races, cultures, or religions.

Division of labour   The organization of economic activity into parts.

Dominant group   The group that holds the most important and powerful positions in a society.

Dominant ideology   Values and beliefs of those in power and who influence society's subordinate groups.

E

Early French Immersion   Instruction in french only during the first years of schooling.

Educational goals   The stated purposes of a formal system of education.

Ego   The I; that which thinks, feels and acts; the self.

Empowerment   Providing students with knowledge, skills, and values required to become social critics who can make and implement effective social, political, and economic decisions.

Equality of educational opportunity   Equal access to schooling, equal treatment within schools, and the potential for equal results.

Ethnography   A type of qualitative methodology that uses a cultural lens to explore and understand the patterns of schooling.

F

Feminist pedagogy   The study of how gendered knowledge and experience are produced and transmitted.

First language maintenance   The continued use and development of a student's first language after the start of schooling in a second language.

First Nations people   Canada's aboriginal population.

Formal curriculum   The courses and subjects to be taught at each grade level as prescribed by those in charge of the education system.

Formal education   The set of organized activities that are intended to transmit skills, knowledge, and values. (See informal and non-formal education.)

Formal organization   A type of group or interaction system in which behaviour is directed towards specific goals.

Free schools   Schools operated by parent and community groups according to a particular philosophy of childhood.

Friendly webpage   A page of text that contains considerate prose, page layout and design, user interactivity and/or navigation, and instructional devices.

Functional theory   Theoretical view that sees education as a structure that contributes to the stability and equilibrium of society.

Functionally literate   Able to read, write, and calculate well enough to get along in one's society.

G

Gender-inclusive curriculum   A curriculum that includes the writings and life experiences of women, their accounts of and interpretations of history.

Generalized other   A generalization based on what others think or do, acquired through socialization.

Generative themes   Freire's notion that curriculum should include themes and social issues relevant to student life couched in student vocabulary, which can lead to reflection, action, and change.

Globalization   The spread and connectedness of production, advances in technology, communication, transportation, and the media—multiple effects on education.

Glocalization   The manner in which the global and the local come together, e.g., as in some text materials.

Governance   Control and operation of the education system.

H

Hidden curriculum   Everything that is learnt by children in school but is not part of the formal curriculum (i.e., social norms relating to competition, achievement, and authority).

Home schooling   Home-based education where instruction is provided by parents or members of the community.

I

Id   Term coined by Freud referring to the individual's biological or unconscious instincts to seek immediate gratification.

Ideal types   A theoretical construct, first conceived by Max Weber, that delineates the prototypical characteristics of society's basic institutions.

Ideology   Values and beliefs implicitly taught by those in positions of power.

In loco parentis   Latin for "in the place of parents," refers to the assumption of parent-like responsibility by the schools.

Independent variable   The manipulated, influential factor in an experiment. (See dependent variable.)

Individualistic orientation   A shared view in which the needs of the individual are more important than those of the group.

Informal education   Learning that takes place outside of school through the process of social interaction.

Informal organization   The patterns of inter-action within a formal organization that emerge on the basis of social and other criteria.

Intended functions   The planned results of an education system or policy.

Interaction theory   View of society as emerging from and maintained by social interaction.

Internalization   A process by which individuals incorporate society's norms and expectations into their own minds.

Internationalization   Cross-border relations between countries in which national economies are overtaken by international economic exchange and interdependence.

Interpretive phenomenological theory   Strain of sociology concerned with the perception of the nature of events and social interaction and on meanings that are constructed and reconstructed in that process.

Intersubjectivity   The process in which individuals interpret the knowledge that they have accumulated through experience, including the knowledge that has been transmitted by parents and teachers.

Involuntary minority   Minority groups that have formed as a result of oppressive internal colonization.

L

Legitimating ideology (legitimation)   A set of beliefs that justifies or supports the status quo.

Liberal feminists   Those who focus on the importance of critical thinking and the conviction that men and women share the same rights and ability to make productive individual choices. Individual dignity, autonomy, equality, and the right to seek self-fulfillment are central to liberal feminist analyses.

Liberalization   The process of removing government-imposed restrictions on the movement of goods between countries in order to create an "open" world economy.

M

Macro, mid, and micro levels of analysis   Studies that focus on larger structural processes, mid-level institutional analysis, or small scale-analysis of social activity or social interaction (as in classrooms).

Male hegemony   The worldview or power structure that is maintained by the dominant class (usually made up of men).

Me   That part of the self that represents internalized social attitudes and expectations.

Melting pot   A society or place where social and cultural assimilation occur.

Mentoring   A conscious relationship between an adult and a student intended to provide general guidance and support to the student.

Meritocracy   A system of stratification based on personal achievement.

Mixed-method research approach   A research approach that combines quantitative and qualitative procedures.

Moral socialization   The process of learning society's normative system, including the organization of injustice and inequality, which is passed on by schools.

Multicultural education   The existence within one society or nation of several groups that differ in ethnicity, race, culture, language, and religion.

N

Narratives   Stories that tell of an individual's life experiences.

Native peoples   Aboriginal, First Nations groups.

Neo-Marxist theory   A theory about the relationship between political and economic forces.

Non-formal education   Organized education and instruction out of school (e.g., piano lessons, scouts).

Norms   Social consensus governing beliefs, attitudes, and behaviour.

O

Open schooling   Education within the regular system characterized by small-group instruction, sometimes in classrooms without walls.

Open-structured schools   Schools that group students according to achievement or interest rather than age and grade.

Outcomes-based education (OBE)   A system of education or instruction that is guided by clearly defined desired results.

P

Paradigm   A conceptual framework.

Patriarchal ideology   A set of beliefs held by a society that preserves the dominance and privileges of men in relation to women.

Pedagogy   The production of knowledge, identities, and values.

Pedagogy of whiteness   Examines and challenges the unquestioned acceptance of whiteness and privilege controlled by the White dominant group.

Phenomenology   Study of events that include the meanings and interpretations of the participants.

Pluralism   A society in which people of all races and cultures are distinct but may not have social parity.

Policy   Written statement that is intended as a guideline for making decisions and acting under specific circumstances.

Political socialization   The role of the school in teaching the values and norms that support the prevailing structure, including the dominant political ideology.

Post-modernist feminism   A focus on the relationship between power and knowledge as defined by the dominant male perspective.

Praxis   The combination of reflection and action.

Primary socialization   Learning that takes place during the early years of a person's life through interaction with primary caregivers (usually parents).

Q

Qualitative paradigm   A research perspective that includes subjective interpretations of events and processes.

Quantitative paradigm   A research perspective that relies on objective recording of events and controlled experimentation.

R

Race   Identity on the basis of physical characteristics such as skin colour, shape of eyes, and hair texture, and other social characteristics such as language, culture, and religion. Race is socially created and is the main force justifying power and maintaining difference.

Reflective practice   An element of teacher education that involves analysis of teaching and ongoing plans for change in practice.

Resistance   Group or individual behaviour that is antisocial and counter to the values of the dominant group. Groups that express resistance challenge the dominant culture and create their own cultures.

S

Secondary socialization   Socialization that occurs within the school through contact with peers, the media, and teachers.

Selection and allocation function   The distribution of individuals into certain roles and positions based on social class, ethnicity, and other ascriptive criteria within the educational system.

Self   An individual's notion of who he or she is.

Significant other   Individual who influences a child's development through constant interaction and strong affective ties.

Social class   An individual's position in society's hierarchy based on possession of whatever criteria (e.g., education, income) are the most highly valued by the dominant class.

Social constructivism   Sees teaching and learning as socially situated, developed through classroom social interaction.

Social context   The societal circumstances in which an event takes place.

Social control   Social pressures that ensure compliance with established norms.

Social learning theory   Focuses on the environmental factors that surround the child.

Social literacy   Being able to "read" one's environment, e.g., the place of technology; think about one's future roles in society.

Social mobility   An individual's upward movement in society's hierarchical system.

Social order   Societal stability and maintaining social equilibrium.

Social process   A sequence of activity driven by social interaction.

Social reconstructivist model   A model of teaching for social change that is anti-racist, free of social class and gender distinctions.

Social stratification   The system of organizing individuals and groups into a hierarchy based on society's values (e.g., education, income, occupation).

Social structure   Society conceived of and organized as a unit distinct from the particular individuals who make it up.

Socialism   Ownership by workers of the means of production.

Socialist feminism   A division of feminism that sees women's oppression as related to gender relations and capitalism.

Socialization   The lifelong learning process through which individuals develop their sense of self and become part of the social group they live in.

Socially constructed   The construction of situations by individuals interacting.

Social literacy   Awareness of what is going on in the world; ability to "read the world."

Socio-technical system   The subsector of society involving the use of technology.

Status competition   Competition between different groups to achieve a higher social status.

Status culture   A particular lifestyle such as language, dress code, association groups, or interests that are deemed desirable by the dominant group in society.

Status groups   A group of individuals who share similar values and lifestyles.

Structures of dominance   The institutions and ideologies used by the dominant class to perpetuate and increase its advantaged position.

Superego The internalized culture and norms of society that govern an individual's socially acceptable behaviour.

Symbolic interactionism (theory) A perspective focusing on how the self and social relationships develop through social experience and communication.

T

Taken for granted perspective Ideas and opinions that are presumed to be "normal."

Technological literacy Knowledge and understanding of the role, functioning, and politics of the use of technology in society.

Technology (of teaching) Blackboards, chalk, pens and pencils, print and non-print text materials (e.g. textbooks), web-based, multimedia ways of packaging and delivering course material.

Theory of liberation A view that educational practice could and should be emancipatory for all.

Tracking Process whereby teachers evaluate, classify, and place pupils into high-, middle-, or low-ability groups. This may result in separate classes for pupils with different levels of ability or the formation of ability groups within a single class.

Transformative intellectual A person who is interested in uncovering the role of education in the struggle for power and meaning in society.

Transitional bilingual program Instruction in a second language for the purpose of replacing the first. (See **first language maintenance**.)

Transmission model A teaching approach in which a body of knowledge is imparted directly from teacher to students.

Typification An interpretation and categorization of individuals on the basis of prior experience and "knowledge" of characteristics; standardized schemes of behaviour.

U

Unintended functions The unplanned but generally regular results of formal education.

Unity in diversity The notion that a society is strengthened and unified by maintaining the cultural diversity of its citizens. The fundamental goal of Canada's federal multicultural policy.

Universalization The process of spreading various products and experiences worldwide.

V

Virtual learning Learning that results from students' interactions with or in computerized and on-line environments.

Visual literacy The ability to derive meaning by connecting an illustration with the text (print or non-print).

Voice Awareness and articulation of people's conviction that they are active agents of change.

Voluntary minorities Groups formed by immigrants who have chosen to leave their native homeland in the expectation of improving their own or their children's lives.

W

White supremacy A set of cultural practices in which White people are systematically privileged or advantaged in society because of their skin colour.

World culture A widely debated view of a culture that reflects dominant Western values, constructed by and maintained through sharing by experts working within international organizations.

Weblinks

Chapter 1

http://www.oecd.org/infobycountry/0,2646,en_2649_34511_1_1_1_1_1,00.html

—Offers international comparative data on key aspects of education systems from various countries.

http://www.cmec.ca

—The home page of the Council of Ministers of Education (CMEC), the national voice for education in Canada, contains links to Canada's provincial ministries and departments of education.

http://www.unesco.org/education/educprog/stat/stat-idx.htm

—Provides data on education from the UNESCO Statistical Yearbook.

http://www40.statcan.ca/l01/cst01/index.htm

—Offers data on the education status of Canadians.

Chapter 2

http://www.whiteprivilege.com/definition/

—Provides a detailed definition of whiteness, in particular, and racialized social privilege in general.

http://www.edb.utexas.edu/wie/tmain.htm

—Provides a list of references and definitions of many of theories and theorists discussed in Chapter 2.

http://wikipedia.org/wiki/Postmodernism

—Provides a detailed account of the term postmodernism and its use in various disciplines.

Chapter 3

http://www.ericsp.org

—An electronic database of over 950,000 records of journal articles, research reports, curriculum and teaching guides, conference papers, and books.

http://www.umanitoba.ca/publications/cjeap

—The *Canadian Journal of Educational Administration and Policy*, a peer reviewed electronic journal, publishes work that raises important questions and promotes debates on problems of educational practice and policy.

Chapter 4

http://radicalpedagogy.icaap/content/issue2_2/schacht.html

—This article speaks to teaching as a political act where a white, heterosexual, male teacher attempts to draw on a feminist pedagogical perspective in courses he teaches.

http://www.library.ucsb.edu/subjects/blackfeminism/ed_phil.htm#top

—This is a multidisciplinary bibliography on black feminist pedagogy.

http://www.holisticeducator.com/liberatorypedagogy.htm

—Provides an interesting account of education as a matter of politics as well as pedagogy.

http://www.holisticeducator.com/liberatorypedagogy.htm

—Recognizes the politics of education, liberatory pedagogy, and critical pedagogy.

Chapter 5

http://en.wikibooks.org/wiki/Introducton_to_Sociology/Socialization

—Introduces students to a clear understanding of the process of socialization and the goals of this process.

Chapter 6

http://www.pch.gc.ca/multi/html/english.html

—Provides links to information on Canada's multiculturalism policy and the Canadian Multiculturalism Act.

http://www.schoolnet.ca/

—Designed to promote the effective use of information technology by helping schools and libraries connect to the internet.

http://www.GlobalEnvision.org/

—Contains units for teachers on various aspects of globalization, including the effects of technological development on education.

General Interest

www.aucc.ca

—Association of Universities and Colleges of Canada (AUCC).
—Includes links to the websites of the provincial and territorial ministries and departments responsible for education.

http://portal.unesco.org/education

—UNESCO global monitoring report 2006 on literacy.

Bibliography

A

Acker, S. (1988). Teachers, gender and resistance. *British Journal of Sociology of Education, 9*, 307–322.

Aikenhead, G. S. (1990). Scientific/technological literacy, critical reasoning, and classroom practice. In S. P. Norris & L. M. Phillips (Eds.), *Foundations of literacy policy in Canada* (pp.127–146). Calgary: Detselig.

Alexander, R. (2000). *Culture and pedagogy.* London: Blackwell.

Althuser, L. (1971). Ideology and ideological state apparatuses. In *Lenin and Philosophy and Other Essays* (pp. 127–193). London: New Left Books.

Anderson, G. (2000). *Fundamentals of educational research.* New York: Falmer Press.

Apple, M. W. (1979). *Ideology and curriculum.* Boston: Routledge & Kegan Paul.

Apple, M. W., & Christian-Smith, L. K. (Eds.). (1991). *The politics of the textbook.* New York: Routledge.

Apple, M. (2003). Is the new technology part of the solution or part of the problem in education? In A. Darder, M. Baltodano, & R. Torres, *The critical pedagogy reader* (pp. 440–457). New York: Routledge.

Arnot, M. (1994). Male hegemony, social class, and women's education. In L. Stone (Ed.), *The education feminist reader* (pp. 84–104). New York: Routledge.

Aronowitz, S., & Giroux, H. (1985). *Education under siege.* New York: Bergin & Garvey.

Aronowitz, S., & Giroux, H. (1993). *Education still under siege.* New York: Bergin & Garvey.

B

Ballantine, J. (1983). *The sociology of education: A systematic analysis.* Engelwood Cliffs, NJ: Prentice Hall.

Banasik, B. (2002). *Teacher turnover in isolated Native communities: A qualitative reflection.* Unpublished masters thesis, Department of Education, Concordia University, Montreal.

Barakett, J. (1979). *Teachers' theories and methods in structuring routine activities.* Unpublished doctoral dissertation, Université de Montreal, Montreal.

Barakett, J., & Leonard, J. (1999). Resisting youth subcultures: Classroom practice and critical pedagogy. *Transformations: The Journal of Curriculum Transformation, 10*(2), 85–93.

Barba, R. (2004). Friendly webpages: Their development and use. In A. Peacock and A. Cleghorn, *Missing the meaning: The development and use of print and non-print text materials in diverse school settings,* (pp. 239–252). New York: Palgrave.

Barman, J. (1987). *Indian education in Canada.* Vancouver: UBC Press.

Bates, A. W., & Poole, G. (2003). *Effective teaching with technology in higher education: Foundations for success.* San Francisco: Jossey-Bass.

Battiste, M., & Barman, J. (Eds.). (1995). *First Nations education in Canada: The circle unfolds.* Vancouver: UBC Press.

Baverstock-Angelus, D. (1999). *Using teacher narratives for reflection, representation and reforms in teacher training programs.* Unpublished masters thesis, Concordia University, Montreal.

Bedard, G. (2000). Deconstructing whiteness: Pedagogical implications for anti-racism education. In G. Dei and A. Calliste (Eds.), *Power, knowledge and anti-racism education* (pp. 41–56). Halifax: Fernwood Publishing.

Belanger, P. W., & Rocher, G. (Eds.). (1975). *Ecole et societé au Quebec*. Montreal: Hurtubise HMH.

Benson, C. A. (2004). Bilingual schooling in Mozambique and Bolivia: From experimentation to implementation. *Language Policy, 3,* 47–66.

Bernstein, B. (1973). *Call codes and control*. London: Routledge & Kegan Paul.

Beyer, L. (1987). What knowledge is of most worth in teacher education? In J. Smyth (Ed.), *Educating teachers: Changing the nature of pedagogical knowledge* (pp. 19–14). New York: Falmer Press.

Bibby, R., & Posterski, D. (1992). *Teen trends: A nation in motion*. Toronto: Stoddart.

Blau, P., & Scott, W. R. (1962). *Formal organizations: A comparative approach*. San Francisco: Chandler.

Bogdon, R. A., & Biklan, S. (1992). *Qualitative research for education: An introduction to theory and methods*. Boston: Allyn and Bacon.

Boli, J., & Thomas, G. (1997). World culture in the world polity. *American Sociological Review, 62,* 171–190.

Bourdieu, P. (1986). The forms of capital. In I. C. Richardson (Ed.), R. Nice, (Trans.), *Handbook of theory and research for the sociology of education.* (pp. 241–258). New York: Greenwood Press.

Bourdieu, P., & Passeron, J. C. (1977). *Reproduction in education: Society and culture*. Thousand Oaks, CA: Sage.

Bowles, S., & Gintis, H. (1976). *Schooling in capitalist America*. New York: Basic Books.

Brady, J. (1994). Critical literacy, feminism, and politics of representation. In

C. Lankshear & P. McLaren (Eds.), *Politics of liberation: Paths from Freire* (pp. 142–153). New York: Routledge.

Bronfenbrenner, U. (1979). *The ecology of human development: Experiments by nature and design*. Cambridge, MA: Harvard University Press.

Bruner, J. (1997). *The culture of education*. Cambridge, MA: Harvard University Press.

Buchbinder, H., & Newson, J. (1994). Corporate-university linkages in Canada: Transforming a public institution. In L. Erwin and D. MacLennan (Eds.), *Sociology of education in Canada* (pp. 473–498). Toronto: Copp Clark Longman.

Burbules, N. C., & Torres, C. A. (2000) *Globalization and education: Critical perspectives*. London: Routledge.

C

Calliste, A., & Dei, G. (2000). (Eds.). *Anti-racist feminism*. Halifax, NS: Fernwood Publishing.

Canada (1982). The Canadian Charter of Rights and Freedoms. In R. Ghosh & D. Ray (Eds.), *Social change and education in Canada* (pp. 367–372). Toronto: Harcourt Brace Jovanovich.

Canada-EU student exchange (2006). *Education for global competencies*. Final Report to Human Resources Development Canada.

Canadian Teachers Federation Report. (1991).

Cardinal, H. (1977). *The rebirth of Canada's Indians*. Edmonton, AB: Hurtig.

Carr, W., & Kemmis, S. (1983). *Becoming critical: Knowing through action research*. Victoria, BC: Dean University.

Carrasco, R. L. (1981). Expanded awareness of student performance: A case study in applied ethnographic monitoring in a bilingual classroom. In H. Trueba, G. P. Guthrie, & K. H-P. Au (Eds.), *Culture and the bilingual classroom* (pp. 153–177). Rowley, MA: Newbury House Publishers.

Carroll, A. (2006, June 7.) Families take on Bill 101 schooling restrictions. *Montreal Gazette*, p. A8.

Carspecken, P., & Walford, G. (2001). (Eds.). Critical ethnography and education. Oxford: Elsevier.

Chennault, R. (1998). Giving whiteness a black eye: An interview with Eric Dyson. In J. Kincheloe & S. Steinberg. (Eds.). *White reign: Deploying whiteness in America* (pp. 299–328). New York: St. Martin's Press.

Chwojka, C. (2006). *Shades of identity: Constructing identities in a multicultural Quebec public school.* Unpublished masters thesis, Concordia University, Montreal.

Clarke, B., & Trow, M. (1966). The organization context. In T. Newcomb & E. Wilson (Eds.), *College peer groups: Problems and prospects for research* (pp. 17–70). Chicago: Aldine.

Cleghorn, A. (1981). *Teacher interaction in an immersion school.* Unpublished doctoral dissertation, McGill University.

Cleghorn, A., & Genesee, F. (1984). Language in contact: An ethnographic study of interaction in an immersion school. *TESOL Quarterly. 18*(4), 595–625.

Cleghorn, A., Mtetwa, D., Dube, R., & Munetsi, C. (1998). Classroom language use in multilingual settings: Mathematics lessons from Quebec and Zimbabwe. *International Journal of Qualitative Studies in Education, 11*(3), 463–477.

Clement, W. (1974). *The Canadian corporate elite: An analysis of economic power.* Toronto: McClelland & Stewart.

Cobern, W. W. (1998). (Ed.). *Socio-cultural perspectives on science education: An international dialogue.* Dordrecht, Netherlands: Kluwer Academic Publishers.

Cohee et al. (1998). *The feminist teacher anthology.* New York: Teachers College Press.

Coleman, J. (1961). *The adolescent society.* New York: The Free Press.

Coleman, J. (1968). The concept of equality of opportunity. *Harvard Educational Review, 38,* 7–32.

Collins, R. (1971). Functional and conflict theories of educational stratification. *American Sociological Review, 36*(6), 1002–1019.

Cooley, C. H. (1956). *Human nature and the social order.* Glencoe, IL: The Free Press.

Corwin, R. G. (1965). *A sociology of education.* New York: Appleton-Century Crofts.

Council of Ministers of Education, Canada. (2004). Access, inclusion and achievement: Closing the gap. Country Report: Canada. Prepared for the Fifteenth Conference of Commonwealth Ministers, Edinburgh, October 27–30, 2003. Retrieved from www.cmec.ca/international

Crago, M., Annahatak, B., & Ningiuruvik, L. (1993). Changing patterns of language socialization in Inuit homes. *Anthropology and Education Quarterly, 24*(3), 205–223.

Culley, M., & Portuges C. (1985). (Eds.), *Gendered subjects. The dynamics of feminist teaching.* Boston: Routledge & Kegan Paul.

D

Dahlberg, G., Moss, P. & Pence, A. (1999). *Beyond quality in early childhood education and care: Postmodern perspectives.* London: Falmer Press.

Danylewycz, M. (1987). *Taking the veil: An alternative to marriage, motherhood, and spinsterhood in Quebec, 1840–1920.* Toronto: McClelland and Stewart.

Darder, A., Baltodano, M., & Tories, R. *The critical pedagogy reader* (pp. 440–457). New York: Routledge.

David-Cree (Katsitsenhawe), L. (2004). *Would you like to hear a story? Mohawk youth narratives on the role of the history of Quebec and Canada on indigenous identity and marginality.* Unpublished masters thesis, Concordia University, Montreal.

Davis, K., & Moore, W. (1945). Some principles of stratification. *American Sociological Review, 10,* 242–249.

Dei, G. (1996). Black/African-Canadian students' perspectives on school racism. In M. I. Alladin (Ed.), *Racism in Canadian schools* (pp. 42–57). Toronto: Harcourt Brace.

Dei, G. (2000). Towards an anti-racism discursive framework. In G. Dei & A. Calliste (Eds.), *Power, knowledge and anti-racism education.* Halifax, NS: Fernword Publishing.

Dei, G., & Calliste, A. (2000). Introduction: Mapping the terrain: Power, knowledge and anti-racist education. In J. Dei & A.Calliste (Eds.), *Power, knowledge and anti-racism education* (pp. 11–22). Halifax, NS: Fernwood Publishing.

Dei, G., James, I., Karumanchery, L., James-Wilson, S., & Zine, J. (2002). *Removing the margins: The challenges and possibilities of inclusive schooling.* Toronto: Canadian Scholars Press.

Dei, G. J. (1999). The denial of difference: Reframing anti-racist praxis. *Race, Ethnicity and Education, 2*(1), 17–37.

Delgado-Gaitan, C., & Trueba, H. (1991). *Crossing cultural borders: Education for immigrant families in America.* New York: Falmer Press.

Diamond, I., & Quinby, L. (Eds.). (1988). *Feminisms and Foucault: Reflections on resistance.* Boston: Northwestern University Press.

Dickie, D. J., & Palk, H. (1951). *Pages from Canada's story.* Toronto: Dent & Sons.

Dickinson, G. (1995). The legal dimensions of teachers' duties and authority. In R. Ghosh, & D. Ray (Eds.), *Social change and education in Canada* (pp. 254–278). Toronto: Harcourt Brace.

Dobyns, H. F. (1983). *Their number become thinned: Native American population dynamics in eastern North America.* Knoxville, TN.: University of Tennessee Press.

Dolby, N. (2003). Popular culture and democratic practice. *Harvard Educational Review, 7*(3), 258–284.

Dreeben, R. (1968). *On what is learned in school.* Reading MA: Addison -Wesley.

Duarte. E. M., & Smith, S. (2002). *Foundational perspectives in multicultural education.* New York: Longman Inc.

Durkheim, E. (1956). *Education and society.* Glencoe, IL: The Free Press.

Durkheim, E. (1961). *Moral education.* New York: The Free Press.

Dyer, R. (1997). *White.* New York: Routledge.

E

Ellsworth, E. (1990). Why doesn't this feel empowering? Working through repressive myths and critical pedagogy. In C. Luke & J. Gore (Eds.), *Feminisms and critical pedagogies* (pp. 90–119). New York: Routledge.

Ennamorato, J. (1998). *Sing the brave song.* Schomberg, ON: Raven Press.

F

Fleming, R. W. (1990). The artifact as text: Being literate in a technological society. In S. Norris and L. M. Phillips (Eds.), *Foundations of literacy policy in Canada* (pp. 53–68). Calgary: Detselig.

Fletcher, C. (1999). Nunavut EMBA information package. Halifax, NS: Department of Anthropology. St. Mary's University.

Flores, B., Cousin, P., & Dias, E. (1991). Transforming deficit myths about learning language and culture. *Language Arts, 68,* 369–379.

Fox-Genovese, E. (1986). Gender, race, class, canon. *Salmagundi, 72,* 151–165.

Frankenberg, R. (1993). *White women, race matters: The social construction of whiteness.* Minneapolis: University of Minnesota Press.

Freebody, P., & Welch, A. R. (Eds.). (1993). *Knowledge, culture & power: International perspectives on literacy as policy and practice.* Pittsburgh: University of Pittsburgh Press.

Freire, P. (1970). *Pedagogy of the oppressed.* New York: Seabury Press.

Freire, P. (1973). *Education for critical consciousness.* New York: Seabury Press.

Freire, P. (1985). *The politics of education: Culture, power and liberation.* Boston: Bergin & Garvey.

Fullan, M., & Stiegelbauer, S. (1991). *The new meaning of educational change.* Toronto: OISE Press.

Fuller, B., & Snyder, C. W. (1991). Vocal teachers, silent pupils: Life in Botswana classrooms. *Comparative Education Review, 35*(2), 274–294.

G

Gaskell, J. (1992). *Gender matters from school to work.* Toronto: OISE Press.

Gaskell, J., McLaren, A., & Novogrodsky, H. (1989). *Claiming and education: Feminism and Canadian schools.* Toronto: Education Foundation.

Gates, S. (2004). Visual literacy in science and its importance to pupils and teachers. In A. Peacock and A. Cleghorn, *Missing the meaning: The development and use of print and non-print text materials in diverse school settings,* (pp. 223–238). New York: Palgrave.

Genesee, F. (1987). *Learning through two languages: Studies of immersion and bilingual education.* Cambridge, MA: Newbury House Publishers.

Ghosh, R. (2002). *Redefining multicultural education.* Toronto, ON: Thomas Canada Ltd.

Ghosh, R., & Abdi, A. (2004). *Education and the politics of difference: Canadian perspectives.* Toronto : Canadian Scholar's Press.

Ghosh, R., & Ray, D. (Eds.). (1987). *Social change and education in Canada.* Toronto: Harcourt Brace.

Ghosh, R., & Ray, D. (Eds.). (1995). *Social change and education in Canada* (3rd. ed.). Toronto: Harcourt Brace.

Giddens, A. (1990). *Consequences of modernity.* Cambridge: Polity.

Gill, D., & Levidow, L. (Eds.). (1987). *Anti-racist science teaching.* London: Free Association Books.

Giroux, H. (1983). *Theory and resistance in education.* Boston: Bergin & Garvey.

Giroux, H. (1989). Schooling as a form of cultural politics: Towards a pedagogy of and for difference. In H. Giroux & P. McLaren. (Eds.). *Critical pedagogy, the state and cultural struggle* (pp. 125–151). Albany, NY: State University of New York Press.

Giroux, H. (1992) *Border crossings.* New York: Routledge.

Giroux, H. (1996). *Fugitive cultures: Race, violence and youths.* London: Routledge.

Giroux, H. (2000). Insurgent multiculturalism and the promise of pedagogy. In M. Duarte and S. Smith. (Eds.), *Foundational perspectives in multicultural education* (pp. 195–212). Don Mills, ON: Addison Wesley Longman, Inc.

Giroux, H., & McLaren, P. (1989). *Critical pedagogy, the state and cultural struggle.*

Albany, NY: State University of New York Press.

Giroux, H., & McLaren, P. (1994). *Between borders.* New York: Routledge.

Giroux, H., & Simon, R. (1989). Popular culture and critical pedagogy. In H. Giroux & P. McLaren (Eds.), *Critical pedagogy, the state and cultural struggle* (pp. 236–251). Albany, NY: State University of New York Press.

Giroux, H. A. (2000) *Stealing innocence: Corporate culture's war on children,* New York: Palgrave.

Glesne, C. (1999). *Becoming qualitative researchers: An introduction.* New York: Longman.

Goodlad, J. (1990). *Teachers for our nation's schools.* San Francisco: Jossey-Bass.

Goodson, I. F. (Ed.). (1992). *Studying teachers' lives.* London: Routledge.

Gordon, R. (1997). Structural adjustment and women in Zimbabwe: Effects and prospects. *Canadian Journal of Development Studies, XVIII*(2), 263–278.

Gore, J. (1992). Feminist politics in radical pedagogy. In C. Luke, and J. Gore (Eds.) *Feminisms and critical pedagogies* (pp. 25–53). New York: Routledge.

Gore, J. (1993). *The struggle for pedagogies.* New York: Routledge.

Government of Canada. (1867). British North America Act. Retrieved from laws. justice.gc.ca/en/const/index.html

Government of Canada. (1982). The Constitution Act. Retrieved from laws.justice.gc.ca/en/const/index.html

Gramsci, A. (1971). Selections from the prison notes. In Q. Hoare & G. Nowell-Smith (Eds. & trans.). New York: International Publishers.

Grant, C. A., & Sachs, J. M. (2000). Multicultural education and postmodernism: Movement toward a dialogue. In M. Duarte & S. Smith (Eds.), *Foundational perspectives in multicultural education* (pp. 173–194). Don Mills, ON: Addison Wesley Longman, Inc.

Grimmett, P. P., & Wideen, M. (Eds.). (1995). *Changing times in teacher education.* London: Falmer Press.

Grinter, R. (2000). Multicultural or anti-racist education? The need to choose. In E. M. Duarte & S. Smith (Eds.), *Foundational perspectives in multicultural education* (pp. 135–154). Don Mills, ON: Addison Wesley Longman, Inc.

Guy-Sheftall, B. (Ed.). (1995). *Words of fire: An anthology of African-American feminist thought.* New York: New Press.

H

Habermas, J. (1968). *Knowledge and human interests.* Boston: Beacon Press.

Hargreaves, D. H., Hester, S. K., & Mellor, F. J. (1975). *Deviance in classrooms.* London: Routledge & Keegan Paul.

Hatch, A. (Ed.). (1995). *Qualitative research in early childhood settings.* Hartford, CN: Praeger.

Hatch, A. et al. (2002). Developmentally appropriate practice: Continuing the dialogue. *Contemporary Issues in Early Childhood, 3*(3), 439–452.

Health Canada. (1998). Government publications: Ottawa. Retrieved from www. justice.gc.ca/en/ps/fm/childafs.html

Held, D., McGrew, A., Goldblatt, D. & Perraton, J. (1999). *Global transformations: Politics, economics and culture.* Cambridge, MA: Polity Press.

Henchey, N. (1987). The new technology and the transformation of learning. In R. Ghosh and D. Ray. (Eds.), *Social change and education in Canada* (pp. 42–56) Toronto: Harcourt Brace.

Henchey, N. (1991). Communication technology and the transformation of learning. In R. Ghosh and D. Ray. *Social change and education in Canada* (pp. 37–48). Toronto: Harcourt Brace Jovanovich.

Hern, M. (Ed.). (1996). *Deschooling our lives.* Philadelphia: New Society Publishers.

Hill Collins, P. (1995). The social construction of black feminist thought. In B. Guy-Sheftall (Ed.) *Words of fire: An anthology of African-American feminist thought.* New York: New Press.

Holmes Group. (1986). *Tomorrow's teachers.* East Lansing, MI: Holmes Group.

Holt, J. (1964). *How children fail.* New York: Dell.

hooks, b. (1992). Representation of whiteness in the black imagination. In *Black looks; race and representation* (pp. 165–178). Boston: South End Press.

hooks, b. (2000). *Feminist theory: From margin to center.* Cambridge, MA: South End Press.

hooks, b. (2003). *Teaching community: A pedagogy of hope.* New York: Routledge.

House of Commons Debates, October 8, 1971, pp. 8545–8548.

Hurn, C. J. (1993). *The limits and possibilities of schooling.* Toronto: Allyn and Bacon.

I

Illich, I. (1971). *Deschooling society.* New York: Harper & Row.

J

Jackson, P. (1968). *Life in classrooms.* New York: Holt, Rinehart & Winston.

Jaenen, C., & Conrad, M. (1993). *History of the Canadian peoples.* Mississauga, ON: Copp Clark Pitman.

Jansen, J., & Christie, P. (1999). *The changing curriculum: Studies in outcomes-based education in South Africa.* Cape Town: Juta Academic.

Johnson, R. K., & Swain, M. (1997). *Immersion education: International perspectives.* Cambridge, UK: Cambridge University Press.

Joseph, G. (1995). Black feminist pedagogy and schooling in capitalist white America. In B. Guy-Sheftall, (Ed.), *Words of fire: An anthology of African-American feminist thought* (pp. 462–471). New York: New Press.

K

Kessen, W. (1979). The American child and other cultural inventions. *American Psychologist, 34*, 815–820.

Kincheloe, J., & Steinberg, S. (1998). Addressing the crisis of whiteness: Reconfiguring white identity in a pedagogy of whiteness. In J. Kincheloe & S. Steinberg (Eds.), *White reign: Deploying whiteness in America* (pp. 3–29). New York: St. Martin's Press.

Klein, N. (2003). *No logo: Taking aim at brand bullies.* Toronto: Vintage Canada.

Kress, G., & Van Leeuwen, T. (1996). *Reading images: The grammar of visual design.* London: Routledge.

L

Laird, S. (1988). Reforming "woman's true profession": A case for "feminist pedagogy" in teacher education? *Harvard Educational Review, 58*(4), 449–463.

Lambert, W., & Tucker, G. R. (1972). *The bilingual education of children: The St. Lambert experiment.* Rowley, MA: Newbury House.

Leahy, W., Cooper, G., & Sweller, J. (2004). Interactivity and the constraints of cognitive load theory. In A. Peacock and A. Cleghorn, *Missing the meaning: The development and use of print and non-print text materials in diverse school settings,* (pp. 89–104). New York: Palgrave.

Lemons, G. (2004). When white students write about being white: Challenging whiteness in a black feminist classroom. In V. Lea and J. Helfand (Eds.), *Identifying race and transforming whiteness in the classroom* (pp. 213–233). New York: Peter Lang.

Levin, B., & Young, J. (1994). *Understanding Canadian schools: An introduction to educational administration.* Toronto: Harcourt Brace.

Lewis, M. (1992). Interrupting patriarchy: Politics, resistance and transformation in the feminist classroom. In C. Luke and J. Gore. (Eds.), *Feminisms and critical pedagogies* (pp. 167–191). New York: Routledge.

Lindsay, B. (1990). Educational equity in cross-national settings. In M. Thomas (Ed.), *International comparative education: Practices, issues, and prospects* (pp. 197–226). New York: Pergamon.

Lipka, J. (1991). Toward a culturally based pedagogy: A case study of one Yup'ik Eskimo teacher. *Anthropology and Education Quarterly, 22,* 203–223.

Lipka, J. (2002). Schooling for self-determination: Research on the effects of including Native language and culture in the schools. (Report No. EDO-RC-01-12). Indian EduResearch.Net, ERIC Digest, Special Edition.

Liston, D., & Zeichner, K. (1987). Critical pedagogy and teacher education. *Journal of Education, 169*(3), 117–137.

Liston, D., & Zeichner, K. (1991). *Teacher education and the social conditions of schooling.* New York: Routledge.

Livingstone, D. W. (1983). *Class, ideologies and educational futures.* London: Routledge.

Livingstone, D. W. (1985). *Social crisis and school.* Toronto: Garamond Press.

Livingstone, D. W. (1994). Searching for missing links: Neo-Marxist theories of education. In L. Irwin and D. MacLennan. (Eds.), *Sociology of education in Canada: Critical perspectives in theory, research and practice* (pp. 55–82). Toronto: Copp Clark Longman.

Lortie, D. (1975). *Schoolteacher.* Chicago: University of Chicago Press.

Luke, C., & Gore, J. (1992). *Feminisims and critical pedagogies.* New York: Routledge.

M

MacDonald, M. (1980) Socio-cultural reproduction and women's education. In R. Deem. (Ed.). *Schooling for women's work* (pp. 13–25). Boston: Routledge & Kegan Paul.

Mackie, M. (1987). *Constructing women and men.* Toronto: Holt, Rinehardt & Winston.

Mackie, M. (1994). Socialization. In R. Hagedorn (Ed.), *Sociology* (5th ed., pp. 89–120). Toronto: Harcourt Brace and Company.

Magnuson, R. (1980). *A brief history of Quebec education.* Montreal: Harvest House.

Manicom, A. (1992). Feminist pedagogy: Transformations, standpoints, and politics. *Canadian Journal of Education, 17(3).* 365–389.

Martell, G. (Ed.). (1974). *The politics of the Canadian public school.* Toronto: James Lorimer & Company.

Martin, J. R. (1985). *Reclaiming a conversation: The ideal of the educated woman.* New Haven, CN: Yale University Press.

Martin, W. B. W. (1975). The negotiated order of teachers in team teaching situations. *Sociologyof Education, 48,* 202–222.

Martin, W. B. W. (1976). *The negotiated order of the school.* Toronto: MacMillan.

Martin, W. B. W., & Macdonell, A. J. (1978). *Canadian education: A sociological analysis.* Scarborough, ON: Prentice-Hall.

McAndrew, M. (1987). *Le traitement de la diversité raciale, ethnique et culturelle et la valorisation du pluralisme dans le matériel didactique au Québec: rapport de recherche.* Montréal: Conseil des communautés culturelles et de l'immigration du Québec.

McEneaney, E. H. (2004). The global and the local in the construction of school science: The case of Canada. In A. Peacock and A. Cleghorn, *Missing the meaning: The development and use of print and non-print text materials in diverse school settings,* (pp. 13–32). New York: Palgrave.

McGrew, A. G. (2000). *Global transformation reader: An introduction to the globalization debate.* Oxford: Polity Press.

McGrew, A. G., & Lewis, P. G. (1992). *Global politics: Globalization and the nation state.* Cambridge, UK: Polity Press.

McLaren, P. (1995) *Critical pedagogy and predatory culture.* New York: Routledge.

McLaren, P. (1998). *Life in schools: An introduction to critical pedagogy in the foundations of education* (3rd ed.). Don Mills, ON: Langerman.

McLaren, P. (2000). White terror and oppositional agency: Towards a critical multiculturalism. In M. Duarte and S. Smith. (Eds.), *Foundational perspectives in multicultural education* (pp. 213–241). Don Mills, ON: Addison Wesley Longman, Inc.

McLaren, P., & Lankshear, C. (Eds.). (1994). *Politics of liberation: Paths from Freire.* New York: Routledge.

McLaren, P., & Leonard, P. (Eds.). (1993). *Paulo Freire: A critical encounter.* New York: Routledge.

Mead, G. H. (1934). *Mind, self and society.* Chicago: University of Chicago Press.

Medicine, B. (1995). A prologue to a vision of Native education. *Canadian Journal of Native Ediucation, 21 (supplement),* 42–45.

Meighan, R. (1997). *The next learning system and why home-schoolers are trailblazers.* Nottingham, UK: Educational Heretics Press.

Mifflen, F. J., & Mifflen. S. C. (1982). *The sociology of education: Canada and beyond.* Calgary: Detselig.

Missionary Register. (June 1828). A periodical published by the Church Missionary Society, pp. 284–85.

Mohatt, G. V., & Erickson, F. (1981). Cultural differences in teaching styles in an Odawa school. In H. T. Trueba, G. P. Guthrie, and K. Au (Eds.), *Culture and the bilingual classroom: Studies in classroom ethnography* (pp. 105–119) Rowley, MA: Newbury House.

Murphy, P. K., & Holleran, T. (2004). Do virtual environments lead to virtual learning? In A. Peacock and A. Cleghorn, *Missing the meaning: The development and use of print and non-print text materials in diverse school settings,* (pp. 133–144) New York: Palgrave.

Murphy, R. (1979). *Sociological theories of education.* Toronto: McGraw-Hill Ryerson.

Myers, R. G. (2001). Globalization, care and educational services for children under six in urban areas. In N. del Río (coordinador), *La infancia vulnerable de México en un mundo globalizado* (pp. 169–193). México, D.F.: Universidad Autónoma Metropolitana.

N

Nathanson, M. (1970). Phenomenology and typification: A study in the philosophy of Alfred Schutz. *Social Research, 37,* 3–4 & 6–8.

National Center for Education Statistics, Washington, D.C., 1994.

Neill, A. S. (1960). *Summerhill: A radical approach to child rearing.* New York: Hart Publishing.

Nelsen, R., & Nock, D. (Eds.). (1978). *Reading, writing and riches: Education and the socio economic order in North America.* Kitchener, ON: Between the Lines.

Ng, R., Staton, P., & Scane, J. (1995). (Eds.). *Anti-racism, feminism, and critical approaches to education.* Toronto: OISE Press.

Norris, S. P., & Phillips, L. M. (1990). *Foundations of literacy policy in Canada.* Calgary: Detselig.

Nunn, E. J, & Boyatzis, C. J. (1998/99). *Child growth and development.* Guilford, CN: McGraw-Hill.

O

Ogbu, J. U. (1991). Low school performance as an adaptation: The case of Blacks in Stockton, California. In M. A. Gibson & J. U. Ogbu (Eds*.), Minority status and schooling* (pp. 249–286). New York: Garland Publishing.

Organization for Economic Cooperation and Development (1996). *Education at a glance: OECD Indicators.* Paris: OECD.

Orpwood, G., & Garden, R. A. (Eds). Assessing mathematics and science literacy. *TIMMS Monograph Series #4.* Vancouver: Pacific Educational Press.

P

Parsons, T. (1967). The school class as a social system. In P. Rose. (Ed.). *The study of society* (pp. 647–665). New York: Random House.

Peacock, A. (1992). *Science in primary schools: The multicultural dimension.* London: Routledge.

Peacock, A., & Cleghorn, A. (2004). *Missing the meaning: The development and use of print and non-print text materials in diverse school settings.* New York: Palgrave.

Peacock, A., & Miller, K. (2004). What changes need to be made in teacher education programs so that teachers can use text materials effectively? In A. Peacock and A. Cleghorn, *Missing the meaning: The development and use of print and non-print text materials in diverse school settings,* (pp. 213–222). New York: Palgrave.

Persell, C. H. (1977). *Education and inequality.* New York: The Free Press.

Porter, J. (1965). *The vertical mosaic: An analysis of social class and power in Canada.* Toronto: University of Toronto Press.

Prophet, R. B., & Rowell, P. M. (1993). Coping and control: Science teaching strategies in Botswana. *International Journal of Qualitative Studies in Education, 6*(3), 197–209.

R

Regnier, R. (1995). Warrior as pedagogue, pedagogue as warrior: Reflections on aboriginal anti-racist pedagogy. In R. Ng, P. Staton, & J. Scane (Eds.), *Anti-racism, feminism, and critical approaches to education* (pp. 57–86). Toronto: OISE Press.

Rezak-Rashti, G. (1995). Multicultural education, anti-racist education, and critical pedagogy: Reflections on everyday practice. In R. Ng, P. Staton, & J. Scane (Eds.), *Anti-racism, feminism, and critical approaches to education* (pp. 3–19). Toronto: OISE Press.

Rich, A. (1985). Taking women students seriously. In M. Culley & C. Portuges (Eds.). Gendered subjects: The dynamics of feminist teaching. Boston: Routledge & Kegan Paul.

Rodediger, D. (1994). *Towards the abolition of whiteness: Essays on race, politics and working class history.* London: Verso.

Rodriguez, N. (1998). Emptying the content of whiteness: Toward an understanding of the relation between whiteness and pedagogy. In. J. Kincheloe & S. Steinberg (Eds.), *White reign: Deploying whiteness in America* (pp. 31–62). New York: St. Martin's Press.

Royal Commission on Aboriginal Peoples (1996). Ottawa, Ontario. Retrieved from www.inac.gc.ca/ch/rcap/index e.html

S

Scholte, J. A. (2000). *Globalization. A critical introduction.* London: Palgrave.

Schön, D. (1983). *The reflective practitioner.* London: Temple Smith.

Schutz, A. (1973). *Collected papers: The problem of social reality.* The Hague: Martinus Nijhoff.

Seidman, K. (1999, May 12.) Laptops or textbooks? *Montreal Gazette*, p. A7.

Serpell, R. (1993). *The significance of schooling.* Cambridge, UK: Cambridge University Press.

Sheehan, N., & Fullan, M. (1995). Teacher education in Canada: A case study of British Columbia and Ontario. In M. Wideen & P. Grimmett (Eds.), *Changing times in teacher education* (pp. 89–101) Bristol: Falmer Press.

Shor, I. (1988). *Freire for the classroom: A sourcebook for liberatory teaching.* Portsmouth: Bayton/Cook.

Shor, I. (1992). *Empowering education: Critical teaching for social change.* Chicago: University of Chicago Press.

Shor, I. (1993). Education is politics: Paulo Freire's critical pedagogy. In P. McLaren & P. Leonard (Eds.). *Paulo Freire: A critical encounter* (pp. 25–35). New York: Routledge.

Short, J. (1968). *Gang delinquency and delinquent subcultures.* New York: Harper & Row.

Shrewsbury, C. M. (1987). What is feminist pedagogy? *Women's Studies Quarterly, 15*(3–4), 6–14.

Simon, R. (1987, April). Empowerment as a pedagogy of possibility. *Language Arts, 64*(4), 370–382.

Slavin, R. E. (1991). *Educational psychology: Theory into practice.* Engelwood Cliffs, NJ: Prentice Hall.

Sleeter, C. E., & Grant, C. A. (1993). *Making choices for multicultural education.* Toronto: Maxwell Macmillan Canada.

Smith, D. (1987). The everyday world as problematic: A feminist sociology. Toronto: University of Toronto Press.

Smith, D. S. (1993). *Parent-generated home study in Canada: A national outlook.* Westfield, NB: The Francombe Place.

Smith, M. K., & Smith, M. (2002). "Globalization"—The encyclopedia of informal education. Retrieved from www.infed.org/biblio/globalization.htm

Smyth, J. (1989). A critical pedagogy of classroom practice. *Journal of Curriculum Studies, 21(*6), 483–502.

Spencer, M. (1979). *The foundations of modern sociology* (2nd ed.). Engelwood Cliffs, NJ: Prentice Hall.

Stairs, A. (1991). Learning processes and teaching roles in native education: Cultural base and cultural brokerage. *Canadian Modern Language Review, 47(*2), 280–294.

Statistics Canada. (1993). *Aboriginal data.* Document 94-327. Ottawa: Statistics Canada.

Statistics Canada. (1996 & 2001). Retrieved from http://www12.statcan.ca/english/ census01/products/standard/themes/ RetrieveProductTable.cfm*http://www.ai nc-inac.gc.ca/nr/prs/s-d2004/02527bbk_e.html

Statistics Canada, (2004). Retrieved from http://www.statcan.ca/english/freepub/ 81-004-XIE/200410/mafe.htm

Steiner-Khamsi, G. (Ed.). (2004). *The global politics of educational borrowing and lending.* New York: Teachers' College Press.

Stigler, J. W., & Stevenson, H. W. (1998/99). How Asian teachers polish each lesson to perfection. In E. J. Nunn & C. J. Boyatzis (Eds.), *Child growth and development* (pp. 90–101). Guilford, CN: McGraw-Hill.

Street, B. (2001). *Literacy and development: Ethnographic perspectives*. London: Routledge.

Stroud, C. (2002). *Towards a policy for bilingual education in developing countries*. Education Division Documents No. 10. Stockholm: Sida.

T

Tabulawa, R. (1998). Teachers' perspectives on classroom practice in Botswana: Implications for pedagogical change. *International Journal of Qualitative Studies in Education, 11*(2), 249–268.

Thomas, R. M. (Ed.). (1990). *International comparative education: Practices, issues and prospects*. New York: Pergamon.

Tom, A. (1987). Replacing pedagogical knowledge with pedagogical questions. In J. Smyth (Ed.), *Educating teachers: Changing the nature of pedagogical knowledge* (pp. 9–17) Philadelphia: Falmer Press.

Tom, A. (1995). Stirring the embers: Reconsidering the structure of teacher education programs. In M. Wideen & P. Grimmet (Eds.), *Changing times in teacher education* (pp. 117–131). Bristol: Falmer Press.

Trudeau, P. E. (1971). Policy on multiculturalism. House of Commons Debates, October 8, pp. 8545–8548.

Trueba, H., Guthrie, G. P., & Au Hu-Pei, K. (1981). *Culture and the bilingual classroom*. Rowley, MA: Newbury House Publishers.

Tufte, E. R. (1997). *Visual explanations, images and quantities: Evidence and narrative*. Cheshire, CN: Graphics Press.

U

UNESCO (2000). *Education for all*. Dakar, Senegal.

UNICEF. (1994). *Children and women in Zimbabwe: A situation analysis*. Harare, Zimbabwe.

V

von Glasersfeld, E. (1995). *Radical constructivism : A way of knowing and learning*. London: Falmer Press.

W

Wagner, H. (Ed.). (1970). *Alfred Schutz on phenomenology and social relations*. Chicago: University of Chicago Press.

Walpole, S., & Smolkin, L. (2004) Teaching the page: Teaching learners to read complex science text. In A. Peacock and A. Cleghorn, *Missing the meaning: The development and use of print and non-print text materials in diverse school settings,* (pp. 197–212) New York: Palgrave.

Weaver, J. (2005). *Popular culture*. New York: Peter Lang.

Weber, M. (1947). *The theory of social and economic organization*. New York: The Free Press.

Weber, S., & Mitchell, C. (1995). *That's funny, you don't look like a teacher!: Interrogating images and identity in popular cultures*. Washington, D.C.: Falmer Press.

Weiler, K. (1988). *Women teaching for change: Gender class and power*. Boston: Bergin & Garvey.

Weiler, K. (1991). Freire and a feminist pedagogy of difference. *Harvard Educational Review, 16*(4), 449–475.

Weiler, K., & Mitchell, C. (1992). *What schools can do: Critical pedagogy and practices*. Albany, NY: State University of New York Press.

Werner, W. (1987). Curriculum and socialization. In R. Ghosh & D. Ray (Eds.), *Social change and education in Canada* (pp. 91–101). Toronto: Harcourt Brace.

Werner, W. (1991). Curriculum and uncertainty. In R. Ghosh & D. Ray. *Social change and education in Canada* (pp. 105–115). Toronto: Harcourt Brace Jovanovich.

Wileman, R. (1993). *Visual communicating.* Engelwood Cliffs, NJ: Educational Technology Publications.

Willis, P. (1977). *Learning to labour.* New York: Columbia University Press.

Willis, P. (1990). *Common culture.* London: Open University Press.

Wilson, J. D, Stamp, R.M., & Audet, L.-P. (Eds.). (1970). *Canadian education: A history.* Scarborough, ON: Prentice-Hall.

Wolpe, A. M. (1978). Education and the sexual division of labour. In A. Kuhn and A. M. Wolpe (Eds.), *Feminism and materialism* (pp. 290–328). Boston: Routledge & Kegan Paul.

Wolpe, A. M. (1988). *Within school walls.* New York: Routledge.

Wotherspoon, T. (Ed.). (1987). *The political economy of Canadian schooling.* Toronto: Methuen.

Wotherspoon, T. (1998). *The sociology of education in Canada: Critical perspectives.* Toronto: Oxford University Press.

Wynne, B. (1988). Unruly technology: Practical rules, impractical discourses and public understanding. *Social Studies of Science, 18*(1), 147–167.

Wynne, B. (1992). Classroom ideas for antiracism through science in primary education. In A. Peacock (Ed.), *Science in primary schools: The multicultural dimension* (pp. 11–27). London: Routledge.

Index

Numbers in italics indicate that the item is to be found in a table, figure, or boxed text.